Ex

Extended Harmonic Techniques

Acoustic Principles for Composition and Musicianship

JACK BALLARD, JR.

Foreword by Warren Pettit

McFarland & Company, Inc., Publishers

Jefferson, North Carolina

This book has undergone peer review.

Library of Congress Cataloguing-in-Publication Data

Names: Ballard, Jack, Jr. author. | Pettit, Warren.
Title: Extended harmonic techniques : acoustic principles for composition
and musicianship / Jack Ballard, Jr. ; foreword by Warren Pettit.
Description: Jefferson, North Carolina : McFarland & Company, Inc., Publishers,
2022. | Includes bibliographical references and index.
Identifiers: LCCN 2022015409 | ISBN 9781476677026 (paperback : acid free paper) ∞
ISBN 9781476643533 (ebook)
Subjects: LCSH: Harmonics (Music) | Combination tones. | Composition (Music) |
Harmony. | BISAC: MUSIC / Instruction & Study / Composition
Classification: LCC MT50 .B185 2022 | DDC 781.2/5—dc23/eng/20220413
LC record available at https://lccn.loc.gov/2022015409

British Library cataloguing data are available

ISBN (print) 978-1-4766-7702-6
ISBN (ebook) 978-1-4766-4353-3

Front cover image © 2022 Maria Averburg/Shutterstock

Printed in the United States of America

*McFarland & Company, Inc., Publishers
Box 611, Jefferson, North Carolina 28640
www.mcfarlandpub.com*

To my family:
wife, Lori,
and daughters,
Erienne and Heather

Table of Contents

List of Figures

ix

List of Tables

Acknowledgments

The list for any kind of research is of necessity long and involves years of input from colleagues, students, family and friends, not to mention plenty of patience through my times of writing, research and questions. Therefore, if I miss any, feel assured they are not forgotten.

Among my colleagues, Warren Pettit exercised great support as we worked together in commercial music at Greenville College at a time where classical music, popular music and engineering were often at odds with each other. I learned a great deal from him in the engineering department on personal projects as well as classroom support in a mutual program. Ralph Lorenz was my advisor in the music theory department at Kent State and was willing not only to read and critique my dissertation work, but above and beyond, read through several chapters and ideas beyond it.

At my university, Jesse Ayers was of great enthusiasm about my composition and theory work. A great composer in his own right, we had that unusual relationship among music writers and theorists that never competed, never maliciously criticized and always appreciated the style and philosophies of the other even when divergent. Kyle Calderhead, math professor, spent hours discussing ideas as our research interests had a much larger Venn intersection than is thought normal between science and art. While one of the ideas got "scooped" before its publication, I strongly encourage him to continue his work in pattern mechanics: some great ideas in there.

I'd like to thank my students, most of which have unwittingly been the recipients of my ideas and conjectures, in principle, outside class and in teaching. My Greenville College music alumni actively applied many of these principles in their music industry work. Several significant Malone University theory students enthusiastically engaged in discussions on waveforms, acoustics and their applications in music technology and production. At the risk of missing some, among them are Eric Hansen and Brad Magyar who have been very supportive. In particular, I would like to thank Mike Seng, who volunteered time helping me develop some practical applications and experiments and was that vital role of sounding board.

Thanks goes to McFarland for taking on this project, and especially David Alff, for his patience as we navigated through reviews, rewrites and formatting questions that were likely obvious in his world though not in mine!

My mother, Marilyn, and my brother, Kelly, both musicians who "get it," have always supported my diverse interests in music. It is not often that brothers work together in music theory but doing a tonal analysis of impressionism in undergraduate theory opened the door to harmonic possibilities that has a legacy in this project.

Finally, my immediate family has been most supportive, especially considering that they did not understand much less show enthusiasm for the principles herein. It is one thing to "love" when you feel emotional toward anything: it is sacrificial love when you support while not understanding why you do and so my appreciation goes further. As professing non-musicians, they encouraged my work without knowing they did many times. In much the same lines, on an infinite level, I thank our Maker whose manifestations include the inspiration and ability to explore this dimension of His works.

Foreword

BY WARREN PETTIT

Music Theory.

Two words that strike panic and fear into the hearts of many a college freshman. But it doesn't have to be that way. Enter Jack Ballard.

The first time I met Jack, I was stunned by the breadth of his interests and abilities. Jazz piano improvisation, mountain climbing and oil painting are only the first of his many talents that come to mind. And, if you'll pardon the pun, I've always considered my friend a "Jack of all trades and master of many." This book is the latest offering from that prodigious and prolific mind.

How to Read This Book

You can decide to be a tourist or an adventurer. A tourist buys a pre-packaged trip and willfully surrenders the moment-to-moment to others. An adventurer embraces the thrill of self-discovery and the responsibility for curating their own experience. This book is the perfect companion for the harmonic adventurer.

Every chapter is a journey into areas of music theory that are both familiar and unexpected. In one chapter, traditional Schenkerian Analysis is the theme and then a sudden segue into the Nashville numbering system appears to turn everything upside down. But not to worry. Jack connects both systems and reveals the similarities. That is the kind of insight you won't find in many other theory texts.

Jack's incredible wealth of musical knowledge and his experience, both traditional and modern, have given him the tools to bring music theory, from around the world, under one cover in a cogent and relatable format.

1

There is no bias; no right or wrong. The joy of music and appreciation of the theoretical architecture that undergirds its construction are the delight of both author and reader.

Enjoy this book and enjoy the adventure.

Warren Pettit is the director of the Contemporary Music Center, Brentwood, TN.

Preface

Wave theory and its concepts applied in acoustics are well known. Ideas of phasing and interactions have had practical and theoretical applications since the Greek philosophers and their legacies in the Arab mathematicians. The applications have had profound influences on instrument construction and musical theory approaches and philosophies. What are less explored are the further implications as wave energy interacts, directionally and obliquely. One might justifiably ask: "Is this a road you *really* want to go down?" Indeed, the more I explored, the more I realized how many different trails I could take and for an initial book had to select a few directions lest it become unmanageable, delayed and even more confusing.

As such, I suggest that the reader consider these principles in new paradigms, especially as they relate to musical applications. One of these that I pass on to my students is that of frequency awareness during mixing, naturally. Ensemble composers, especially those in orchestra, avant-garde or electroacoustic styles, are aware of these interactions as they combine instruments of varying frequency spectra. It is not enough to assess the combination of a "cutting" oboe sound versus as mellower horn but to understand how additive synthesis contributes to instrumental separation (see my MS on Basic Arranging: Principles of Separation and the "3-D" model).

As a result, much of what we take for granted as musicians or even as humans must be reconsidered in light of audio interaction. From the two or three-component phasing model, we find that there are literally "wheels within wheels," forming a matrix that colors any audio experience we have at any given moment.

Introduction

The innovations in composition over the last one and a half centuries have led to new and exotic perspectives on harmony and its constitution. The advents of serialism, atonality, impressionism, modern jazz, and other stylistic trends have encouraged modern society to reassess its perception of music, and by extension, harmony and resolution. The implications of a unique harmonic system goes beyond chromaticism as the perspective gives new views on tonal systems, such as what may be a justification for the minor triad, the blue notes, harmony as a lateral extension of melody, and psychoacoustic perception.

To fully appreciate such a culture of complex harmony requires education as well as appreciation. We can see this in the greater public acceptance shown with response to avant-garde and atonal techniques used in film scoring, for example. Once an audience understands the purpose behind a piece, listeners are not only disposed to listen to it politely but can amicably appreciate the significance of the composition.

Generally, the more chromatic tones a chord contains, the more perceived dissonance in the sound. This affects the ensuing resolution, making it stronger with relation to a more consonant chord. This has nothing to do with objectivity when we consider that various styles such as progressive jazz rely on relative dissonance as a point of resolution, not tension. In this context, certain paradigms in tonal music infer that: (1) half steps are inherently dissonant, harmonically and melodically; (2) half steps are melodically useful for resolution and may be manipulated as such; (3) half steps can harmonically add to the strength of a chord's relative dissonance. In ethnic music, such as the "blues," quarter-tone and other microtonal steps can produce even more tension.

Even extreme chromaticism can be a basis for consonance at a surprisingly tonal level. Questions are left unanswered by conventional thought, for there are "non-traditional" approaches that may be looked at in the light of traditional as well as extended harmony. We must consider that even if half steps are merely ways to enhance dissonance, tension-release situations, and voicing conflicts, there still may be elements that allow for the use of harmonic half steps that are consonant even in the context of tonal music.

For example, why does a major seventh chord sound more consonant than many other chords in spite of a half-step/major seventh between the seventh scale degree and the octave root? Similarly, why does an added ♯11 maintain the consonance—albeit lush—of a major seventh chord with extensions while its relationships contain a dissonant tritone and major seventh with the root and perfect fifth, respectively?

For one thing, harmonics play an important role in sonorous perception by reinforcing a chord's harmonic functions and sonority or negating them. From Heinrich Schenker's work to that of Olivier Messiaen and others,[1] the "resonance" of the harmonic series can produce both clearly audible and non-perceivable yet influential harmonics.

What is commonly known is that a fundamental note will produce a variety of harmonics according to a certain order. This order as it relates to the chromatic scale is based upon the even ratios of soundwave divisions, as shown in Figure 1.

*frequency's intonation is imperfectly notated

Figure 1. Harmonic series in notation (actual frequencies vary)

Harmonics based upon other tones in the major triad are less considered by the listener. For each single tone that is generated, a series of harmonics based on the level of the resonance in the original oscillator and environment is produced as well. This helps explain relationships between notes and the traditional classifications of consonance and dissonance.

Generally, these discrepancies are close enough for aural acceptance, excluding the interval mentioned above between the sixth and seventh harmonics. In an ensemble situation where fixed instruments are in the minority, tuning often has a completely different meaning as chords change from progressive or linear to vertical or harmonic vantage.

Each note in the triad or any chord also generates its own harmonic series. This explains why a major seventh chord is consonant, not through the relationship of the major seventh with the root but in spite of it. It is consonant through its perfect fifth relationship to the third of the chord, and because it sounds strongly in the third's harmonic series as its fifth. Similarly, an *"add9"* chord is consonant, in spite of the whole steps on either side of the ninth, because of its perfect fifth (harmonic) relationship with the resonant and expressed fifth. Both examples are the result of the harmonically consonant relationship of a perfect fifth to tones in the primary and secondary levels of the harmonic series (the resonant fifth and major third). By extension, an expressed major seventh chord contains a fundamental note (the seventh), which resonates *its* perfect fifth (at the octave): the augmented eleventh chord. Granted, this is further away from the root of the chord and may be considered less consonant but only because of its resonant relationship with the root, not the other played notes.

Therefore, in a dissonant context, the effect and analyses of chromatic tones are those of alterations to a tertian chord. Chromatic tones in a diatonic context may be *either* dissonant or consonant. Given that a non-diatonic tone such as the augmented eleventh is harmonically consonant, we can by extension infer consonance to other chromatically related tones in the diatonic scale.

This book proposes that chords may be extended into the third and fourth octaves of the tertian system, hereafter referred to as "hyperextended" chords. The sources for this thesis lie in the harmonic series, inter-harmonic relationships, and the related principle regarding note separation: the farther two notes are apart, the more consonant their relationship is. It is also clear that the relationships of these tones to lower, more resonant and audible tones, may lend credence to their classification as "consonant." Resonance adds new, compatible tones, and additive synthesis based on phasing effects interact with the played tones as well as their respective harmonics, resulting in a matrix of interactivity. The results include an explanation for the consonance of the elusive minor triad, voicing and arranging from a vertical or harmonic perspective, and a system of classifying the sonority, or *Klang* of each chord. How these impact the listener and how the composer applies these principles are dealt with in the last chapters. Finally, we conjecture upon how these matrices and resonance have impact into other fields of wave interaction.

Theoretical Precedence and Other Historical Indicators

The traditional and non-traditional uses of extended chords are well documented in both theory and example throughout the late nineteenth and twentieth centuries. As composers began to explore harmony beyond "accepted" uses, extended chords were acknowledged as vertical sonorities, rather than as incidental chords based on the coincidence of harmony and contrapuntal writing. How and why they are used is an interesting study, which ranges from dissonant to consonant, functional to non-functional, and even tonal to post-tonal and atonal.

When composers began to explore harmonies non-functionally, they emphasized harmonic effects rather than linear principles of tension and resolution. For example, Maurice Ravel's *Pavane pour une infante défunte*[2] uses parallel dominant seventh chords without resolving them and treats the chords as a melodic collection of lateral sonorities whose effect mimics various harmonic series. Other pieces reflect ethnic and other influences such as the blue tonality of American jazz and the pentatonic-derived fourths and fifths of American folk music. Scale-related tone clusters, quartal and quintal chords, polytonality, and other perspectives came into vogue in tonal music as the twentieth century progressed. Atonality, dodecaphony, and other attempts at non-functional tonality introduced a new aspect with regard to sonority and redefined what made up an aesthetic listening experience but reflected the same principles of sonority ultimately in new contexts of consonance.

"Resolution" within a tonal context contains these chords as "altered tones," usually found in authentic and related cadences, and as approach tones within a chord or progression. A second area relates to those that access a new perspective in harmonic consonance or non-resolution. However, as "consonant" is a relative term, in this case we will examine and discard uses that are so harmonically advanced that "consonance" has no real meaning, are non-tertian in approach, imitative of microtonal perspectives (such as the blues), or atonal in effect and intent.

Finally, we shall examine the use that this book proposes: consonance for its own sake within a tonal perspective. The phenomenon of the hyperextended chords is to be considered beyond the vast majority of the uses that seem prevalent. Its validity remains in the area of using sonority for its relatively consonant sake and disregarding the potential of each of these intervals for dissonance in both tonal contexts that need resolution and other harmonic contexts that need none. As applied in various pieces the implications of such consonance rely on the following situations:

- The context of the chord in the piece, progression, or harmony determines the depth of consonance.

- The chord is resolved to, rather than provides tension for ensuing release.
- The chord is not transient (as in "non-harmonic" or "non-progressive" chords).
- The chord is resonant, within the context of the harmony.
- The chord reinforces the harmonic series presented by the bass or lower notes.
- The voicing plays a vital role, as upper tones must conform within context to the resonance of the lower tones for "consonance."

Notation and Methodology

Approach

Because the thesis relies heavily on aural, psychoacoustic, and contemporary compositional approaches, the arguably irrelevant (although tempting) recent discoveries made possible through technology will be avoided, at least initially, in the first section of this book. The acoustic principles supporting the existence of hyperextended chords are best served through physically observable phenomena found in the writings of those scientists and theorists whose work relied most heavily on immediate computation, physical—not virtual—experiments, and observations. Although written in the nineteenth century, Hermann von Helmholtz's *On the Sensations of Tone*,[3] for example, made amazing inroads into the field based upon minute observation, computation, and deduction, rather than by relying heavily upon technology. Heinrich Schenker and Matthew Shirlaw drew conclusions based upon observable harmony that does not change, regardless of the technology available to enhance, observe, or analyze it.

The implication offered by these and other theorists is that such observation and conclusions may be reached by anyone during any given period of time regardless of the technology available. This is important, for although psychoacoustics and physics are consistent elements of the human condition that transcend culture or time, the composers and theorists alike were and are bound by their own paradigms, environments and technologies, no matter how innovative. Thus, while "intent" is entirely subjective and likely to be erroneous, the period and style in which a composer writes may dictate whose perspective is most accurate. The relatively "consonant" quality of Ravel may be most evident through the eyes of a critic of his time, although it is subject to the approach of an analyst living in another time period.

Notation

Because these sonorities can transcend style and culture, we use several ways of designating these tonal concepts, keys, and modes. The methods of notation, fonts, and analyses are selected based upon the unique character of the musical style or approach. For example, hand-written-style fonts are most appropriate to jazz and popular styles, and Schenkerian analysis has a basic set of graphics unique to its approach. In most cases, the selection of the method will be clear and familiar to those knowledgeable of the style or approach but it will generally adhere to the following systems. All examples and reductions are in concert pitch for ease of comparison and analysis except where noted and of course in facsimiles.

Font

The book uses the Macintosh "Opus" set of fonts in the text for classical music and analysis. It adheres to the Sibelius "Inkpen" series for use with jazz styles and analysis in the text and non-text examples. This method of changing fonts will help differentiate between these cultural contexts and interpretations.

Chords in the examples identified with the jazz context will use the "Inkpen" series. The text, for readability's sake, will adhere to the "Opus" method in both contexts.

Sources for Arabic theory will range from original in Arabic script when possible, to Latin transliteration for clarity's sake and understanding that the majority of the readers will be most familiar with English. Those who read and understand Arabic are strongly encouraged to peruse the original manuscripts referenced, especially as there are more sources in this area that have not been translated at all, and I do not read or write Arabic well at all.

Chord Symbols

Since jazz is a chord-oriented medium that relies on the sonority of the chord as well as melodic lines for resolution, its method of chord designation in tertian analysis is extremely accurate and has effectively challenged figured bass and Roman Numeral analysis for primacy in some types of theoretical interpretation. While jazz chords can effectively indicate sonorities in many types of tonal classical music, figured bass is less easily applied to jazz for purposes of readability and simplicity.

For this reason, the convention of using widely accepted symbols inherent in jazz is used throughout the paper to designate the tertian approach of chord designation. Even in jazz, there are several accepted methods. Jazz musicians often use a shorthand. They may substitute the "minus" sign for the abbreviation "minor," or a more ambiguous "alt" for dominant seventh chords with altered fifths, for example. This shorthand method invites equivocation among musicians not familiar with the culture and performance practice and is more open to interpretation among those who are. As such, shorthand jazz notation is perfect for the style but difficult to analyze conclusively outside of the interpretive media of jazz, popular, and other ethnic styles.

Influences from Broadway and other cultures added specific elements to this shorthand, which left no question as to the chord desired by the arranger. The addition of these influences is best used for this paper in its references to traditional tertian analysis. This includes the following designations (using a C root chord as an example)[4]:

- The basic chord is designated outside parenthesis. Superscripted, parenthetical designations indicate the addition and/or adjustment of individual notes.
- "C" alone always refers to the C major triad, of three pitch classes (major scale degrees $\hat{1}$, $\hat{3}$, $\hat{5}$, or C, E, and G).
- The term "min" always refers to the minor chord, with all its implications of standard tertian order deriving from the natural minor scale: "Cmin" or "Cmin7"
- The term "maj" is only used when the chord in question includes a seventh and successive tertian notes (ninth, eleventh and thirteenth), all of which are generally derived from the major scale: "Cmaj7" or "Cmaj13." It is never used alone without the seventh and extended additions.
- The symbol "+" refers to an augmented triad, when placed next to the root designation: C+.
- The symbol "o" refers to a diminished triad, or if the seventh is added, a fully diminished seventh chord: C°7 = C, E♭, G♭, B♭♭. For this book, the commonly designated symbol ø to denote a "half" diminished seventh (Cø7 = C, E♭, G♭, B♭) will not be used. Instead, a less ambiguous but equally common designation, Cmin7$^{(-5)}$, will be used.
- While Rameau's figured bass used accidentals regardless of the designated note, to avoid confusion the parenthetical designations "♯" and "♭" are replaced by "+" and "-," respectively, to indicate a raised or lowered tone with relation to its natural placement. Otherwise an "A♭7$^{(\sharp 9)}$" may refer to an incorrect B♯ on

top rather than the intended and correct B. "A$\flat$7$^{(+9)}$" is acceptable in the associated chord-based cultures and theoretically more correct.

- Main designations, including all function and color tones, will be placed in standard script. Parenthetical alterations will be superscripted.
- Note and frequency designations will be sub-scripted thus: C_{528}.

Terms

I will use Hugo Riemann's term "*Klang*" and its German plural, "*Klänge*," to designate the general sonorous impact a chord makes, compositionally, psychoacoustically, and aesthetically. This includes the sonic impact of harmonics generated by a note, the chord tones expressly written, and the harmonic series reinforced by those expressed notes including those that denote timbre. Robert W. Wason and Elizabeth Marvin, in their introduction to their translation of Riemann's "Ideen zu Einer 'Lehre von den Tonvorstellungen,'" define Riemann's word as a "tonal complex above and below the pitch in question."[5]

Confusion exists when defining the terms "harmonic," "overtone," and "partial." According to the Merriam-Webster Online Dictionary, "harmonic" is defined as a "component frequency of a complex wave (as of electromagnetic energy) that is an integral multiple of the fundamental frequency."[6] By contrast, an overtone is generally understood as *any* higher frequency sympathetically vibrating with the fundamental pitch, such as those more random overtones found in acoustically "noisy" instruments. The term "partial" is generally thought to be synonymous with "harmonic," with various sources considering them alternatively including or excluding the fundamental. In this book, only the term "harmonic" will be used as the method refers to sympathetic harmonic overtones whose derivative frequencies are whole number ratios of the fundamental frequency.

Analysis

Except where otherwise noted, the designation "HE tones" refers to "hyperextended tones" as defined in this paper, and it indicates the non-diatonic chordal tones derived from the example given. Roman numerals indicate relative position and function where necessary, as in accepted tonal practice. When applicable, other approaches of analysis, such as Schenkerian, Rameauian, and others will use methods found in common practice.

Harmonics and Ratios

As there are often several perspectives and reference points regarding the notes as present in the harmonic series and ratios, two aspects need to be mentioned. First, to avoid confusion, ratios are not given with regard to simple intervals but to each harmonic's relationship with the fundamental and to each other (e.g., 5:4 is the ratio in frequency of the fifth tone to the fourth tone as they relate to each other and the fundamental, or "first" tone). Second, designations of harmonics are referred to with the fundamental as f_1. Thus, the first partial (second harmonic) as produced by the fundamental, f_1, is designated in this paper as f_2, the second partial (third harmonic) as f_3, and so forth. This system will facilitate the application of the ratios and avoid confusion: the ratio of the first harmonic to the fundamental frequency, f_2 to f_1, is 2:1, for example.

1

Justifying Thirds
as a Basis for Analysis

Intervals and the Divisions of Vibrating Medium

Conventionally, most authorities derive the intervals from the progressive nature of the harmonic series or the related division of the "monochord" (see Figure 2), a philosophy that goes back to Zarlino and before, to the Arabian and Greek theorists (see Chapter 21 for more detail). The relationship of the harmonic series to the equal-tempered system has its own flaws and causes disagreement between the notes and intervals as produced in relationship to each other and as produced in the series. Tunings become flawed in the disagreements between harmonics, harmonies, and the current system of tempered scales, and some of these are more aberrant than others.

The progression of intervals based upon a continuum of consonance generally adheres to the following order as they occur in the harmonic series and complex frequency ratios, increasing in relative dissonance:

- Unison (frequency ratio of 1:1)
- Octave (2:1)
- Perfect fifth (3:2)
- Perfect fourth (4:3)
- Major third (5:4, and its less consonant inversion, minor sixth[1])
- Minor third (6:5, and its less consonant inversion, major sixth)
- Major second (9:8)
- Minor second (16:15)

It is no coincidence that this order is virtually the same as the order of consonances developed from the monochord.[2] The tuning methods through the monochord justified intervals on a progressive level. Its method of division allowed the string to display intervals that could

Figure 2. Intervals in the harmonic series

be arranged according to consonance and ratio, both of which could be developed according to mathematical or practical philosophies.

Theorists seem to agree that the perception of consonance in tonal music, and in particular a major triad, is based upon its alignment with the harmonic series, as well as the level of simplicity in the mathematic ratios. Regardless of how composition is approached, the resonating tones of timbre and presented notes are components too important to be completely ignored.[3]

Even at the time of early tonality in the sixteenth century and continuing for some time, the theory community accepted the idea of structural thirds in relation to the bass and their inversions related to the bass as well. This idea also acknowledged that the *Klang* was the same in effect, regardless of the inversion. Jean-Philippe Rameau's $\hat{1}$, $\hat{3}$, $\hat{5}$ and related to the triad by being placed in what we would call "root" position. This is important, for it assists any consonance implied by directly reinforcing the harmonics f_4, f_5 and f_6.[4] Ian D. Bent and Anthony Pople point out the mathematical and practical observations Rameau made to support this.

> At the heart of his theory are the three "primary consonances," the octave, fifth and major third, and the fact that they are contained within and generated by the single note. (This he saw first through mathematical subdivision of string lengths ... and later, through the observed overtone structure of a sounding body, or *corps sonore*.)[5]

Herbert Westerby's commentary on Rameau reinforces his view on this relationship of the triad to the harmonic series. He noted that Rameau emphasized "the exploitation of the principle of Inversion of Chords, one which had probably been suggested by his study of the phenomena of harmonics in the works of Zarlino, Kircher, and Mersenne"[6] among other theorists.

Johann Lippius developed his concept of the musical triad as a combination of three tones and three "dyads" or intervals of two notes, combined.

The harmonic, simple, and direct triad is the true and unitrisonic root of all the most perfect and most complete harmonies that can exist in the world. It is the root of even thousands and millions of sounds, because each of them should ultimately be reducible to the parts of the triad, either by unison or by octave.[7]

Rameau presented this "perfect chord" (the major triad) and used the "third interval" to promote a philosophy of tertian harmony. In his *Treatise*, Rameau states unequivocally this approach:

Without considering the octave, which may be regarded as a replicate of the bass ... the perfect chord is made up of three different sounds. The distance from the first to the second is equal to the distance from the second to the third, as may be seen from the three numbers 1, 3, 5; there is a third from 1 to 3 and another from 3 to 5. In order to form the seventh chord, we need only add another sound to the perfect third between 5 and 7, and this last chord differs from the perfect chord only in the seventh added to it.[8]

The Minor Triad and Stacking Thirds

The development of the minor triad is arguable: by all logic, it should not exist as a consonant chord, much less as the basis for other consonant chords. Riemann held that the minor triad was derived from a so-called "undertone" series, that is, the inversion of the harmonic series.[9] In this series, each underlying tone has a harmonic common with each other in a sort of inverse progression (e.g., an "F minor" undertone series contains notes that have a C common within each note's harmonic series: thus, C_3 is f_5 for $A\flat_1$, f_3 for F_2, and f_1, f_2, and f_4 for C_3, C_2, and C_1). David Howard and Jamie Angus follow others when describing its appearance as a minor third between f_5 and f_6 of the harmonic series. Their approach develops the minor triad from that point.[10]

Still others—Paul Hindemith and Heinrich Schenker as two notable examples—viewed the minor triad as a "clouding" or an aberration of the naturally consonant major triad. The classic "Picardy third" of the eighteenth century reinforces this view by demonstrating a brightening or a resolution of a minor tonality in the major triad at the end of a piece in a minor key. One could argue that this "corrects" the initial clouding of a major triad resulting in the minor as described by Schenker and Hindemith. This principle has implications in the perspectives of both the minor triad and the blue third. The minor triad as seen from this perspective has practical and theoretical support within the tertian structure by showing this as a deviation from the major triad, Rameau's "perfect" chord. However, we will examine the minor triad in its own right and the blued third as different entities in later chapters, introducing the approach of using harmonics as a justification for its sonority and consonance.

A tertian view of chord structure generally builds progressive tones within the order of thirds. Variations are limited to successive major or minor thirds, and by using the tertian order as a template these variations can be stacked variably as the situation and level of consonance or tension requires. The consonant triads and chords depend upon the interaction between the chord tones themselves as well as their relationships to the fundamental.

Rameau's treatise developed the tertian organization through the first octave, then into the second octave. Early justification of extended chords focused on the lateral tension and resolution techniques found in counterpoint. Moritz Hauptmann viewed "the ninth, eleventh and thirteenth are merely as of suspensions, that is, so to speak, of the early evolutionary form of all discords."[11] Hauptmann was not alone. Many of the early tonal theorists held that any chord beyond the triad could and should be justified as functions of non-harmonic tones rather than consonant sonorities. The infamous Kirnberger-Marpurg discussion was only one battle in a war of harmonic perspective. Even the seventh chord, dominant or otherwise, was originally discussed as the result of a suspension or non-harmonic tone, as shown in Figure 1-1, from Walter Piston's *Harmony*.[12]

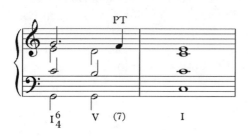

Figure 3. Dominant seventh chord as the result of a non-harmonic tone

In another example, Schenker acknowledges the existence of the V9 chord, which he asserts has too many internal anomalies to be viable as a vertical sonority. These anomalies found within the chord are the diminished triad, the dominant seventh, and the seventh chord on the seventh scale degree, which may be theoretically unjustifiable but aesthetically acceptable.[13] This is not to say Schenker discounted the idea of function. He reduces a diminished seventh-chord (vii°7) to the underlying V7 chord, as the resolution is dependent upon the V7, not on the seventh scale degree or its diminished chords themselves. This is similar to Piston's approach of sub-positioning the vii° as we will see later.[14]

Schenker continues to build the chords through the thirteenth: "In fact, such phenomena are again based on a pedal point, in most cases in conjunction with the dominant V; and it is thus in all cases the power of the pedal point, not the sum of the intervals heaped above it, that creates a unity."[15] He continues to justify extended harmony within the traditional two-octave span as a function of relations to a pedal point. It also seems that this concept of the pedal point and the shifting chords above it might have been a basis for Schenker's later concept of prolongation. Schenker's "function of relations" must be considered alongside his aversion to vertical sonority and his development of lateral movement and resolution.

The opposite point of view identifies the vertical sonority as a function within itself. Arnold Schoenberg discounted the idea of suspensions or non-harmonic tones at all. He said, "There are in fact 'no non-harmonic tones,' no tones foreign to harmony but merely tones foreign to the harmonic system ... these are of course, by definition, harmonies—something that sounds similar to the more remote overtones."[16] David W. Bernstein states that "...by denying the possibility of non-harmonic tones, Schoenberg entirely rejected the distinction between essential and non-essential dissonance."[17] Such an approach justifies harmonic effects on a strictly vertical basis. This is at odds with early composers such as Palestrina, whose conventional approach obsessed with inter-voice relative consonances; and post-tonal composers as Copland, who at times composed "pan-diatonically," that is, presenting effective melodic lines without any compositional regard for vertical or harmonic interaction.

While Schoenberg in his atonal approach did not often need chords for resolution's sake, his stance still underscores the idea of "color" or sonorous effect as ultimate reasons for harmonic structure. This concept of color supports the vertical aspect of music regardless of progression or purpose. The principle of vertical sonority is also true of tonal music, and a perspective of sonority changes tonal analysis from horizontal movement to vertical movement. Riemann's *Klänge* philosophy becomes vital with this approach.

As harmony progressed and composers became more adventurous, the concepts of "consonance" became subjective and yet in another way, objective. The objectivity was approached by composers who understood what the implications of extended resonance and harmonics might be, and their implications of effect. Strauss, Holst, and other late–Romantic adventurers began to push the envelope by extending harmonies—still within certain tolerances and resolutions—but relying more on texture and effect while retaining ideas of tonal composition practice.

2

Tertian Chord
in Harmonic Perspective

A Perspective on Functionality

Thus practice to evaluate chord consonance based upon tertian harmony—that is, chord structure is based upon succeeding thirds—has become the basis for most tonal harmonic analysis. This method's versatility in tonal music allows it to be used in a wide variety of styles and cultures, even in some music of non–Western traditions. It has been shown to describe harmonic and melodic resolution as well as internal construction with regard to consonance and dissonance within the harmonic perspectives of the style analyzed. American popular music, such as jazz, rock, blues, and folk, relies heavily upon tertian organization for compositional, performance, and analysis.

To summarize, the triad is the fundamental chord component, and ensuing extensions develop upon its harmonic basis of thirds. The seventh tone was added to provide dissonance and a point of tension that resolved to a different, more consonant triad. In use it has developed into an accepted vertical sonority itself, depending upon the context and construction. Additional notes added non-harmonic tones, then harmonic extensions to the three- and four-note octave chords, namely the Î1, and in various uses and capacities.

Below is a diagram breaking down traditional tertian organization of two octaves into new categories, based on tuning, harmonic series, and function. These notes may be outlined in a tonal context as follows in Figure 4.

Figure 4. Tertian organization

20

"Root" or "Fundamental" Tones

These are scales degrees $\hat{1}$ and $\hat{5}$. Scale degree $\hat{1}$ never changes, obviously, since that is also the name of the chord, harmonic fundamental, the fundamental bass, and the root in tertian harmony approach (e.g., $\hat{1}$ in C♯ major is C♯). This also relates to the approach by Rameau, Hindemith, and others in that the fundamental bass is vital, providing the harmonic reinforcement of higher tones and their relationships to that bass and its harmonic influences.

Because of the principle of the fundamental bass and its harmonics, $\hat{5}$ is sounded or implied whether it is played or not due to the physical harmonic characteristics of $\hat{1}$. It is also the second harmonic, which is most noticed or perceived after the fundamental. Root tones do not change, except the fifth as an altered tone, which in turn changes the character of the chord within the dominant function as noted below.

"Function" Tones

Function tones are those scale degrees that dictate the actual sound and function of the chord, and they include scale degrees $\hat{3}$ and $\hat{7}$. If function tones change, then the entire chord changes its *Klang* and functional or contextual use. Color and altered tones in the chord may be added or changed but they will not normally change the functional *Klang* of the original chord.

"Color" Tones

Degrees $\hat{9}$, $1\hat{1}$, and $1\hat{3}$ enliven the chord, and by using them judiciously with addition and voicing, the composer can make the chord sound everything from stark to shrill to lush. They do not change the character or fundamental *Klang* of the chord although the harmonic differences change. Chords that use these degrees are often called extended chords or extended tertians, since "color" tones extend beyond the octave (e.g., ninth = octave plus a major second). Such extended tones can be added or deleted as appropriate to the style or composer without changing the function or overall tonality. Color tones are added diatonically and begin within the diatonic context. To increase dissonance as well as add color, they are often altered chromatically. Two exceptions to this are the eleventh chord in the major *Klang*, and the thirteenth in the natural minor *Klang*. In both of these cases, the naturalized or diatonic tone creates a non-contextual dissonant minor ninth in relation to the third and fifth, respectively. To alleviate this half-step tension, both are raised by a half step (most often as a raised 11th in a major, or 13th in a minor, key relatively).

William Mitchell says that the chromatic alterations are aberrations to the diatonic scale, and when treated as such are more understandable in two ways. "Interpolation refers to those instances in which the chromatic half step is introduced between diatonic tones.... Replacement occurs, often as an abbreviation of interpolation, when a chromatic variant is substituted for a diatonic element...."[1]

It is important to note that such chromatic changes of extended chord tones are not considered "altered" tones as defined below, even if they are changed by a half step in either direction. In the case of the lowered thirteenth, which is enharmonically equivalent to the augmented fifth, the perfect fifth is played in the bottom triad of the chord's structure—not just implied in the harmonic series—providing additional dissonance in the minor ninth between the two notes. The augmented fifth is played in the augmented triad and the perfect fifth here is implied in its octave: two different chords.

Such chromatically enhanced color tones contribute to the dissonances created by dominant seventh chords to produce the dominant function more effectively, often in an advanced tonal context where the resolution to tonic is to a non-functional dominant seventh or dissonant sound (see Figure 5).

| #19, #23 | #15, #19 | #15, #23 |
| C7c13+♭ | C7c13-♭ | C7♭9-♭ |

Figure 5. Chromatically enhanced color tones

(Note: Chords shown may contain the enharmonic equivalent for clarity.)

"Altered" Tones

Altered tones do not fit into the above categories but are chromatically changed dissonances from and relating to specific naturally occurring counterparts. The most common altered tones, as defined by jazz artists and other chord-based instrumentalists, are scale degrees $\hat{5}$ and

$\hat{9}$, which must be raised or lowered by one half step. They may occur in four combinations or as a total.

+5-9   +5-9   +5+9   -5-9   ±5 ±9

Figure 6. Manifestations of altered tones

These half steps provide the minor second tensions inherent in extended dissonance, similar to but with more definition than our chromatically enhanced extended tones. By definition, altered tones are added to provide additional dissonance for resolution to a dissonant chord in the case of a harmonically advanced style (such as jazz) in the same ways as described above regarding altered color tones. Altered ninth chords are not traditionally used with anything but a dominant seventh chord, while simply altering a perfect fifth in a triad will change the triad to something completely different. As David Lewin in his adaption of Riemann's work showed in his transformation theory, this is a completely different technique and result, as opposed to altering a chord while maintaining a function (refer to Figure 7)[2]:

- A lowered fifth will change a minor triad to a diminished triad.
- A raised fifth will change a major triad to an augmented triad.
- A raised fifth against a minor tonic triad will merely change it to the first inversion of the submediant, enharmonically.

A lowered fifth against the major will imply a non-triadic function: namely whole-tone cluster, with the implication of a second tone between the root and the third.

Figure 7. Transformation of triads

None of these cases exclude the dissonance inherent within a dominant seventh, whether in a tension that needs resolving (such as the expanding/collapsing resolution of the inner triad's interval of a fifth) or the blues context where the tension produces a desired relatively consonant effect. Transformation processes by definition require the change of a chord into a completely different form and/or root: altered chords maintain the original function.

3

Sub-position

Another perspective relating to tertian chords and their uses was that of "supposition."

Supposition in musical terms, not to be confused with the medieval philosophy, is also listed as "sub-position," a term that describes the meaning far more effectively. In essence, it refers to the presented tones in a tertiary context that extend to seventh or even ninth chords, with the understanding that function as well as *Klang* depend upon perspective and context. Functionally, the theory provides an added tone, one diatonic third below the played tones. It is this tone that actually defines the function of the remaining tones above, even though it is implied, and not often played.

Rameau and Piston in their treatises on harmony wrote of "odd," unstable dominant and dominant class chords. They may be considered "odd" simply as our ears—as theirs, within their cultures—are tuned to various modifiers. Equal temperament, for one thing, would be somewhat jarring in its infancy of Rameau's time but tolerable to Piston's and to today's listener, especially those of jazz who consider the V7 a derivative of blues tonality and not as a functional dissonance.[1] However, a student of Harry Partch or a choral vocalist, whose ears are finely tuned to harmonics and the interaction between instruments or parts, would return to that "jarring" dissonance of Baroque culture against equal temperament.

Rameau's perspective emphasized the relationship of the V7 to vii° diminished chords, with the V7 being the underlying, if not actually played, function of the vii° diminished. His perspective implied that the diminished triad was anathema to functional harmony, as the tritone increased the harmonic instability, and could only be seen as either a function of the dominant 7th or as particularly dissonant melodic movements.

Dissonant Perspective in the Diminished and Augmented Triads

Everything about the diminished triad fights against what constitutes consonance: a minor third against the harmonic major third (in this case, two of them between 1 and 3 scale degrees, and between 3 and 5 scale degrees), and the intolerable instability of the diminished fifth, which strives against the harmonic perfect fifth.

Rameau's perspective was that any diminished seventh chord is really the function of the upper end of a dominant chord that has had a minor third "superpositioned" over a stable dominant triad. Therefore, the fifth scale degree of the key (or the root of the V^7 if one wishes a differing point of view) is *sub-positioned* under the vii° triad. Note his reduction and analysis of Zarlino's vii°-I resolution includes the "implied" $\hat{5}$ SD—what Rameau referred to as the "fundamental" bass— even though it is not written in Zarlino's piece[2]:

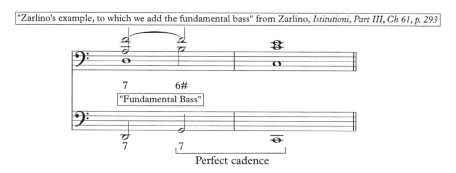

Figure 8. Rameau's analysis of Zarlino

Piston seems to agree but with Schenker's inference carried this idea beyond the V7 and the vii°. In his paradigm, the fully diminished vii°7 chord, with its *three* stacked minor thirds, adds also two diminished fifths for a combined dissonance of five intervals. To complete the resolution of extreme tension to consonance, all:

Figure 9. Dissonances in the V°9 chord

Piston makes his view clear that the vii° triad is simply a function of an incomplete dominant and justifies the fully diminished seventh chord as the superposition of a dominant chord. He referred to the complete dominant as a "V°9" chord, with the "sub-positioned" V making the dominant seventh, with the diminished 9th of the V7 chord providing the fully diminished 7th of the related vii°7 chord. As with many substituted chords, the top four notes of the V°9 chords in C: $G^{7(-9)}$ (jazz notation for a "V°9") may be isolated as the vii°7 (e.g., B°7, or fully diminished 7th by removing the G). His term for this development of extended or related chords is "superposition" in which the upper notes are added to develop a chordal function in the top, often discounting the bottom (bass) note. Again, the implication is that the fifth scale degree (G in the key of C) is "present" on a functional level, through composition, harmonic implication, or voice leading.

In an earlier manuscript on arranging and harmonic movement, I pointed out the relationship of chord progression and movement and it is worth mentioning briefly.[3] Using both the sub-positioned tertian chords, and the actual 5-1 resolutions of the bass or root of the chords, we get a large array of possible movements. The strongest, through voice leading as well as the familiar unstable-to-stable *Klang*, is the V7-I progression with the following strong whole and half step voicing leading:

5-1   7-8   4-3   2-1

As a general principle in most tonal music (there are exceptions in modal, pentatonic and ethnically derived scales and tonalities), stronger resolutions include half-step relationships, with the close interval creating a strong tension as well as a more satisfying release. Further, it implies that the "weaker" resolutions are those that have fewer half-step tensions, such as linear whole-step relationships. Those with weaker resolutions would have fewer of the above combinations found in the authentic, V7-I, cadence, such as a v-I, v-I or even v°-I (by virtue of a diatonic bass movement). Others are slightly stronger, with half-step resolutions but lacking the sub-positioned tone resolution of 5-1, it is also not as strong as a full V7-I.

Functionally, it is important that we understand that these chords may be used as a "dominant class" chord, that is, one that through both linear and harmonic resolution, moves to a I chord in tonal progressions. A classic example in both classical and jazz circles is the so-called "turnaround." In jazz, this progression is compressed into a "sub-progression" to further a song's construction or used to complete the repetition commonly found at the end of a 12-bar blues section. Note how the entire turnaround given in Ex. 10 consists of V-I progressions of various types. Even the awkward resolution to an unstable i° and thence its movement by a diminished fifth movement in the bass can still progress to the iii chord, the diatonic key being somewhat forgiving to the ear, and Rameau's "fundamental" bass sub-position give a great deal of harmonic "forgiveness" for the listener.

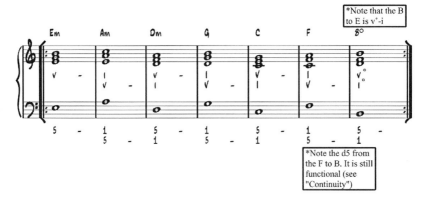

Figure 10. The jazz "turnaround"

4

Acoustic Justification

Implications of the Tuning Systems

The arguments for various tuning systems are as numerous as the years multiplied by the cultures in which they have had an impact. The justification of any particular system relies on several factors:

- The relationship of pitches to each other melodically.
- The relationship of pitches to each other harmonically.
- The relationship of pitches to the harmonic series of the lowest pitch or the fundamental bass.
- The construction of instruments with "fixed" strings and/or pitches.

Any system is worthless except to acousticians if it does not affect the ear in interpretable ways. The value of a system to the listener depends upon the following factors: (1) the physical limitations of the ear when discerning variable frequencies; (2) the interpretive ability of the listener; and (3) the nature of the music to which one is listening.

The consonance of melodic lines developed before the idea of harmony. Monophonic lines were convenient and tuned in practice according to the ear and the custom of the singers. In various traditions around the world, melodic lines are heavily influenced by the construction of the instruments. The monochord allowed for adjustments of the original ratios, and this allowed the variety of tunings available in different cultures. Probably the most common result can be seen in the various lutes from multiple ethnicities (e.g., *rubebas*, guitars, *balalaikas*, sitars), many of which have frets and thus are actually constructed with a fixed tuning in mind.[1] Treatises ranging from Arabian to medieval European sources identified what the tunings were for any given situation in which such an instrument was necessary through the expression of the ratios.[2] Due to the immutable construction of the instrument, once frets were imbedded in the neck of an instrument, this tuning was as technically fixed as that of any keyboard and provides insight into the musicology of ancient as well as modern cultures.

Harmonic structures likewise developed from the stringed instruments, and the ratios of string lengths to each other were adjusted according to mathematical reduction as well. Generally, if the numbers of the ratio were smaller or more closely related (e.g., 1:1, 1:2), the intervals were more consonant. The octave was considered more consonant than the fifth because its ratio was simpler. The octave's ratio of one half-length of a string to the total length, or 2:1 is numerically simpler than the fifth's ratio of one third to the half, or 3:2. In turn, the fifth is more consonant than the third as the ratio of 3:2 is simpler than 5:4.

As musicians found that such relationships were often inconvenient or even impossible in practice, adjustments were made to compromise certain intervals. As the centuries progressed, advances were made in the perception of intervals as well as in compositional techniques. In all of these cases, the tuning system required the adjustment of "consonant" and what were perceived as "dissonant" intervals.

A myriad of tuning systems, such as "just" tuning, different types of "meantone" temperament, and finally the all-encompassing, if slightly out of tune, equal temperament system, provided means to adhere to or compromise the harmonic series, according to whatever best realized the performance of the contemporaneous music. "Just" intonation referred to the development of the scale based on the whole number ratio of the harmonic series (e.g., C to D would be derived from a harmonic ratio of the whole numbers 9:8, D to E 5:4, etc.). The "quarter-comma meantone" approach began with the scale construction as derived from the Pythagorean system based on harmonically perfect fifths. In this case the syntonic comma left at the end of the Pythagorean enharmonic octave was distributed equally among four successive fifths, producing a harmonically accurate major third. This resulted in a more versatile tuning standard that allowed closely related keys to be used but still in tune. The equally tempered system has been praised and vilified for being out of tune with the harmonic series but its strength lies in the fact that all keys in its case are *equally* out of tune from the harmonically pure standard, and thus tolerable.

Mitchell believes that chromaticism, in its best form, cannot be fully realized without the benefits of equal temperament.

> The history of intonation is an absorbing, and in various respects a controversial subject.... Equal temperament resolves these and related kinds of pitch incompatibility by envisioning a just or pure octave divided into twelve equal semitones. The result is a completely enharmonic octave made up of universal pitches rather than the specific pitches of earlier tuning methods.[3]

The third aspect is a fundamental difference and arguably outlines the same differences between theory and practice. With harmonic resonance as a consideration (which it must be whenever more than one note is played), the intervals may be aligned with those naturally occurring through the harmonic series. The series does align with the natural divisions of the monochord but when theorists began adjusting it, dichotomies arose between the series and the resulting interval pitches.

All of these considerations would not matter without the development of fixed tunings and related perspectives in performed harmony. The fixed tuning concept impacts fretted instruments and keyboards of various types whose construction required a fixed approach to tuning.[4] Wind and brass instruments also depend upon breathing and embouchure techniques for proper intonation, and musicians adjust at each moment to whatever tuning method is desired or present. Finally, vocalists, string ensembles and chamber musicians are "notorious" for adjusting intonation at any given moment, and it is often impossible for an ensemble to determine which of the "Big Four" tuning methods— Pythagorean, just, quarter-comma meantone, or equal—is used at any given time unless expressly determined by the player, the director and/ or the style.[5]

Harmonic Resonance

Olivier Messiaen wrote a short treatise explaining his method of composition, responding to the public's misperceptions and demonstrating his technique of harmony, melody, and general composition. One of his approaches is worth mentioning here. He developed one cluster of chords from a harmonics perspective and derived both notes and voicing from the resonance inherent in a single note. In his *Technique de mon langage musical*, he discusses the derivation of a chord using a cluster with the intervals of the ninth, raised eleventh, raised twelfth, and major seventh using functions of the harmonic series. He also uses these chords without the supporting fundamental and triad. He organizes the chord tones in a cluster and thus seems to develop the internal intervallic relationships as well as an actual derivation of resonance.[6] For the purposes of this book, it is also interesting to note that he did not derive new approaches in chord construction from this in a tertian sense but maintained the cluster voicing and did not justify each *individual* note except on a harmonic or resonance basis.

Whereas Schenker proposed that the harmonic series only includes up to the fourth partial as functionally heard (where the fundamental bass is designated as f_1), Messiaen extended this perception of audible harmonics to include partials up to f_{11} (F♯ when f_1 is C) on a practical basis, and beyond that in theoretical bases. He refers to the new harmonics as added notes and the resulting effect of these notes played simultaneously as an *accord de la resonance,* or "agreement of [the] resonance" (Figure 11).[7]

He inserts the G♯ and B in a very non-tertian approach and voicing, more directly in line with the harmonic series and not on a tertian theoretical basis. In this particular instance, he does not extend the concept to the augmented fifteenth or raised twenty-third, although the raised nineteenth is plainly visible. Notice that the B is included, not in relation to the lower harmonics or tertian structure but strictly as a function of extended harmonics, in this case f_{16}.

Figure 11. Messiaen's accord de la resonance

In his Figure 220 (shown here in Figure 12), he also shows the effect of "inferior resonance," not unlike Riemann's undertone series approach.[8] Here the voicing (D-G) indicates a series of interfering or combining "overtones":

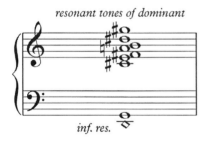

resonant tones of dominant

inf. res.

Figure 12. "Inferior Resonance" (Messiaen, Figure 220)

Aside from producing the overtones of the G and D, this clash of a perfect fourth interval produces additional harmonics. Again, the voicing is an interesting approach, but it retains the same order as in his example derived from the harmonic series. A chord resonating with the harmonic series is found in both G and D, these bass notes being low enough to provide the arguably audible tones of both series. In this case, the actual fundamentals are provided as well as implied, emphasizing each series. This, and other "resonant" approaches have implications in the development of harmonic matrices and the justification of hyperextended tones, as we will see.

Paul Hindemith's Perspective

Giselher Schubert writes of Hindemith,

> As a theory of musical material, Hindemith's *Unterweisung im Tonsatz* investigates aspects of pitch from an acoustic perspective and sets out theoretical principles governing the melodic and harmonic relationships of pitches. Hindemith takes two acoustic phenomena as his starting-point: the harmonic series and combination tones.[9]

While acknowledging the role music theory has in historical style, Hindemith felt that to be bound by tertian harmony could discount aspects of resonance necessary to proper composition, not to mention listening, interpretation, or comprehension of music.[10] Still, the tertian harmony system is an approach that can work for the majority of, if not all, tonal music. Even the pre- and post-tonal music styles have vertical elements that can be approached from such a perspective.

To further Hindemith's philosophy, one must acknowledge the limitations that conventional tertian approaches have toward extended harmonies. In its traditional form, the justification of chromatic tones as only non-harmonic belies both intent and advanced effects regarding the *Klang*. There is a need to develop a vertical approach that is inclusive of chromatic tones as consonances as well as aberrations.

Reiterating Schoenberg's perspective, the chromatic tones within a diatonic—not to mention tonal—context must somehow be justified as harmonic chord tones and not just as substitutions or ornamentations. The contexts of chromatics include purpose, progression, and effect. Even these will clarify and be clarified as the vertical aspects of chromatics are taken into consideration. The analyst determines the level of consonance, dissonance, and their roles in tension and resolution.

The Resonance of Progressive Fifths

Schenker and Shirlaw both reiterated the development of harmony using natural resonance as the base. Their perspective relevant to this book is found in the philosophy of harmonic and progressive relationships. The outline of fifths as resonant pitches is integral to the support of hyperextended tones as consonances (see Figure 13). Schenker stated:

> The consequences for the relations of the tones among one another are of the greatest importance. To the Question: Which two tones are most naturally related? Nature has already given her answer. If G has revealed itself as the most potent overtone[11] emanating from the root tone C, the potency and privilege of this close relationship is preserved also in those cases where, in

the life of a composition, C meets G as an independent root tone: the ascendant, so to speak recognizes the descendant. We shall call this primary and most natural relationship between two tones the *fifth-relationship*.

If the fifth-relationship is the most natural relationship between two tones, it will also remain the most natural if applied to more than two tones. Thus the sequence of tones ... shows a relationship of fundamental and permanent validity.[12]

Figure 13. Schenker's series of progressive fifths

Shirlaw's discussion centered around the use of a central resonating point. He quotes Gioseffo Zarlino:

"The Octave is the mother of all consonances." And not without reason. For the Fifth (or 12th) is not merely the third upper partial tone of the harmonic series but arises from the harmonic division of the Octave:...This fact gives to the Fifth a peculiar tonal property, viz., it must be related to the Octave in order to ascertain its tonal significance.[13]

This integration of the fifth within the resonance of the octave is the foundation for his view, which emphasizes the growth of triads from a fundamental bass.

Suzannah Clark observes, "The capacity for each new tone to project its own overtone series forever yields fresh fifths, making each tone other than the first (the tonic of the scale) both a created fifth and a creator of a (new) fifth.... [N]ature in its purest form yields an infinite array of replications."[14] Schenker limits the permutation of this "mysterious five" element, through his philosophy of harmonic abbreviation. This limitation is acceptable when referring to a single note or concept. Nevertheless, in tonal music, especially music with extended tonalities, these tones in fifths are not just implied through the harmonic series but are often written. Once an instrument has actually played a note, it adds fresh harmonics of the new expressed tone to the sonority.

This relationship of consonant fifths is justified in Schenker's musical worldview in spite of his nominal rejection of the ninth, eleventh, and thirteenth chords as vertical sonorities. However, the consonance of such harmony is developed or justified, Figure 14 shows a way to organize them into thirds for the sake of tertian perspective.

Therefore, if each perfect fifth is resonantly justifiable by each tone expressed, then the F♯ and C♯ (as shown in Schenker's explicit

Figure 14. Schenker's fifths in tertian form (Cmaj13$^{(\#11,\#15)}$)

renderings) and by extension the G♯ and D♯ are also justifiable because of the same extending relationships.

While Schenker expressed this concept within the context of resolution, he also made it clear that a linear grid of justifiable fifths develops from that overtone perspective. These relationships are consonant by their relationships to each other on a vertical basis as well, and by extension to the fundamental bass, C. Shirlaw outlined this organizational structure with the G, D, and A triads as justifiable by extension.[15] If we were to produce such a relationship and include each as a justification of consonance to each lower fifth and higher fifth from it, then the chain is justifiable as a resonant whole.

There is an aspect from mathematical fractal theory in this in the concept that higher organization is analogous to lower organization.[16] Arguably, each overtone produced by a lower element, beginning with the fundamental, can in turn be its own fundamental on a harmonic basis. This becomes more evident if each overtone is reinforced through explicit notes played. In any case, a system based upon Schenker's fifths can become complex once all notes and their relative harmonics are considered.

In the tables below (Tables 1 and 2), a random fundamental pitch was selected (C_1) to demonstrate the redundancy of harmonics within a vertical situation—corresponding to Schenker's resonant fifths philosophy—and extending it into the eighth harmonic. The first grid below shows the relationships as indicated on a keyboard or in standard notation. The seventh harmonic is a partially raised major sixth with relation to the fundamental.

The first column indicates the harmonic series as generated by C_1. As each harmonic is actually generated, it produces additional harmonics as if it were a new fundamental. The top row refers to each harmonic implied by each of these "new" fundamentals.

	f_1 harmonics	Partial	2	3	4	5	6	7	8
Series on C^1	C	C	G	C	E	G	A+	C	D
Series on C^2	C	C	G	C	E	G	A+	C	D
Series on G^2	G	G	D	G	B	D	E+	G	A
Series on C^3	C	C	G	C	E	G	A+	C	D
Series on E^3	E	E	B	E	G♯	B	Cx	E	F♯
Series on G^3	G	G	D	G	B	D	E+	G	A
Series on $A+^3$	A+	A+	E+	A+	C♯+	E+	Fx+	E+	F♯+
Series on C^4	C	C	G	C	E	G	A+	C	D
Series on D^4	D	D	A	D	F♯	A	B+	D	E

	f_1 harmonics	Partial	2	3	4	5	6	7	8
Series on C^1	0	12	19	24	28	31	33.5	36	38
Series on C^2	12	24	31	36	40	43	45.5	48	50
Series on G^2	19	31	38	43	47	50	52.5	55	57
Series on C^3	24	36	43	48	52	55	57.5	60	62
Series on E^3	28	40	47	52	56	59	61.5	64	66
Series on G^3	31	43	50	55	59	62	64.5	67	69
Series on $A+^3$	33.5	45.5	52.5	57.5	61.5	64.5	67	69.5	71.5
Series on C^4	36	48	55	60	64	67	69.5	72	74
Series on D^4	38	50	57	62	66	69	71.5	74	76

Table 1: Harmonic implications on a C_1 fundamental tone

A second grid shows the same fundamentals presented in cycles per second (Hz, using C^4=528Hz).

	f1	*f2*	*f3*	*f4*	*f5*	*f6*	*f7*	*f8*	*f9*
f1	33	66	99	132	165	198	231	264	297
f2	66	132	198	264	330	396	462	528	594
f3	99	198	297	396	495	594	693	792	891
f4	132	264	396	528	660	792	924	1056	1188
f5	165	330	495	660	825	990	1155	1320	1485
f6	198	396	594	792	990	1188	1386	1584	1782
f7	231	462	693	924	1155	1386	1617	1848	2079
f8	264	528	792	1056	1320	1584	1848	2112	2376
f9	297	594	891	1188	1485	1782	2079	2376	2673

Table 2: Comparative numbers (measured in Hz)

The "series'" noted in the leftmost column corresponds to the harmonic series f_1, and each entry is treated as its own fundamental. The various shades show the common harmonics in Hz. Not only does this chart show frequencies that naturally occur—and in many cases are audible, according to Messiaen and others[17]—but they are actually reinforced several ways. The boxes below in Table 3 show C_{33} reinforced with, to and from multiple harmonics. The arrows connecting G_{792} demonstrate how the same frequency from four different series mutually support each resonance. Then, each harmonic is in turn reinforced by its own as well as other like frequencies from other series.

It should be understood that this only demonstrates the principle and will vary based on the frequency spectrum of any given instrument, the acoustic conditions, the general frequency range of the played tones, and the amplitudes of each.

	f1	f2	f3	f4	f5	f6	f7	f8	f9
f1	33	66	99	132	165	198	231	264	297
f2	66	3 132	198	9 264	330	396	462	528	596
f3	99	198	297	396	495	594	693	**792**	891
f4	132	264	396	528	660	**792**	924	1056	1188
f5	165	330	495	660	825	990	1155	1320	1485
f6	198	396	594	**792**	990	1188	1386	1584	1782
f7	231	462	693	924	1155	1386	1617	1848	2079
f8	264	297	**792**	1055	1320	1584	1848	2079	2376
f9	297	594	891	1188	1485	1782	2079	2376	2673

Table 3: Reinforcement of harmonic tones

Therefore, the justification in harmonic terms for the consonance of the raised fifteenth, twenty-third, and nineteenth can occur in both the fifths relationship as described in Schenker or as a resonance common to that of the harmonic series partials emitted from the fundamental bass and *its* partials. In this case, the augmented fifteenth of a C chord corresponds to $C\#_6$, or 1144.5, which is f_6 of C_1's fourth harmonic, E_3, and f_4 of C_1's sixth harmonic.

An argument may be made that this harmonic in both cases is badly "out of tune," and using the higher harmonics as described above to justify it is too weak a principle to be used in the thesis. However, tuning and perceptions of tuning may be equivocal. By adding and reinforcing each fifth in Schenker's approach, we modify the development of harmonics in a vertical sense on an ongoing basis. By itself, the harmonic series is not strong enough to justify the C# against the C, although it does help. Referring to the examples above, we reiterate that the harmonics at least to f_4 are audible and distinctly play a part in the consonance of the chord structure and voicing. Each expressly played part's second harmonic is distinctly audible and justifies its reinforcement, no matter what note it is and no matter what relationship it has to the fundamental of the *Klang*.

The Harmonics of the Triad

A simple triad matches the harmonic series up to f_5 of the fundamental. Playing these notes reinforces the series and produces overtones as well. A C triad sounding with whatever voicing one chooses will produce overtones that suggest the added *Klang* of C, E, G, B, and D as an avenue of consonance, hence the pleasing resonance of a Cmaj7 or even Cmaj9 chord. By developing a chord as a tertian context, we can also justify consonant and progressive tertian extensions: building by thirds but justifying by discerning resonant perfect fifths as shown in Figure 15:

Figure 15. Justifying subsequent notes using perfect fifths

By using Schenker's argument, each perfect fifth acts to justify a subsequent note one perfect fifth higher, and by adding notes in a tertian context, we can justify notes as consonant far higher up the series than with merely the series produced by the fundamental and the fundamental of each subsequently expressed note. This is important in evaluating the relative consonance of different chords, especially as we will see with the minor triad in a later chapter.

5

Psychoacoustic Considerations

Two interpretive perspectives enter into our discussion. First, one must consider the actual skill and human perception of what constitutes sound, tone, frequency, and the interactive elements of each that make up music, much less harmony or melody. At what point does the human psyche actually discern pitches, and arguably more important, the aesthetic differences between two close frequencies? For example, Westerners may conclude that the more accurately harmonic North African pentatonicism is "out of tune," and the converse is possibly equally true. However, Westerners who have grown up with a "just" or other tuning system may not perceive the compromises in an equally tempered system to the point where it actually bothers them.

Denis Diderot's *General Principles of the Science of Sound* (1748) states this issue at an early point in tertian history:

> [H]ow many people with sensitive ears are unaware of the relationship of the vibrations that form the fifth or the octave to those that produce the fundamental! Does the mind have this knowledge without realizing it, much as it judges the size and distance of objects without the least notion of geometry, although a kind of natural and secret trigonometry seems to play a large role in judgment it makes?[1]

Hermann von Helmholtz reinforced this in his treatise on acoustics:

> Any one who endeavors for the first time to distinguish the upper partial tones of a musical tone, generally finds considerable difficulty in merely hearing them.... I will remark in passing that a musically trained ear will not necessarily hear upper partial tones with greater ease and certainty than an untrained ear.[2]

In this case, the question is how close are the frequencies of the disparate tuning methods as far as human perception is concerned? If the difference is negligible, then the actual issue has minimal concern: any tuning method may be used to justify the inclusion of harmonics, the resonance of harmonics with relation to any presented tone, and the impacts these have psychoacoustically. Robert W. Wason and Elizabeth West Marvin comment: "Riemann believed that the ear would adjust according to relativity only but cannot really relate a difference between various tunings. It is this premise that allows him to develop transformation theory, as his theory requires only relation, not absolutism."[3]

Riemann himself said,

> Those who advocate the introduction of school instruments in pure intonation are of the opinion that the surrogate intervals of temperament blunt the ear's ability to distinguish exact intonation—that is, that they damage that organ.... Since the creation of a truly exact equal temperament is scarcely possible anyway ... in other words, our imagination knows nothing of the tuning difference [between] D and D but rather equates both, and imagines D as lower fifth of A and at the same time also as upper fifth of G.[4]

Riemann believed that the ear would adjust according to relativity only. In effect, when one is immersed in one tuning, it is difficult for the ear without training to discern or understand a difference between that and another tuning except by comparison.

Helmholtz also had an interesting analogy based on colors: the partials are to timbre what the individual colors are to white light. We perceive a single "institution," but in reality we see the composite without discerning the "partials" that make up the institution.[5] Riemann also alluded to this: "We can add that the *imagination of pitch level* can also be associated with the *imagination of tone color*, for example, in the reading of a score that indicates the disposition of the individual instruments."[6]

This light analogy tends to relate to an internalization or mental conceptualization while hearing to actually determine timbre or pitch, or combinations thereof. This combination of psychic and physical operations may also include environmental education and experience as well as innate predispositions in aural perception.

Pitch Placement Operations

According to Howard and Angus, the issue of pitch has to do with the "placement" as well as the "temporal" theory and is probably a mixture of the two. The phenomenon of the "missing fundamental," that is, the perception of a single pitch whether or not it exists, is based upon the neurological ability to identify the fundamental based upon the perception of its harmonics, whether naturally or artificially produced. The order of harmonics seems to be necessary for the human brain's reduction of a complex sound into pitch. This phenomenon is shown in its simplest form in Figure 16a. The C triad shown is voiced as a $^6_1$ inversion. The un-played but sounding fundamental appears at C_4. Figure 16b shows a compositional technique where the voicing attempts to emulate a "missing" fundamental on a practical basis. This technique is particularly effective where the timbre of the instruments is focused on each fundamental, such as a flute choir or a vocal ensemble. Notice how the notes imitate the upper harmonics of the series.

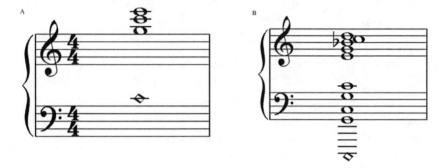

Figure 16. Implied fundamental in a triad and a complex (C9) chord

There is a direct correlation between this subjective pitch perception and perceived amplitude. The Fletcher-Munsen curve shows that the perception of lower frequencies increases as the overall volume of the complex sound increases.[7] There seems also to be a discrepancy of the perception of pitch again varying from person to person, based upon other influences such as amplitude and timbre, actual and implied harmony, and the influx of other related or unrelated frequencies.

Leo L. Beranek demonstrated these principles in 1954. The year is important, for the fidelity of the technology at hand (analog processing, tube amplifiers, cabling standards, etc.) actually emphasizes his observation:

> [O]ne finds it difficult to understand why some small radio sets and loudspeakers sound reasonably well. One reason is that the lowest bass notes are actually supplied either physiologically or psychologically because several of their harmonics are present in the signal. The [fundamental] pitch of a sequence of frequencies such as 400, 600, and 800 cps is apparently that of a 200-cps tone. However, if the frequencies 500 and 700 cps are added, the [perceived] pitch will drop to that of a 100-cps tone ... this happens even without harmonic distortion in the sound-reproducing system because most music is relatively rich in harmonic content.[8]

In current recording studios, the addition of a speaker whose resonating capabilities register below 100 Hz (a "sub-woofer") harmonically supplements these higher frequencies that are enhanced in the system's other speakers.[9]

It is clear that the "harmonic content" of music has the greatest impact upon the perception of a single pitch, whether expressly notated or merely present in the number and strengths of the harmonics present. The diminishing of the fundamental in a "bright" tone demonstrates this principle as the energy present is apportioned to the upper frequencies. For example, the resonance of a distorted guitar sound (whether overdriven, distorted, or otherwise manipulated to present additional harmonics and/or noise) sounds incomplete when amplitude emphasizes the higher harmonics. A bass doubling an octave lower than the functional chord's fundamental adds richness to the chord and the guitar sound. As a result, effective writing for rock doubles the guitar riff, chord structure, and even rhythmic feel in the bass. Distortion and overdrive added to a guitar create so many overtones—harmonic and otherwise—that the third is usually eliminated in practice, resulting in the so-called "power chord" or E5 chord (also written E[no 3rd]). Fundamental support is drastically reduced.[10]

This is even more pronounced when one considers the multiple harmonic series present in actual harmony, relative to the complexity of the chord or harmony at any given time. Bernstein's article on Georg Capellen states,

> Capellen claimed that a chord may be generated by two (and sometimes even three!) concurrent fundamentals. When two fundamentals are sounded simultaneously...each engenders its own overtone series up to the ninth partial. Capellen asserted that when overtones in the same register are a half step apart, the conflict is resolved in favor of the partial closest to its own fundamental.[11]

This acoustic generation has implications in the psychoacoustic field, since the mind's experience needs to reconcile the conflicting overtones, timbre, and compositional frequencies.

This information may be flawed in its presentation to the brain, much less the interpretation. Beranek states that "The point of excitation on the basilar membrane is surprisingly broad, and it seems that the shape or peak of the frequency (often referred to as 'Q' [bandwidth] to sound engineers) is sharpened through neurological influences."[12] Arguably, the physical aspect—the educational process of repetition— reinforces learning elements. As the brain recognizes these patterns on a fundamental basis, it learns to recognize them as a "pitch" by a process of fine-tuning in the physiological aspects.[13]

Therefore, can we really consider it an "adjustment?" There is a finite number of cilia and therefore areas of frequency response along the basilar membrane, just as there is a finite number of bars on a marimba. Thus, on both levels, there is a certain amount of quantizing in the physical resonance of the inner ear alone, much less how it is interpreted. Both are attributable to "forgiveness." The premises in this book do not discount intonation and related systems but assume that education, culture and natural ability can be shaped to "forgive" more in interpretation of frequency.

Relationship as a Fundamental Perspective on Consonance

Riemann implies that the anticipation of a note or resolution is a significant part of the actual sounding of the note, and it determines the perspective with which it is received.[14] Recent visual illusion experiments by Mark Changizi show that the brain has the ability to predict future events within the context of sensory input. His work demonstrates the mind's propensity for what he calls the *perceiving-the-present prediction*. He also thinks it is possible that "one's brain is singing along, so to speak, in such a way that one is listening to the music in the present, rather than delayed by a tenth of a second or so. (Which requires that the brain anticipates the music)."[15] A musician simply playing in time is a function of this, once one considers that pianists and drummers plan the timing of impact to coincide exactly at the moment they desire, even considering the jazz and Romantic nuances of "driving" and "laying back." In any case, this "anticipation" can be called in at varying moments according to genre, personal style and skill.

There seems to be general agreement among theorists that there are several aspects of "harmony" as it is generally defined. The earliest approaches differentiated between practice and theory. Many of the issues throughout the history of theory have involved the schism between those views that work mathematically and those that work practically. Riemann, for example, discusses the idea that harmonies are not necessarily justifiable from a theory or mathematical perspective but are nonetheless acceptable because they have an aesthetic basis for existence.

This idea of relationship plays heavily into the idea of consonance. Without a context into which to put a note, chord, phrase, or even movement, there is no way to apply a definitive classification of "consonant" or "dissonant." Resolution, and therefore the idea of variable consonance, depends heavily on the context and the brain's ability to predict resolution in its analysis of the present *Klang*.[16]

6

Continuity as a Function of Context and Consonance

"Combining a suitably revised form theory and a flexible Schenkerian theory produces a profound theory of form along Schenkerian lines.... The principal postulate of such a theory is that *form and fundamental structure are essentially the same thing*—that they are the same kind of musical entity, viewed from different perspectives."[1] Charles Smith's principle of integration becomes more important when one considers that form is an overarching framework of duration, and fundamental structure is the Schenkerian organization of harmony and pitch. By defining these as such, we can see their individual, analogous components—rhythm, harmonic progression and motive—can work together in different roles to achieve different effects.

Within this context is the development of a linear perspective, combining form, melody and even the horizontal aspect of harmonic resolution. However, form itself is the issue, here. The "form," whether we call it fundamental structure or sectional form, is a series of tension and resolution, and by extension, deviations from an environment to assimilation to the environment. This holds true somehow in tonal, pre-, post- or a-tonal contexts, whether the composer intends it or not.

This idea of resolution implies a "home base" of some sort, however one defines it. The interesting thing is that such resolution can work in harmonic, melodic and rhythmic fields to support each other. In the traditional, Rameauvian perspective, this is called the "cadence," but we do not wish to limit it to this one instance, for it occurs, intentionally and otherwise, in other areas. What is most interesting is the idea of "continuity." Understanding that each cadence brings to an end a section of music, where is the listener's desire to continue? If there is "closure" to the musical issue at hand, there seems wanting the need to continue.

The Music in Section

This sectionalizing of the music is clear in its major forms, such as the sonata, symphony or strict theme-and-variations. Breaking it down even further, periods and phrases contain sections within the motives. Each can be considered a Schenkerian microcosm of tension and release for whatever context the composer is striving. While this paper will emphasize the means by which continuity happens, an overview of continuity as it might exist in form may be beneficial.

The theme-and-variations form is arguably the most highly sectionalized form in Western music. Each presentation of the theme actually stops at the final cadence of the theme or its variation. Nonetheless, each variation may stop or start as a function of continuity. Even the simplest forms, such as AAA or through-composed forms show from antithetical sides the ideas of continuity. An AAA form urges continuity through repetition and a through-composed song with its *lack* of repetition inversely requires some sort of continuity to provide a resolution to the whole. The AABA form also lends itself to "continuity," for though it is highly sectionalized, each section contextually implies an "urge" to move forward, either in repetition or through the instability of the "B" section and its subsequent resolution to yet another "A."

In similar ways, the clear cadences of the concert forms bring to closure sections of introduction. But development or contrasting sections in each will also show short pieces of cadence. There is a close relationship between the sectionalizing in jazz pieces and concert forms, especially in development or improvisational sections.[2] What allows these individual pieces to perpetuate the composition is the position of the tension-and-resolution, repetition, and what Larson called "contextual stability."[3] Simple and complex song forms, as well as the more complicated concert forms, all use various means of continuity.

A second sectionalized form, the classic presentation of the *sonata allegro* form brings out this problem in continuity throughout the entire presentation but especially in the more highly structured exposition. As the two main themes are presented in their entireties, they close unequivocally on their respective tonics. As with the more concert-oriented forms, the listener often perceives the song on multiple levels. Each theme may be listened to as a "song" (section) within itself or each section within the context of the entire piece. At this level, the motive or even theme is present in its exposition and as such may be retained in the memory long enough to become significant, should the piece incorporate development. There are also harmonic and rhythmic dimensions as the listener will begin to place emphasis on variations within the environment of the song, or section. The anomalies inherent within the development section with relation to the exposed theme drives the listener's interest.

These dimensions remain in place as the listener listens on progressive "macro-levels." The skills and education of the listener come into play as the song is examined. For instance, the next level may be only the four-bar phrase that a typical musical comedy song is made of. After that, the listener may perceive both sections and deviations from the song's environment in the simple song form imbedded in the overall structure: AABA of the refrain, for example. Finally, on the highest level, a listener will perceive the sections between the intro, verse, refrain and coda, if present, by the deviation from the prevailing environment.

These depend on the listener's experience, innate skill and education. In most cases, perception of the environment is the standard by which subsequent deviations are measured: understanding the components of the environment is not necessary to perceive anomalies. With this in mind, we can see that the listener will recognize a B section easily as a sonic anomaly within the context of persistent "A-ism" if you will, which permeates the other parts of the refrain or exposition.

Several aspects of continuity may be present. *Harmonic continuity* represents the technique by which harmonic resolution is used to propel the piece. *Rhythmic continuity* depends on the rhythmic feel, completion or polyrhythmic aspects. *Melodic continuity* refers to the listener's tendency to "predict" the direction or resolution in the linear aspects of a piece. *Syllogistic continuity* brings into play the cognitive, experiential and educational aspects of the listener as the brain is actively engaged on a more frontal level. Finally, *environmental or contextual continuity* is demonstrated throughout all examples and aspects as it shows how the brain's concept of the immediate surroundings provide an expectation of continuity, accepting the concept that "there is nothing new under the sun." Obviously, if all aspects are present, the strength of the concept of continuity is at its highest but even if single or incomplete elements exist, the idea of continuity can occur, resulting in new perspectives based upon context. This is important to provide context for consonance, tuning and harmony.

Harmonic Continuity

The harmonic element is the simplest and most obvious. While a resolution most obviously wants to continue to the tonic, nonetheless, a harmonic setup can fool the ear and "unsettle" the resolution implied by the tonic by using a sort of deceptive cadence. In "The Man I Love" (Gershwin, 1924), the harmonic continuity is fulfilled by the presentation of the common jazz phrase of ii-V-I (ii°-V-i in minor, or its variants as in this example, vii°/V-V7-i). This unsettles the tonic resolution afforded by the A' section and prepares for the classic bridge in a related but contrasting key, C minor:

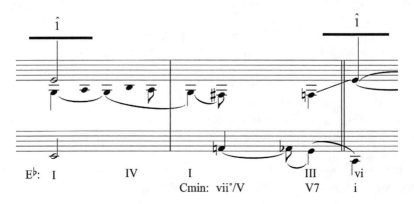

Figure 17. Harmonic continuity

The key phrase is "in context." This ii-V-I progression clearly resolves but its unique placement at the end of a phrase provides continuity in two ways, in spite of the resolution. First, the actual resolution overlaps, occurring at the top of the next phrase. This is common in many popular tunes, especially in rock, where the repeat of the all-important riff often coincides with the last note (Figure 18):

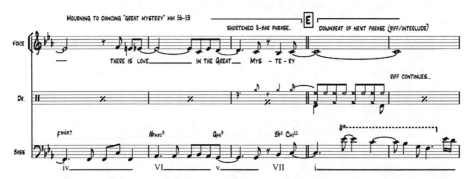

Figure 18. "Great Mystery," performed by Mourning to Dancing (Mourning to Dancing. Audio recording. *Great Mystery*. 2007, 2015. "Sigh As You Close the Book." Music and Lyrics by Jack Ballard, Alliance, OH: Kiwibird Music. Used by Permission.)

The ii-V-I offset progression is not only common in rock and Tin Pan Alley tunes but provides a solid basis for many other jazz styles, even—or especially—such styles as bebop, cool and related sub-styles. Many jazz tunes from the bebop and "cool" jazz era of the '50s and '60s are classic examples how the ii-V-I offset promotes harmonic continuity within phrases and inside entire sections. However, as we will see, it must rely on rhythmic continuity to develop cohesiveness in the larger structure.

In Figure 19, note how the chord structure (with defining fundamental bass) progresses through each major section, resolving but allowing the downbeats to redefine the role of the tonic chord in each ii-V-I:

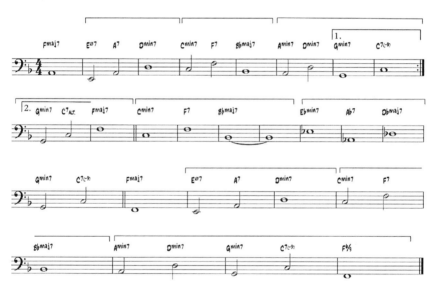

Figure 19. Typical bebop chord progression (For an example of a released song and the recordings of various interpretations, see Parker, Charlie. *Confirmation*. The Real Book, Sixth Edition [Hal Leonard Corp]. New York: Atlantic Music Corp., 1946.)

The brackets indicate the ii-V-I progressions and the double bars indicate two bar sections within four-bar phrases. Note how although the progression is clearly a harmonic resolution to the tonic, the staggering of the progression against the phrase actually requires continuity by virtue of the overlap. We also see this in Schubert's lieder (see next page).

Here we see the dominant sustained rather than transient and the tonic chord in the context of the new phrase. This one act of continuity

Figure 20. "An Schwager Kronos" (Schubert) (Schubert, Franz. *200 Songs in Three Volumes*. Volume III. Translated by Gerard Mackworth-Young, edited by Sergius Kagen. New York: International Music Company, 1961.)

prevents the tonic from having its own place as a complete resolution: it is relegated to the new phrase. Again, this overlap of harmony over form relates to contextual stability allowing the bridging between two sections.

Rhythmic Continuity

A second important method of continuity has to do with the rhythm of the piece whether in concert or popular styles. This determination of a rhythmic feel, or "groove" in the popular music vernacular, will project continuity through the cadence.

Particularly in a jazz or popular song context, a consistent rhythm is a standard by which syncopation and other rhythmic anomalies are measured, whether implied, expressed, or even unintentionally generated by the listener. The cessation of the section or song in melodic and rhythmic senses implies some sort of resolution. The dissonant, loud jazz chord at the end of many big band charts may be the final tension: the audience applause is the resolution and completes the cessation of rhythmic continuity.

This rhythmic continuity also belies the tendency for cessation at the tonic. In the same way that harmonic continuity forces the tonic to be considered outside of its normal perspective, rhythmic continuity helps by also overlapping form and mixing "hits" with continued rhythmic feel juxtaposed with form. Without rhythmic cessation, perceived or literal, the tonic becomes again a victim of context and its rhythmic instability contributes to its tonal instability. This is most evident in the context where the instrumentation contributes to the perception of rhythmic continuity, such as in jazz or rock with the rhythm section. Even underlying passages can support the impression a listener has that the groove, or rhythmic feel continues. Note the accompanying part in "The Man I Love":

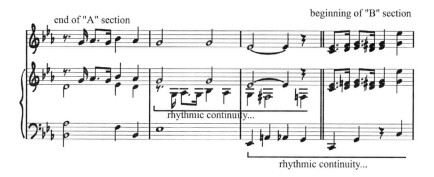

Figure 21. Rhythmic continuity in accompanying parts ("The Man I Love") (Gershwin, George and Gershwin, Ira. *The Man I Love*, P.D., 1924.)

The classic blues form also shows continuity through both harmonic and rhythmic methods:

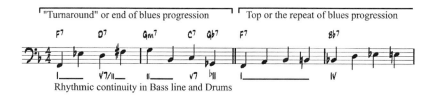

Figure 22. Rhythmic continuity in a blues progression

Lest one think that such rhythmic continuity is limited to a "groove-oriented" style such as jazz, symphonic dance or popular songs, Robert Morgan points out the idea of a hierarchy of rhythm based on event placement and duration analogous to Schenker's approach to linear pitch.[4] The above Schubert shows one type of rhythmic continuity in that the rhythmic motive is repeated. As is clear in many theorists' writings[5] once a motive is repeated, it becomes expected, "anticipated," or fixed in the mind as a melodic "home base." Whether a composer determines to repeat it once again or not becomes the next issue. In this case, the motive continues in a rhythmic pattern throughout the next phrase. The Schubert shows continuity in the repetition of the accompanying motive but also in its continued establishment of a consistent "groove." This groove is found in concert music, especially in dance-related forms. The incessant rhythmic in Ravel's *Bolero* propels the otherwise highly sectional repetition of the main theme:

"Bolero" repeated rhythmic pattern/feel (Ravel)

Figure 23. "Bolero" rhythmic figure

It stands to reason, then, that in the same way that contextual stability in harmonic consideration contributes to the perception of resolution throughout a section, this perception of a rhythmic hierarchy also minimizes the perceived effect of any kind of cessation on a micro level.

A clear example of rhythmic continuity is found in the melodic of Holst's "Jupiter" movement of *The Planets*. The melody feels like "the song that never ends," and although it melodically completes, the rhythmic impetus underneath interacting with the melody supports its propulsion to the next iteration:

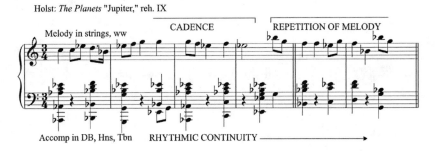

Figure 24. Rhythmic continuity in Holst's "Jupiter," reh. IX

Melodic Continuity

The harmonic and melodic tendencies in "The Man I Love" and the Jupiter theme contribute to a third continuity principle: that of melodic momentum, or "continuation," in Larson's term. As an AABA song, "The Man I Love" is highly sectional, as we will see below. The "trick" is fooling the ear into believing that each section is *not* the end but a continuation to the next section. In this case, the timing and direction of the resolving line will contribute to the instability of the final.

In the case of this Gershwin tune, examine the scalar descent at the end of the second section, A':

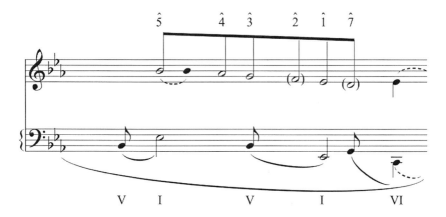

Figure 25. Melodic continuity

The descending line, while culminating in a melodic tonic, continues into the tonality of the contrasting key (C minor). The actual culminating tone is the C, the root of C minor, and is led to this point through the implied tone, $\hat{7}$ (the harmonic fifth of the V in C minor). In this particular song, the melodic continuity is weaker but is strongly supported by the other two criteria. This descending line is particularly important, for the structure supports the "auralization" of implied tones. Larson states that "[i]n a melodic step, the second note tends to displace the trace of the first, leaving one trace in music memory; in a melodic leap, the second note tends to support the trace of the first, leaving two traces in musical memory."[6] Thus, in our *Urlinie*, the "memory" of the tonic is supplanted by the real or auralization of the following seventh scale degree, returning to the E♭. However, our E♭ now has no longer the same position it had in the A' section: it has been "demoted" to a $\hat{3}$ in C minor.

Typical in many English folk songs is the propensity to skip scale degrees and to bridge into the refrain. Vaughan Williams wrote settings for folk songs that support these melodic continuations. See Figure 26 at top of next page.

The melody is somewhat modal, for although it ends on a satisfying "A," the strong note is an "E" throughout. The basic pentatonic structure encourages an "auralization" of the melody, whether actually written in this arrangement.[7] A reduction of the melody shows also auralized melodies in the above bars 6 and 7.

Continuity is shown in a slightly different light given the modal nature of the melody. The high point is the E, supported by Vaughan Williams' E minor chord, in the third bar above. The E may act as a modal "I" but transfers to the octave and descends to a clear A minor at

Figure 26. Vaughan Williams, "The Spanish Ladies"

the end of the refrain. The continuity is found in this transfer of octave, which helps propel the melody toward the end with its descending line. This is especially interesting in light of the octave's tendency to confuse the first and second harmonics with actual played notes.

Syllogistic Continuity

A final reason for continuity is simply the expectation of something more to happen. The AABA form of the musical comedy song is highly sectionalized, with complete cadences at each one of the sections (see top of next page).

There are clear interruptions before bars 30 and 40. We have shown above how continuity can work within this context on harmonic, rhythmic and melodic bases. There is also a simpler explanation. The education of the listener—formal or experiential—plays into how the listener

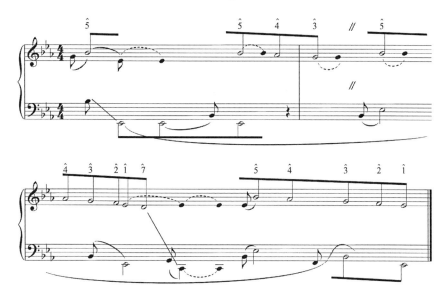

Figure 27. Sectional continuity. Gershwin, "The Man I Love" (Schenker reduction)

perceives the music, on a macro- or micro-level. The motivic, sectional and multi-movement structures are made of individual "pieces," each of which is arguably complete. The context in which the section is placed has everything to do with this aspect of continuity and the education and experience of the listener go far in interpreting the purpose of any given moment. (Many an audience has been fooled into generating misplaced applause at the close of Holst's "Jupiter"!)

"The Man I Love" is a single song in a musical comedy. Its musical "completion"—in section and in its entirety—works on three syllogistic levels: within the song between the sections, within each section and within the continuity of the drama. We have explored the first two within the context of harmonic, rhythmic and melodic continuation.

The last is simply that it is part of a drama, and a formulaic one at that. In fact, it may be argued that the musical comedy found its prototypes in the Gershwin events of the early 1920s and those from light operas of the 1800s. "Lady Be Good," the musical from which "The Man I Love" comes, may also be considered an early prototype of the modern romantic comedy film. A romantic comedy film's plot reflects the typical frustrated love and sexual tension, miscues, embarrassing moments and successful romantic conclusion at the end of a performance of "Lady Be Good."

The audience would know, much as today's film audience knows, that the romantic comedy has really only one end in mind however the plot may twist in the middle. That expectation carries the spectator through whatever satisfying musical conclusions or scenes as they end, usually in the chase to the airport as the lover realizes what he/she is missing out on. This is not unlike the expectation a concertgoer has when listening to a symphony. A symphony has four movements and the expectation of a second following the first, the third following the second and an emphatically concluding fourth carries the listener through each cadence in the same way it carries through each exposition or development. This is one reason why a musical comedy or a theme-and-variations hangs together in spite of the chunky form: it is not *expected* to end at any one of these sections. It seems that many seem interminable because composers acknowledge the inability to write a successful conclusion as they continue to come with new variations: it seems a shame to simply end when all are waiting for continuity.

Cognitive Anticipation

On a micro level, however, the brain deals with sections in much the same way. The educated anticipation of what is "supposed" to happen supersedes the foils an enterprising composer may throw into the mix. This may be because of the short latency in stimuli response and perception.[8]

It is possible that the stimulus-response latency requires the brain to "think" ahead, anticipating the next event in the song. Music is, after all, sequential by nature on macro- and micro-levels, even down to the periodic soundwaves that dictate a pitch. This micro-level is integral to the perception of pitches, their perception individually as the ratio of frequency to time contributes to a single pitch as well as the interaction of multiple frequencies in a resultant *Klang*.

Such multiple levels of perception play heavily into a listener's enjoyment of a piece. The complete periods of the musical comedy refrain and its ability to stand alone as a song without the verse call into question the effective methods for applying continuity as a principle. This is also true of its concert counterpoints, in the Schubert lieder, and the "periodic" symphony. Even in a nebulous mass such as the tonal fantasia, the sections of completion within the piece allow for the idea of continuity as a principle.

The four aspects of continuity described above—rhythmic, harmonic, melodic and syllogistic momenta—can be applied to the most chopped up forms in concert (or popular) music. Even the theme-and-variations method in classical and blues forms, with its propensity for completeness at the end of each repetition, benefits from some aspect of continuity. Other aspects may be examined, such as intensity, performance effect, dynamics and texture, which can indicate or support an incomplete cadence's propensity for progressive propulsion. There is potential for new analysis techniques through continuity.

7

Tone-Sustaining Issues

The sustaining of frequency to the point of auditory perception in a melody often determines the perception of pitch and thus harmony. This perception is subjective but there are mitigating factors that help determine, including harmonics, continuity and context, and envelope. One reason a so-called "audio-to-MIDI" function in notation software and digital audio workstations (DAW) is problematic is the lack of intuitive artificial intelligence in a computer algorithm, which cannot tell distinguish between intended notes and incidental frequencies. Moreover, it cannot tell the "intent" or purpose of any given note, chord or frequency at any given moment for it is not given on a linear basis and cannot understand context, culture or style (Ex. 28).

> Note: a computer cannot tell if the notes in are played (m. 1) or resonated (m. 2)

Figure 28. Played notes vs. harmonic resonances

It is much worse than a human listener, who with "built-in" intuition who still has problems discerning "intent." A computer cannot tell whether the first five audible and distinctive harmonics are played notes, sounding resonances or psychoacoustically implied tones. When one considers that Messiaen and others believed that distinctive harmonics extended up to or beyond f^{12}, it complicates the matter further.

Short Tones

A short, vertical tone, such as in an orchestra "hit," has no melody to speak of, since any changing lateral motion literally does not exist, without progression. Context is everything, much as the letter "a" can mean anything without the context of surrounding letters, and even within "cat," the three letters have little meaning beyond an indicator. While "cat" can imply a feline animal, without placement, not to mention

56

overall intent and context, it can also mean "cattail" or "cat tail" strictly based upon the placement of each letter within additional "information." From that point, it can provide further information within a sentence, paragraph or even book (in context, "cat" by itself can evoke a child's book, or an Edgar Allan Poe story).[1]

If our synthesizer sound called "orchestra hit" is made up of a C chord, with its played and perceived tones, it can also imply multiple things, depending upon the context of progression. In the same way, the tone itself must be long enough to not only produce a periodic sound-wave but one long enough to interact with other tones and be perceived by the ear and brain, otherwise there will be no real perception of pitch much less context. As with continuity in all of its approaches, length, context and perception all combine to provide cohesive information.

Therefore, there is only the short perception of harmony, as all tones resonate and interact *only* vertically, should they play at the same time. An exception may be argued with independent interaction between lines such as in pretonal music, where the absence of a third or more voice prevents a completed chordal matrix. But in this case, they no longer occur simultaneously: they are heard independently, at most melodically, and thus with far less harmonic context.

Perception may include the residual element of continuity and Larson's "trace." Much like the concept of film scoring "hits," the brain processes visual and audible cues at different speeds. This allows a composer to place and perform orchestra hits within a surprisingly wide margin of error: the observer will line them up with a great deal of forgiveness, depending, of course, upon the length of both media's hits.

Figure 29. Bach, JS. *Praeludium in Dmoll* (BWV 851, from MS) (Bach, JS. *Praeludium in Dmoll* (BWV 851, from MS)

In spite of the shortness of the notes and the tones themselves, the repetition of the *alberti bass* and similar moments in Bach's keyboard pieces (such as his *Praeludia*) serve to mimic a sustained texture and thus uses repetition as a way to sustained tone. I have demonstrated his *Praeludia* to classes, demonstrating minimalism, by repeating each chord representation several times, changing the sustain of a keyboard to the short duration of a xylophone and increasing the tempo by a factor of six. The individual notes are lost, and the harmonic rhythm becomes evident as the repetition permeates instrumental and acoustic resonances, generating sustaining harmonics, and filling the *Klang* of each chord throughout its duration.

Another exception may be made regarding individual parts with differing tones and by extension, volume. However, in the context of harmony, it must be remembered that tone is first a perception, and second, contributes to the overall harmonic spectrum. So ultimately, it does not matter what instrument produces the frequencies, as long as we consider the aggregate. It is possible for disparate instruments to make up the same frequency spectrum at any given moment, to produce a similar sound.

Finally, volume will color the harmonic perspective and matrix, as phasing changes the color with frequency amplitude from resonant sources and changes in individual frequencies. If an oboe with a spectrum that emphasizes B_{990} plays in unison with a flute and a clarinet that—regardless of their fundamental—have spectra that also emphasize B_{990}, that frequency will stand out as a significant color in the total harmonic matrix.

A tone must be long enough for frequencies to interact. Long tones will be long enough to interact due to the sustain portion of the envelope's elongation of the periodic soundwave. Normally, this is not an issue as anything long enough to be perceived as a "tone" will last long enough to phase, however short. While the idea of "long" is arbitrary, for the purposes of this book a "long" tone should be long enough where phasing creates an audible tone, for our purposes, 30 Hz or above. Depending on the frequency, it may be present but not detected by the listener, hence, our 30 Hz, which builds in a margin of error.[2]

Shorter tones will create incidental phasing, superimposing chord tones and creating difference tones and resulting harmonic matrices. In this case, the matrix will function as a short-lived harmony, even if low frequency oscillation such as beat waves are not present due to the shortness of the tone.

Time is of consideration here, as it takes more than one superimposed period to create phasing, much as periodic soundwaves are needed to create frequency or pitch. As fewer cycles pass through in a second (comparatively, given a consistent speed of sound) in a lower frequency, there are fewer "opportunities" for phasing interaction not to say perceptible LFOs and difference tones.

Clearly, as higher frequencies create a higher resolution and more waves per second, an LFO or difference tone has more "chance" to be produced through phasing interaction. The ratio for frequency to time, may be described as follows.

Two or more audible frequencies are superimposed and the difference tone must be higher than 30 Hz or the theoretically lowest audible frequency, given some margin for individual perception. The lower frequency must be equal to or higher than 30 Hz for there to be an audible frequency. The higher frequency must be high enough to produce an audible difference tone of 30 Hz or more (>60 Hz). The higher frequency's duration must last for at least enough cycles to produce an audible difference tone, which we will designate as one second, or 30 cycles.

So a 500 ms burst of frequencies at 60 Hz and 30 Hz will produce a 15-cycle phase with a difference tone at 30 Hz. But a 100 ms burst (6 and 3 cycles, respectively) will technically or theoretically produce a 3-cycle phase, still at 30Hz but undetectable. A 1:2 cycle is in phase and modifies the existing wave shape without producing a distinctive difference tone due to harmonics and the natural confusion of the ear to distinguish harmonics and played tones.

At what point do we say it is too short?

$$f_1 - f_2 = f_d > 30_{Hz}$$
$$f_1 = 60Hz$$
$$f_2 = 30_{Hz}$$
$$\text{Ratio of } f_{Hz} : 10_{ms}$$

$$\frac{10_{ms}}{(60_{Hz} - 30_{Hz}} = 333_{ms}$$

Figure 30. Determining phasing time

Therefore, a 30 Hz difference tone must occur for at least 333 ms to be considered effective. A higher frequency, such as our previous examples of a C triad, produces a difference tone of C_{264}:

$$G_{792} - C_{528} = C_{264}$$

$$\frac{10_{ms}}{(792_{Hz} - 528_{Hz}} = \frac{10_{ms}}{264_{Hz}} = 37.8_{ms}$$

Figure 31. Phasing time for higher frequencies

High difference tones yet will produce something even shorter. It is important to consider that these are not necessarily detectable by the listener but an arbitrary indicator of the formation of a matrix.

Therefore, a very short "hit" in musical terms will have the same harmonic matrix as a long note. Our "orchestra hit," which is actually long in this context, has the necessary duration for both a matrix and for listener detection, especially when one considers the built in reverberation in the General MIDI or industry standard sound.[3] Even the lowest tones are long enough and supported by their octaves to be reinforced and register a harmonic matrix.

Envelope

One of the considerations is the amount of energy applied and absorbed by the vibrating medium. This, of course, depends upon the size and mass of the medium. The formula for moving mass is basic physics; we will concentrate on the acoustic aspects as it applies to music and to our harmonic matrices. But the important thing to consider is how media reacts to any initiating energy of any instrument, whether struck, bowed, or buzzed.[4]

As any body set in motion is affected by mass, inertia and the applied energy, these dynamics interact to produce vibrating frequency action. A piano and a flute, for example, have similar harmonic spectra in the upper registers (C^5 and higher) but sound very differently because of the way a struck, strung instrument reacts versus a metal-encased column of air that is blown, react to applied energy. In some cases, the stiffness of the material—ironwood in a xylophone compared to a more flexible metal bar in a vibraphone—produces initial frequencies that are quickly dampened.

Synthesizers are programmed by imitating the harmonic spectrum of and instrument, as well as its *envelope*, sometimes referred to by programmers as the "ADSR" for its components. The envelope is the initiating and resonating of vibration in a medium, whose mass, stiffness and initiating action define its sound on a temporal basis.

The four components are:

- *Attack*—initial application of energy, which takes extra to move the mass from a static state to one in motion
- *Decay*—Once energy has been applied to get the mass in motion, extra energy is no longer required to maintain that motion
- *Sustain*—The consistent application of energy to maintain vibration
- *Release*—Residual energy within the vibrating medium (kinetic vibration) when external energy (sustain) is removed

A vehicle progressing from a stop sign on a level ground is a good analogy.

- To get the car (around 1.5 tons in weight) moving extra gas is required, and added until the vehicle is at the desired speed (*attack*).
- Once the car is moving at the desired speed, the operator backs off of the gas (*decay*) as the extra push is no longer needed for acceleration.
- Once at consistent speed, a minimum of gas/accelerator is needed to maintain the speed of the vehicle (*sustain*).
- Once the driver lets off the gas, the car coasts (*release*)

Energy, Time and Frequency

The higher the energy, the more resonance in a physical body, and thus, generally, the higher frequencies have high amplitude and thus interact in phasing. For example, a cymbal, rolled with a soft mallet, sounds brighter when the operator applies more force. Each is brighter with more energy, so that a cymbal roll tends to a brighter sound when more energy is applied through the roll. A cymbal roll adds resonance to existing vibration with each time the mallet strikes; this is why it works in a composition as a way to increase momentary intensity.

In Ex. 32a and 32b, examine the comparative timelines and spectra for each instrument. Note the shape of each spectrum based on amplitude and presence. Note the organization of the chart, with the relative frequency in the y-axis and time in the x-axis. In 4a, the piano, a G_{396}, shows a sudden attack propagated by the striking of a string with a hammer. Frequencies up to 8 kHz are present at the beginning. However, the piano has an immediate decay due to the high tension of the string and no sustain (consistent application of energy) to speak of, and the release does not only show the diminishing of overall amplitude but as one can see on the diagram, an exponential decrease in higher frequency as time progresses. Figure 32b, "pop horns," have a sharp attack and an initial decay but while the presence of harmonic remain consistent due to a strong sustain (from continuous breath or backpressure), there is a slight attenuation from the initial attack.

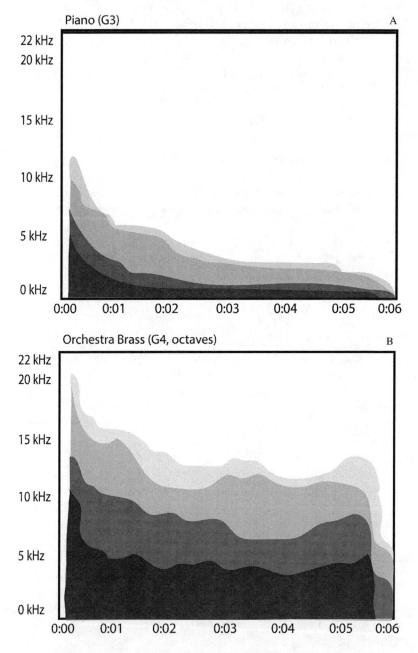

Figure 32. Comparative spectra of piano and orchestra brass

In Figs. 33a and 33b, the string sounds show a slow attack as the bow takes time to excite vibration in the string. We see little decay as a result and as the bow continuously applies energy to the string, a consistent array of harmonic amplitudes.

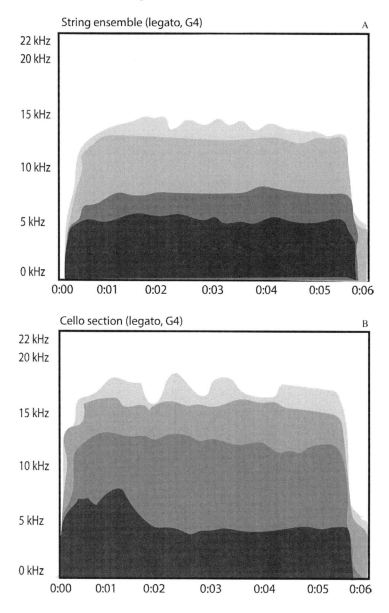

Figure 33. Comparative spectra of cello and string ensemble

In Figure 34 below, we find a correlation between resonance and amplitude in the comparative brass. A similar ensemble, plays at two different amplitudes (based upon the appropriate measure per style: "pop" which is louder and edgier, vs. "the orchestra brass in Figure 32," which in this case is a sustained chorale and thus softer and mellower):

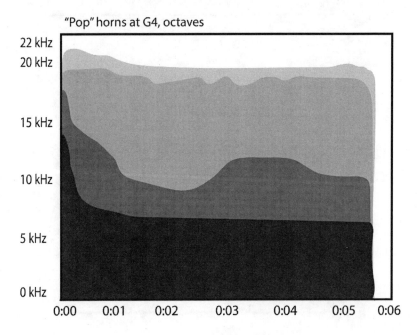

Figure 34. Spectrum of pop horns

In musical practice, our dynamics determine tone as well as instrument sound. The more energy that is applied to the vibrating medium, the more the mass reacts until more material resonates, creating higher amplitude in higher harmonics, making them and difference tones more audible. A classic example is the change in tone from a French horn's "mellower" sound at soft levels to the designated "brassy" tone. While the air column, configured by the shape and length of the bore, resonates more strongly with lower frequencies, the "brassy" designation directs the player to play loud enough so that the metal of the instrument itself oscillates.

A violin's sound ranges from a muted string with the high frequencies suppressed, to a brittle edginess, with the added sound of the bow scraping across the strings. The instrument's resonance has as much to do with the vibration of the construction and material of the resonator body as the string-and-bow action itself.[5] Ralph Vaughan Williams'

Fantasia on a Theme by Thomas Tallis[6] is notable for its interweaving and exchanges of tone colors throughout two string orchestras and a string quartet. These three colors range from the more strident natural string sound in solo instruments, to an orchestra with mutes for a darker sound, to an unmuted ensemble sound.

Figure 35. *Fantasia* interweaving

The antiphonal approach to the writing directs the "echoing" orchestra to use mutes and play at a lower level. The mutes dampen the strings vibrating action to attenuate higher harmonics for a mellower sound, while the other orchestra, unmuted, also plays at a higher dynamic. When the groups play antiphonally, the echo is enhanced with the softened tone; when together, it provides a darker tonality to the *tutti* effect.

8

Principles of Separation

Introduction

Through the considerations of interaction, we can determine how and how much any particular note, not to mention parts and instruments, can contribute to the melodic or harmonic purposes of a composition or performance. Dimensions of separation can help define how to separate voices, or instruments and conversely how to integrate them for harmonic effect.

Aggregate Components of Compositional Separation

Dynamics of separation can be organized into a three-dimensional space model. Engineers as well as composers may find this beneficial in mixing and writing, as the combination provide avenues of melodic, harmonic and rhythmic separation.

- "Height" analogously considers frequency separation and the harmonics as well as the placement of the notes themselves.
- "Width" or time-based separation identifies placement of each note or melody in the context of the timing, phrase development, and the envelope or shape of each oscillator or instrument
- "Depth" or amplitude separation is simply how loud each part or note is relative to the others

"Vertical" or Frequency Dimension

There are two components based on this concept as shown in Figure 36 on the next page.

Instrumental location in the above diagram is defined as that where

67

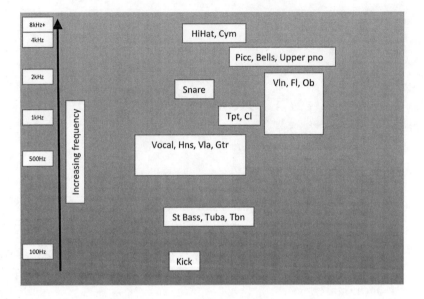

Figure 36. Vertical separation

the instrument of concern is primarily located. A violin's range is from G_{396} to as high as G_{7040}, although an arbitrary note may be selected for our illustrative purposes, around C_{2112}. An electric or acoustic bass in its main function in a pop style ranges from as low as C_{132} (with a classical extension or B_{124} with a five/six string version) to E_{330}. Voices, guitar and piano often function as mid-range, as lead or as harmonic support, from C_{264} to C_{1056}.

A second concern is the frequency spectrum of any given instrument. A sound engineer recognizes that an electric bass in a heavy metal rock band may have a higher comparative amplitude at mid-range (ca. 400–800 Hz) than in jazz or hip hop styles; it is appropriate for that style but many engineers prefer a duller tone more in keeping with modern pop and hip hop, emphasizing the lower frequencies from 100 Hz to a maximum of 300 Hz.

These color the consideration of the instrument's ranges, as the spectrum emphasizes harmonics outside those actually played. The "EQ" or frequency "Equalizer" function of a sound board can modify these in varying detail according to frequency selection, bandwidth and amplitude (plus or minus "0"). Separation of frequency must take both of these in consideration, so that the resonance of the instrument is maximized and used at its maximum benefit for the aggregate presentation. However, these principles can apply to any sound: instrumental, natural, electronic or artificially constructed.

There are several qualifiers. As mentioned, different styles dictate specific approaches in mixing when working with frequencies. The sense of harmony can change. A fuller, muddier or lush sound is better attained by "crowding" harmonic frequencies together, intentionally ignoring the principles of separation we are discussing. Often, specific lines and melodies need to be brought out. By avoiding harmonics/frequencies in the immediate area of the melody, a melodic line can be heard separately from the cloud of harmonics, or a texture whose harmonic cloud extends widely.

Time-Based Dimension

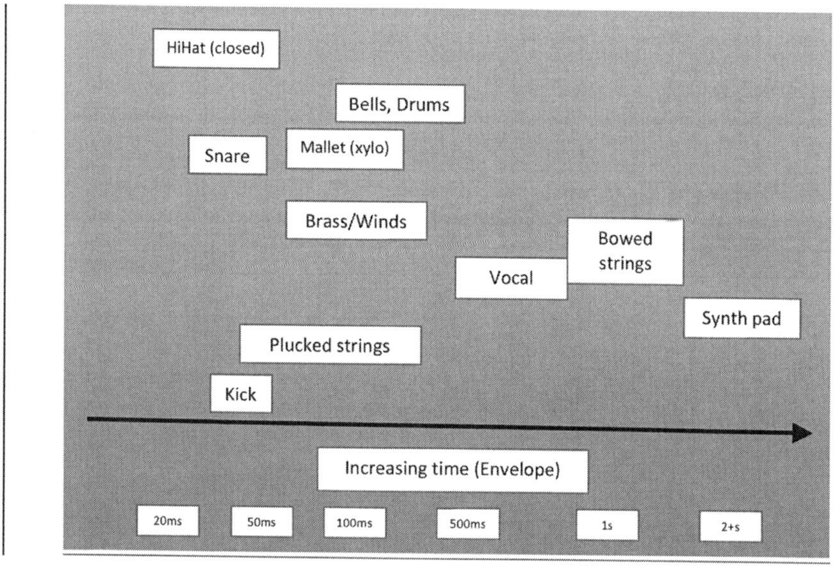

Figure 37. Time-based separation

A "horizontal" or time-based perspective deals with the duration, envelope and placement of sound events. Strategically based, these events can emphasize frequencies at given times as well as separate out from other lines or texture units. Considerations in this dimension include repetition, duration and envelope.

Repetition

As noted earlier, repeated notes basically have the same effect as long or elongated notes but this becomes more evident on a faster, even as quickly as on a millisecond basis. A rolled mallet instrument involves the repeated attack of a mallet against the oscillating body, most times maintaining a vibration before the release mode of the envelope. This is an active, measurable action, perpetrated by the musician.

A second is a similar action on a microtemporal basis in a violin as the hair of the bow repeatedly catches and releases a string. This catch generates potential energy, releasing kinetic energy and generating a complex waveform along the string. Subsequent "catch-and-release" moments maintain the wave motion and multiple harmonic vibrations. In a similar fashion, the buzz of a brass player is the start-stopping of a flow of air, exciting the standing wave inherent in the cavity of the instrument. It is the same action as the vocal chords in a singer.

Depending upon the length, repetition can be part of the environment. Once a person becomes inured to an object, it becomes background or part of the environment. In this case, pure repetition becomes background. Note the worker in a flower shop or in a horse barn: in either case, initial exposure to the smell will allow a person to react one way or the other. However, repetitive days, hours, minutes or seconds of smelling the same thing inures a person to that smell, until no longer does a flower shop smell "nice" (as subjective as that is) or "nasty."

A psychoacoustic phenomenon is the sonic wearing down of the ear's cilia, which are specifically and finely tuned to corresponding frequencies. For this reason, industry practice recommends that studio engineers keep "mixing" sessions to four hours at 84dB: the ear simply gets physically tired of constant information input, to say nothing of the brain's capacity to process it.

Combine this with specific frequencies, such as minimalistic music, tinnitus or artificial stimuli, and frequency-specific sections of the basilar membrane begin to be unresponsive. They literally lie down because they are too tired to respond. A sound engineer under this condition is in a situation where certain frequencies become literally a "pedal" tone, sustained and unrelenting as music shifts frequencies around it.

Compositionally, a producer working on an entire album in the key of C sees a psychological, physical and psychoacoustical impact on the ability to respond objectively. Consumers listening to said album or film goers listening to the same theme in the same key over and over get tired of hearing the same key. Worst, the same frequencies impact the listener: C permeates the air with C_{132} and all its harmonics, not to mention others played in sympathy.

Environment

A second type of situation where the listener can have a difficult time in identifying elements involves the environment. When a person is immersed into an environment, an instinct of self-preservation takes an inventory of the surroundings to ascertain danger, opportunity or interaction. This can be as conscious as an intelligence operative scanning a restaurant for an enemy or as subconsciously as a student walking into a classroom.

Once the student sits, the initial sonic input (and other elements, such as lighting) becomes muted. It is still there but is in the background and is no longer taken note of: the white noise of the projector overhead, the cough of a neighbor in a season of illness, the crackling of paper and the swish of clothing from classmates, or the tapping of keys or smartphone input. Any perceived change in the environment is then noted. It is in the environment or "texture" that any new sonic information is noted, for the person identifies it on a basic level as a threat or opportunity. Among the sea of audio information above, the student will note an unusual ringtone, another student tripping on the way to the desk, or the professor walking in. This also refers to the absence of sound: the projector turning off its fan, for example.

The musical style of minimalism uses this principle relentlessly, as does certain aleatoric or atonal pieces. John Cage's infamous 4'33" relies on the environment to provide the entirety of the piece. The author's composition for choir, percussion and celesta, *Cherubim Bells*, takes note of the environment as follows, relying on it for acoustic compositional contribution rather than interference:

> Composer's Note: Although this piece can be done conventionally, half the choir should "stage" whisper the rhythms of each part at the same time the other half sings the pitch of the same part…. If possible, the venue itself should be absolutely free of external, non-acoustic noise (HVAC turned off for this tune, for example), otherwise sibilant effects may not be heard. The more reverberant the venue, the better: the long rests are designed for this.[1]

Texture as Environment and Instrument

While it has historically been convenient to identify "instruments" as a single producer of a tone and as organized groups or ensembles, in combinatorial writing the composer shifts paradigms to better categorize the sounds. This approach helps identify electronic, vocal and soundscape sources as well as conventional instruments.

Several things come into play here, as we will examine below. As we have seen, interaction of notes creates an immense complex of frequencies, whose extent reflects amplitude and resonance. But there are also elements of time and human perception. While we "hear" these frequencies, it is difficult to identify them consciously, if at all; we get an impression, a cloud, as it were. We see a color, and not an aggregate of light frequencies: the whole is literally much more than the sum of its parts.

There comes a point where this identification is shrouded even more so in the repetition of notes, sequentially or melodically. At this point, we must give up the idea of note presentation much less melody and identify the effect as a "cloud" of harmony, or texture. However, there are other ways to separate: a texture simply becomes one more collective avenue of separation, or even an instrument unto itself as we will see.

Other avenues of separation delve into lateral or time-based perception as well. Some of these are long-term, measured in phrases and compositional periods and well known to any improviser or composer. Others are as minimalistic as to be measured in amplitude and time under decibels and milliseconds. In its simplest form, we looked at the comparison of chordal harmony and the "cloud" of harmony in a complex textural feature, such as polyrhythm and cyclic construction as heard in African and gamelan performances.

The mind—unless actively choosing to do so—does not separate out the different instruments and indeed it is impossible to do so when the envelope and frequency spectra as well as range are similar. A "displacement" theory[2] identifies the inability of the mind to separate out melodies when the frequency spectrum and envelope are identical or related. In the opening bars of the last movement of Tchaikovsky's Sixth Symphony, the principle is clear as the strings sonically portray a descending chord cluster with an apparent melody, not unlike a jazz chord and its voicing. However, the individual parts show a very different composition:[3]

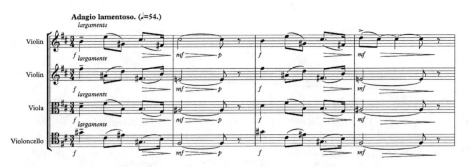

Figure 38. Sixth Symphony, mvt. 4 (Tchaikovsky)

Figure 39. Aggregate *Klänge* in Tchaikovsky's Sixth Symphony

The term "wavestacking" has often been used in various software to identify techniques of combining disparate instruments into new sounds. By understanding this pragmatic approach to a synthesizer's emulation of acoustic instruments, we can better understand the roles of instrument combinations. For example, a popular combination superimposes an acoustic piano sound with a string "patch" or synthesis. This provides a piano with sustain, or a string "pad" with a better-defined attack. The first gives a warmth to a piece with a slow tempo, sparse notation or minimal instrumentation; the second provides definition to a rhythmic piece while still maintaining a string tonality.

It is glib to name a synthesis patch, for example, "brass ensemble," understanding that it is a combination of brass instruments. However, popular and electronic musicians recognize the patch as having a specific sound, specific to the application at hand; it just happens to have a name that has allusions to its sound. Its sound happens to recall a "brassy" collective but specifically as only synthesizer programming can make it.

A second example is the overused, so-called "Orch Hit," literally a collection of orchestra-type instruments, each assigned to, or reinforcing the harmonics of a major triad, from A_{55} to A_{3520} as well as noise elements in the percussion. It is a sound well known in techno, dance, hip hop and rap cultures, as well as other electronica, as being an easily reproduced "sample" file. By understanding this pragmatic approach to a synthesizer's emulation of acoustic instruments, we can better understand the roles of instrument combinations.

Under this consideration, we can classify a "texture" as an "instrument." In some ways, this is not unlike the technique often termed "granular synthesis," in which case "packets" of sound, motifs, groups, rhythms, etc., are kept intact but rearranged as needed. Such a "texture" may be a collective of instrumental parts whose aggregate effect renders the parts indistinguishable but more of a type of unit.

Under this definition, it becomes easier to classify texture among the other elements, within the context of separation. All components of a piece can together and interactively be allowed to be heard separately or combined against a backdrop of environment.

- Frequency—a harmonic texture has the elements of played and harmonic frequencies that may range widely or limited, based on the context of the composition, sound cloud, or environment

- Duration—A texture, by definition, may hold as an effect from an environment.
- Length of each component, packet or grain will determine the static nature of the environment and its strength.
- If the texture changes noticeably, it ceases to be considered "environment" as an environment in our application must be static by definition.
- If it changes, its harmonic components create a harmonic "progression," not to be confused with a "chord progression," although they are related.
- Amplitude—Amplitude will vary based upon the components but while give an aggregate volume level in relationship to melodic and other instrumental elements and vary in its makeup through assigned volume and envelope.

In popular music, writers and producers use a principle of adding instruments to create growing intensity. For example, rock songs often begin with a drum pattern that underscores the subsequent groove and/or riff. Two measures of drumbeat provide a consistent "groove" or rhythmic feel, with minimal variation. The ear attends to the groove for the first measure, then places it as a background when the next instrument enters, often a guitar or electric bass. The listeners focus then is on the new, the change in the "groove environment," as it were, which is no longer noted. Repetition, especially on a regular basis as in a drum pattern, becomes background.

It should be noted that other principles in arranging can use this idea of environment. When the drums "fill" or lead into another section, ceases altogether, or when it stops the groove in vertical "hits," the listener attends to the distraction, as the "environment" or groove is interrupted. Any change in the environment is immediately noted.

Rhythmic Duration

One aspect is that given the change in amplitude for each impact, short tones will be heard among long tones of the same frequency. In this case, the sudden bursts of amplitude in an otherwise static tone or even texture unit (TU) combine to bring forth these tones in their specific frequencies.

On a practical basis, look at Vaughan Williams' *Fantasia on a Theme of Thomas Tallis*. In m. there is a *pizzicato* in one string ensemble against the same *arco* notes in another ensemble. Yet, both parts are heard: the *pizzicato* because of the higher amplitude in the attack, and the sustain supporting the tone in the *arco*. See Figure 40.

Figure 40. Short sounds help separating similar instruments and spectra

Phrase Cooperation or Interaction

In jazz, gospel, and other popular music styles, "call-and-response" or "phrase-and-fill" are common. This shows a distinct, long-term example of linear, or time-based separation. Classical music composition often identifies this approach as primary and secondary melodies on a linear, not concurrent, basis.

In the case of jazz, the main melody plays and as it is often sung, played by a wind instrument, or written as if it were, there are distinct breaks between phrases. An improvisatory instrument will overlap the ending and beginning of the next phrase but providing a literal "filling" of improvised melody between the two. Each is heard, and moreover, the fill is stylistically complimentary to the main melody. This technique is also used expressly in the ensemble arranging, along with "hits" (see above regarding short tones' audibility among a larger harmonic texture.). See Figure 41 on the next page.

Depth—Amplitude, or Volume Designations

The best known example of separation is that of amplitude. Simply put, the louder instruments will be heard above the others. What

Figure 41. Melody and fills provide support and separation

is notable about this, in the context of our discussion, is that the background often becomes a variable texture unit (VTU). A VTU is important because it contains a harmonic progression, changing matrices as the chords and lines change. But it is nebulous in its compositional role as a support, not a focus.

This begins with the bass and kick in popular music, and with the

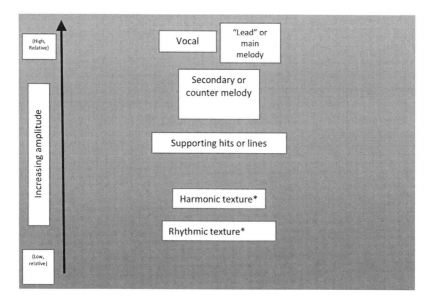

Figure 42. Amplitude separation. * = multiple instruments

tuba and basses in orchestral music. Keyboard, harp, and other instruments that spread over the audible range contribute to this array. The mid-range instruments provide the tonal direction, as supported by the lower frequency instruments' harmonic series. Sometimes this goes awry as internal non-harmonic tones change the matrices, or the composition intentionally creates tension through dissonance. In keeping with a linear principle outlined below, higher instruments tend to ornament or double lower tones, again supporting harmonics. However, as will be seen, these are now high enough to only reinforce audible harmonics of the first two, maybe three, orders (octave, fifth and second octave). This is an acoustics reason for doubling the melody in the high instruments. The high instruments need some sort of tonal foundation to give body: any less will sound thin, reedy and unsupported. Lower octave instruments are given extra body, as the high instruments support the harmonic series in the octave. The above, with the noted exception, are relegated to the background, moving and shifting with internal lines, harmonic support and matrices.

Because of the amplitude difference, focus is on the "lead" instrument line or lines, as the case may be, and the listener will not particularly notice the background support and texturing. One other exception exists with the linear or time-based separation, and the "fill" principle. With the absence of the lead in the "fill" areas, the background now comes into focus and a secondary melody, supported by other dimensions or not, becomes the focus as within the context of the texture, it is louder than the other.

We have three levels in this example: lead, secondary, and texture, with the secondary fading in importance against the textural background while the lead is present.

9

Linear Concepts

Harmonic Separation and Consonance

Putting aside the concept of harmony for harmony's sake at this point, we can look at the interaction of lines, as did the pre-tonal composers did until the eighteenth century. Even though we have emphasized harmonic interaction, primarily from the tertian construction perspective, that is with three or more tones organized in thirds, line-to-line analysis can reveal some interesting concepts for composition as well. There are a couple of things to keep in mind.

First, consonance increases as notes separate. The reason for this reflects the general lack of interaction between each note's harmonic series as we will see below. Second, the top note is arguably within the harmonic series of the lower note, if placed high enough in its series. Thus, in line with our concept of consonance voicing and its compatibility with the harmonic series, the upper note reinforces an existing resonance of the lower note, and can even force or amplify the harmonic, even if existing resonance of the original oscillator precludes that. Once we consider microtonal scales, the concept of consonance embraces a great deal more than a single tertian octave. Relative consonance and voicing are also dependent upon location and the perception of hearing.

We hear tonality in the mid-range (between 300 Hz and 1000 Hz on a practical compositional basis, 3200 according to Rossing and Houtsma[1]) since it has the best combination of harmonics that support chordal resonance. One reason a triad based upon a tone around 100 Hz (say, C_{132}) is "muddy" is that the harmonics produced are most evident in the mid-range, not to mention the overwhelming presence of timbre clusters existing very loudly beginning with f^{12} chromaticism and higher microtonal resonances.

If we take this to an extreme, we examine extremely low but still "audible" pitches. As stated earlier, human hearing extends down to 20 Hz, and to about 30 Hz on a practical basis. However, are we truly

79

hearing this? A series of clicks occurring at 30 Hz may be considered a "pitch" by some but experiments demonstrate pitch's subjectivity based on length, intensity and frequency range (300 Hz–3200 Hz).[2,3] Once we get below a certain point—again arbitrary as pitch is subjective—it becomes difficult to identify whether we are hearing the pitch fundamental or the interactive harmonics its resonance generates. A perfectly controlled system (with no acoustic or elective resonance) generating a 30 Hz sine wave is virtually inaudible to most people, and is subject to its intensity or physical SPL. Eventually, depending again on the frequency and level, a person may identify "something" but not necessarily a pitch compared to a presence or a sense of low power. "House," EDM or hip hop effectively use this concept in the synth bass to help define their unique stylistic signatures.

By itself, it is not a problem, with the harmonic series merely being reinforced by proper voicing for consonance and matching the rest of the series. However, it becomes an issue when we add the rest of a simple triad alone, E_{165} and G_{198}. Here we produce additional harmonics belonging to these roots, with difference tones and any resonating harmonics:

C_{132}	C_{264}	G_{396}	C_{528}	E_{660}	G_{792}
E_{165}	E_{396}	$\mathbf{B_{495}}$	E_{660}	$G\#_{825}$	$\mathbf{B_{990}}$
G_{198}	G_{396}	D_{594}	$\mathbf{G_{792}}$	$\mathbf{B_{990}}$	D_{1188}

As we will see, these harmonics are present as part of the matrix belonging to the C triad. What makes things complicated is that these are the six "audible" and identifiable harmonics (including the fundamental) that Helmholtz claimed was evident in all acoustically produced tonal sounds. At this range, the tones, as prominent as they are, cannot fail to produce combination tones from the clashes of B to C (2 cases) and G to G♯. Higher harmonics (C_{1056} and above) are also stronger in auditory perception in this range simply because it is more accessible by the listener in the mid-range than a vague clustering of timbre-defining frequencies.

A related issue for consideration is a line or chord that is too high. In this case, the resonance and harmonics are lost, as the upper (timbre) harmonics are lost to the range of human hearing. The same triad placed very high, (C_{2112}, E_{2640}, and G_{3168}) does not contain the audible character or timbre as it would in mid- or lower frequencies. Much of the defining character, the timbre, is lost at the upper end of human hearing. It is thus relegated to almost a simple sine wave as far as human perception goes, keeping in mind that the audible or distinctive lower harmonics are out of the mid-range:

$$C_{2112} \qquad C_{4224} \qquad G_{6336} \qquad G_{8448} \qquad E_{10560} \qquad G_{12672}$$

At C_{2112}, any frequency higher than f^9 is difficult to hear as an actual sound for all except the child whose natural exposure hasn't lost the ability to hear higher frequencies. Something as "low" as f^{10} at circa 21 kHz is above the range of human hearing, and the harmonic is considered by some to be well within the range of detectable tones if the fundamental is in a lower range. Note this does not apply to phased difference tones of hypersonic frequencies, nor those that are medium-dependent, as we will see in later chapters.

So once two instruments, even those of differing harmonic spectra, begin fundamentals above C_{2112}, the unique harmonics that define the instruments' timbres exist but are inaudible, basically rendering each instruments' sound much closer to the other, barring envelope, artificial resonances or wavestacking below that frequency. See Figure 43 below, for a Fourier analysis diagram, depicting the complex array of sine wave frequencies in a "simple" square wave. The 14th harmonic is shown superimposed over the aggregate square wave as an example. The majority of harmonics are not distinguishable but together demonstrate and complete the shape of this square fundamental wave. One can imagine how complex the Fourier analysis of an acoustic instrument may be.[4]

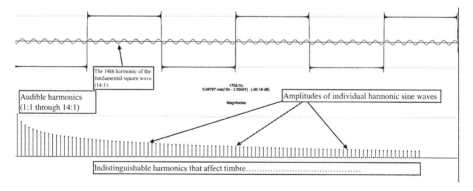

Figure 43. Fourier analysis of a square audio wave

This particular waveform emphasizes specific amplitudes of only the even harmonics (H[1], H[2], H[4], H[8], etc.), which defines its unique tone.

The fundamental frequency of the example above is only 90 Hz. The last frequency pictured (not the last sounded) is actually 22.52 kHz, well above the limit of human hearing. Were we to eliminate all harmonics above the, say, 20th harmonic, the nature of the waveform would be completely different as the characteristics of its timbre change drastically. The tone would be "rounder" or duller (as per Helmholtz's descriptions) without the higher frequencies to give it any brightness. There may also be a shifting of amplitude apportionment as the energy is redistributed to the lower harmonics and fundamental.

This "round" or dull tone also occurs on a practical basis at higher fundamental frequencies, for it becomes immaterial whether a harmonic is suppressed, eliminated, or simply is not heard. In the above display, a fundamental at 1.05 kHz (about $C_\#^5$) would lose any audible timbre-influencing harmonics at the 19th harmonic, or 20.45 kHz. The last visible harmonic (the 247th) has a frequency of a staggering 266.1 kHz! That is 228 timbre-defining harmonics lost to the listener.

For a compositional example, see movement 2, "Complaint," from the author's *Concerto No. 2 for Piano, Orchestra and Jazz Continuo*,[5] where the interplay in thirds between the upper piano and the soprano saxophone's upper octave has stripped spectra of timbre harmonics to the point where each instrument has spectral characteristics similar to the other. Therefore, the interaction of harmonics between two melodic parts, while not to be discounted in other octaves, are best for this reason demonstrated in the mid-range.

Figure 44. Spectra sound similar as higher harmonics disappear from aural range

Proximity and the Interplay of Harmonics

To review: higher harmonics are inaudible and may be considered increasingly "stripped" from pitches whose fundamentals are above C_{2112}, and pitches lower than C_{264} have increasing presence of harmonics as even the higher ones are lowered into the optimal listening range. This creates "muddy" and "thin" sounds, respectively. The primary issue is the relationship in octaves of the parts in this case. The example given below, from Bach's *Wie Wunderbarlich* (BWV 244), shows its original form.

Figure 45. *Wie wunderbarlich* **(Bach)**

For this purpose, we change the octaves of two parts in relationship to each other, using only the alto and soprano lines. (Once we consider more parts, we begin working with triads, and other more complicated chords and interactions.)

Far apart, the more individual lines are distinct, and the *perception* of harmony is fairly low. The harmonics of the lower melody have little or no impact on the notes or the harmonics of the upper voice.

Figure 46. Far separation = little harmonic perception

The opening notes ($E\flat_{157}$ and G_{3168}) have harmonics as audible to H^{12} well separate from each other, with $E\flat_{157}$ harmonic H^{12} at 1884 Hz, well below the fundamental of G_{3168}. Any difference tones that might reinforce harmony are too high and out of tune to create a fundamental harmonic base: $G_{3168} - E\flat_{157} = E\flat_{3011}$. With this absence of harmonic interaction or fundamental support, the lines are perceptibly independent of each other.

As the lines approach, the lines become less distinct and harmony perception increases. The harmonics of each voice begin to overlap, especially as the contours begin to approach at points. The opening notes are now $E\flat_{314}$ and G_{1584}, with H^{12} of $E\flat$ at 3768 Hz, well above the fundamental of G. This includes harmonics from H^5 to H^{11} as well. The difference tone is now lower and provides an additional triad support, at $E\flat_{1270}$. There is more audible perception of harmony in this case.

Figure 47. Closer soprano and alto parts

Closer together, we hear more perception of harmony as matrices interact and primary, note-defining frequencies are less distinct (see top of next page).

In Figure 48, closer lines diminish linear and melodic clarity but increase the perception of harmony, with opening notes at $E\flat_{628}$ and G_{792}. All harmonics of the lower note are above the fundamental frequency of

Figure 48. Matrices interact

the upper note, providing a complete interactive, if simple, matrix, and the difference tone is a solid $E\flat_{164}$.

Figure 49. The closest lines equal the greatest interaction and harmony

When the lines are closest possible, without compromising notes or contour, there is the least idea of melodic line but the highest degree of harmony. In this case, the harmonics of the bottom line are not only interacting but are completely entangled with those of the upper voice, as each relative partial is literally the same intervallic relationship with its relative partner (f^2-f^2, f^3-f^3, etc.) as its fundamental.

This makes Billings' and other "shaped-note" writers of the same century as Bach particularly interesting, as the arbitrary octave shift of the singers and their parts maintain a consistent chord structure. It is important to remember that any octave shift on the singers' parts is generally by choice, and so there is a good chance that the original octave is being sung by someone. This provides more of an octave reinforcement of parts, rather than a complete overhaul of octave placement. Thus, the final product is a lusher chord structure that still maintains chordal integrity.

10

Harmonic Permutations
of Chordal *Klang*

Introduction

While the overtone series and its counterpart, the so-called undertone series, have been explored ad nauseam over the last several hundred-odd years, the exploration of chord tones' relationships in a resonating context has yet to be fully developed. As chord tones interact with each other, they form interactive relationships that develop new pitches and reinforce others, forming a complex matrix that explains many facets of the resulting chordal *Klang*, or sonority. These relationships can be shown structurally in a theoretical and mathematical diagram, theoretical examples, and through acoustical analysis. Asmus declares that, "It would appear that the difference tone phenomenon occurs often in music performance and may have distinct effects on perceived tone quality."[1] He does not specify how this may occur, as the focus of his study was on the physical and psychoacoustical properties of the phenomenon.

That it has been accepted that inversions contain the "essence," or the sonority of their root positions has been part of the canon since at least Lippius. One with any kind of musical ear can identify a triad's root and its *Klang* regardless of inversion. An F Major triad still has the F "sound" regardless of whether an A or C is at the bottom of the presentation. Why this occurs goes beyond cultural bias, as shown in studies of African vocal music,[2] much of which is learned by rote and thus relies on natural, acoustic inclination as well as culture and training. Even untrained musicians who harmonize naturally understand aurally the triad that three-part (for example) harmony attempts to construct and they can adjust their parts in it to conform within that context, usually regardless of inversion. Cazden attempted to explain the ideas of consonance and dissonance by compiling the various theories dealing

86

psychoacoustic and acoustic aspects but failed to go beyond using harmonics as a primary arbiter. While he mentions combination tones as an avenue of perception, he does not go into how it impacts the construction and perception of simple, much less complex, chords. "In short, the properties' consonance and dissonance do not and cannot apply to intervals ... [but], encompasses the relevant and differential degrees of blending, fusion and coincidence among fundamentals, partials, combination tones and inharmonics [*sic*]."[3]

This chapter shows the interdependency of harmonics and combination tones, developing a matrix system proven by physical resonances. Going beyond culture and psychoacoustics lie issues in phase principles, "wavestacking" and additive synthesis, difference tones and additional harmonics that permeate our perception of what constitute a chord's sonority. Inversely, culture and psychoacoustics are directly impacted by these elements as styles, instrumental timbre and tonal qualities change to enhance or subdue them as shown in the tuning philosophies of diverse ethnicities.

One aspect these tests have shown is not necessarily the consistency within *Klang* of like types but the resonance within the just tuning system upon which each chord is based. Thus, the systematic and theoretical development of structural systems in this book will be based upon the resonance produced by each chord, no matter its length or tonal pervasiveness. It is expected that the results will show that while tolerance of tuning systems dictate certain aesthetic and cultural responses, the "forgiveness" a listener imparts upon a vertical sonority is actually greater than many assume. It is more than a mere adjustment of the cents of each tone but the wide variance of the implied and actual partials, and combination tones between them.

Approach

The concept of combination tones and harmonics as a perspective on fundamental tones have been applied to music theory expressly by such theorists as early as Helmholtz, and Schenker, and as late as Cazden and Hanžek. Helmholtz in particular explained the system extensively but didn't draw conclusions based on the resulting sonority or their implications so much as commentary upon the justification of intervals. He did say, however, that chords did produce multiple interactions, producing additional combination tones that could be heard. Cazden emphasized the relationship of the perception of consonance to the presence of combination tones of both types.[4] Patterson noted that the manipulating of harmonics had profound impact on the fundamental as well as the timbre characteristics.[5]

Helmholtz' conclusions, based upon physical observations, were limited in the ranges of amplitude and frequency. Modern technology can see beyond these limitations of the human ear, as valid and applicable as such observation may be, and can deconstruct a complex signal into its frequency components' details. There is some indication that human sensory and even aesthetic perception go beyond audible range as detected by the ear, and can even perceive ultralow and high frequencies, although not hear them or identify them as actual tones.[6] This is one of the foundations of the arguments regarding the benefits and disadvantages of digital versus analog recording technology, and their various renditions and resolutions. Thus, acoustically based approaches or aural observation alone cannot serve to complete experiments whose implications go well into psychological and supra-aural perception.

The Development of Structural Organization

In the nineteenth century, Helmholtz wrote *On the Sensations of Tone*, in which he outlined his observations on difference tones and resonance. In general, he referred to complex tones and while alluding to "simple tones" (e.g., fundamental sine waves), he believed there were no resonating implications inherent, even within the interactions of two or more tones. We have technological and other measurement capabilities that he did not have access to, and combined with his mechanical and physical observations, reinforce his conclusions and show their omissions.

A tone may theoretically have no harmonics at all (such as sine waves in a completely controlled environment with absolutely no chance of resonance) but once a tone becomes aurally or electrically detectable, the acoustic and electric environments begin to influence it. First, combining tones will produce phasing occurrences in a mathematically ordered way, which may be enhanced by their interactions in any acoustical or virtual acoustical environment. "Virtual" acoustics may include resonances generated by certain software, based on the algorithms of the programming, or electronic resonances inherent in the sound equipment. The results are often termed "combination tones," and may be calculated by subtracting the frequencies involved ("difference" tones) or adding them ("summation" tones). These tones have been shown to be audible and measurably present, not just psychoacoustic.

Phasing in superimposed waves is a well-known phenomenon that has seen application in composition, instrument construction and architecture since the early parts of the last millennium, and acoustic and electronic sound synthesis. While we examined the simplistic superimposition of one instrument over another, phasing in a wavestacking context involves the superimposition of one simple or complex wave over one or more others, adding each wave's sound pressure level (SPL). By adding a *modulating* wave, of selected amplitude or frequency to a *carrier* wave, a third wave may be produced of a completely different nature, especially if the resulting pulse wave is fast enough to produce additional, audible tones. This was the basis for Yamaha's innovative DX-7 synthesizer (released to the public in 1983 but prototypes existed as early as the mid–70s).[7]

Even in the simplest terms, such as a sine wave in which no "corrupting" anomalous frequencies are theoretically present, phasing will produce difference tones. Difference tones may be determined by the simple formula:

$$f_a - f_b = f_\Delta$$

Figure 50. Difference tones

where f is the frequency of the initiating oscillation of a and b in Hertz and f_Δ is the resulting difference tone. Compare the following readouts of a single sine wave at 528 Hz (a common designation of C_4) and a combination of C_{528} and E_{660} (E_4):

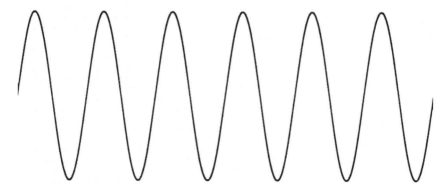

Figure 51. C_{528} sine wave

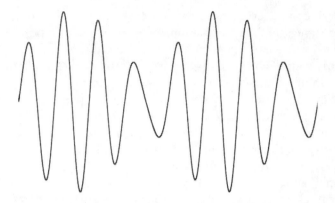

Figure 52. C$_{528}$ and E$_{660}$ played simultaneously

According to the system of Fourier analysis, complicated timbre may be deconstructed into a series of sine waves of individually increasing frequency, using additive synthesis principles to generate additional tones. Notice how the addition of the above frequencies also produce a lower frequency through phasing, or the addition of wave components according to corresponding amplitude.

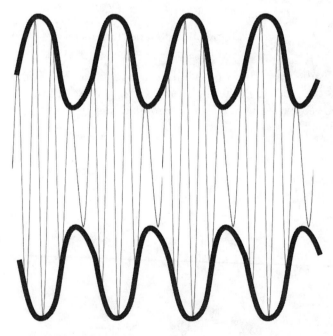

Figure 53. Difference tones through additive phasing

With the above in mind, compare the additional combinations within a C triad:

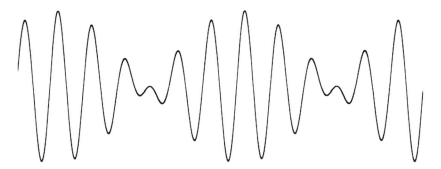

Figure 54. E$_{660}$ and G$_{792}$ played simultaneously

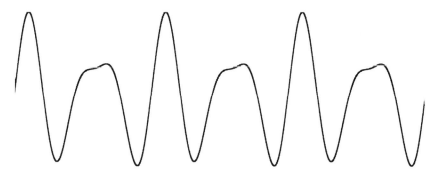

Figure 55. C$_{528}$ and G$_{792}$ played simultaneously

And the entire combination of triads includes all of these combinations:

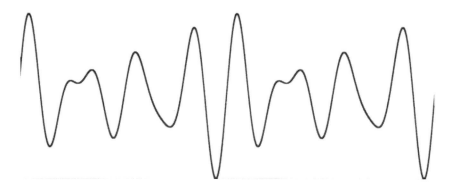

Figure 56. C triad wave

While the argument goes on as to whether difference tones are the result of acoustic or psychoacoustic phenomena, the above indications show pulses within pulses that occur through additive synthesis.

The best-known difference tones relate to those produced by the different combinations of the tones in a simple major triad. Thus (Numbers refer to cycles per second in Hz):

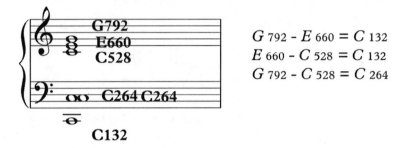

$$G\ 792 - E\ 660 = C\ 132$$
$$E\ 660 - C\ 528 = C\ 132$$
$$G\ 792 - C\ 528 = C\ 264$$

Figure 57. Musical representation of C triad, root position

Therefore, these tones sound and reinforce at least the root of the triad one and two octaves below. Again, difference tones are well known. However, we can also do a comparison of the triad's inversions, as well, showing a relationship between the three positions that center on the root:

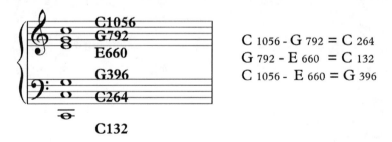

$$C\ 1056 - G\ 792 = C\ 264$$
$$G\ 792 - E\ 660 = C\ 132$$
$$C\ 1056 - E\ 660 = G\ 396$$

Figure 58. Musical representation and voicing of C triad, E, G, C or first inversion

These examples imply several things: first, the root is not merely the bass note, as shown in each position but is reinforced by the difference tones, to varying degrees, *regardless* of the position. Therefore, the relationship of each tone within the position is more important in presenting the *Klang* than the perspective of the top or bottom notes. This also has implications in voicing as shown by Schenker,[8] where its consonance relates to its conformity with the harmonic series.

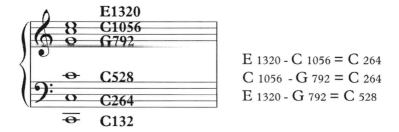

$$E\ 1320 - C\ 1056 = C\ 264$$
$$C\ 1056 - G\ 792 = C\ 264$$
$$E\ 1320 - G\ 792 = C\ 528$$

Figure 59. Musical representation of C triad, second inversion

Second, the sound of each position and its relevant consonance directly relates to the number and strength of the underlying difference tones of the root. A wave's readout of the root position and second inversion show similar characteristics and the oscilloscope readout shows an almost identical pattern resulting from these combinations. In closed voicing, two positions show a surprising similarity, all related to permutations of the root as displayed in the difference tones. We may infer in this case that the *Klang*—*not* necessarily the direct relationships of the played tones or their compositional or linear approach—of the root and $\frac{6}{4}$ positions are more consonant than that of the $\frac{6}{3}$ chord. These characteristics in their simplest forms of intervals and triads allow for a new classification of chords according to consonance with the criteria being difference tones and their related harmonics. All tertian (and by implication, any sonority, quartal, quintal, atonal) may be considered within these criteria.

Most importantly, these results and displays demonstrate why the C major *Klang* is consistent through each of the inversions. Moreover, it demonstrates another reason why voicing with both the harmonic series and mid-range grouping (e.g., the seconds and thirds of a voicing placed between 300 Hz and 1 kHz) maximize the perception of chordal *Klang*.

Reinforcement of the Harmonics

The first criterion is the direct reinforcement of the harmonics. The multiple techniques of sonic analysis underscore the necessity of external resonances to expand upon and develop secondary harmonics. The C major triad is the simplest example of chord structure within the context of the above tones.

The following diagrams show the "played tones" as those expressly presented by an oscillator, at equal amplitudes. These produce harmonics in various relative amplitudes, based upon the spectrum production of the initiating oscillator, such as an instrument. These are indicated along lines specific to each played tone. These are "possible" harmonics but are consistently present outside the oscillating medium as acoustic dynamics (outside an instrument's resonator) react resonantly to the audio excitation. Thirdly, the difference tones of each combination are presented to the left of the played tones, and finally, their respective harmonics line up to each difference tone's right. Lines presented to the right from each played tone and from each difference tone indicate its respective harmonics series. Solid lines show relationships between tones of the same frequencies. Smaller, lighter lines indicate relationships between the same tones in different octaves, also color-coded.

Thus, the root position of the C major triad will appear in just tuning:

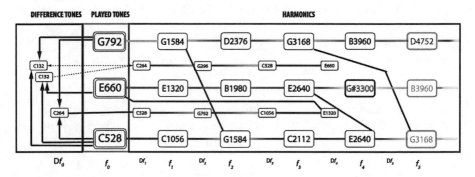

Figure 60. C Triad matrix, root position

This basic representation shows only the tones involved; it does not imply amplitudes. Subsequent three-dimensional lattices also included additional difference tone combinations from the harmonics that are shown on spectrographs below. Note that the tones are not just represented but often obliquely supported and reinforced through additional harmonics and phasing. For example, in a triad environment C_{528} shows the following additive support of two difference tones of harmonic f_3 from C_{132}.

There is a prevalence of the note B in the harmonics, which has implications in additional consonant chords. The following charts show how primary (played) and secondary (harmonic) tones reinforce each other:

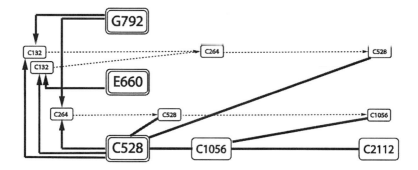

Figure 61. C triad matrix, C_{528}-class reinforcement

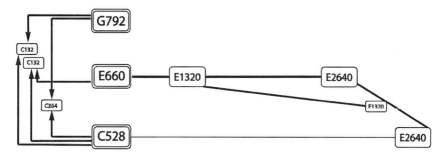

Figure 62. C triad matrix, E_{660}-class reinforcement

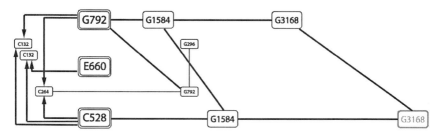

Figure 63. C triad matrix, G_{792}-class reinforcement

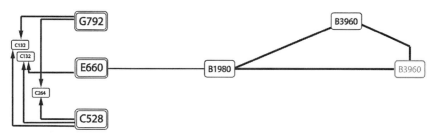

Figure 64. C triad matrix, B-class reinforcement

Consonance Issues

Inversions

One of the concerns in music theory is the interesting phenomenon regarding the pervasiveness of the *Klang* in spite of inversion. While some chords change the perceived *Klang* according to context or perspective, nonetheless, even these are found to result from respelling or contextual bias.[9] For example, an F^6 chord is also the inversion of a D^{min7} chord; diminished and augmented triad chords are simply respelled inversions of each other.[10] Most, however, clearly represent a single overall *Klang*, albeit depicted differently. The consonance itself may even change with the inversion but the *Klang* is still clear, if modified. With the C triad, inversions 1 ($\frac{6}{3}$) and 2 ($\frac{6}{4}$) recall the C root *Klang* but vary in several ways.

Ironically, the least consonant sonority is the first inversion, not the second as perceived in traditional Rameauvian theory. That view generates the $\frac{6}{4}$ chord as a non-harmonic function of the dominant, with an incidental unstable vertical sonority that needs resolving through the 4-3 and 6-5 scale degree resolutions. Justifying the $\frac{6}{4}$ chord as a vertical consonance as found in jazz and other popular styles may be shown in several ways.

First, examine the structure of the $\frac{6}{3}$ chord below, showing a weaker difference-tone organization than the root position. The fifth is represented as well, weakening the overall presence of the root from three to two tones. A second weakening characteristic is the shift from C_{132} to C_{66}, one that has less tonal perception, and one with a different relationship to aural perception.[11]

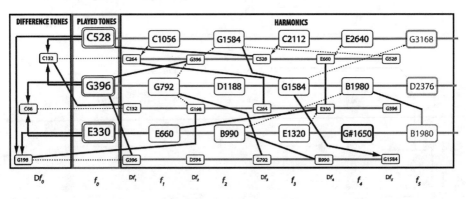

Figure 65. C triad matrix, 1st inversion

This also impacts the resulting matrix of harmonics, bringing in additional reinforcement of the G_{198} series, including D_{594}, which occurs in this case far lower (Df_2) than it does in root position (D_{1188}, also f_2) and is more reinforced (D_{1188} and D_{2376}, both at f_5). So, in first position, we hear a weakened root, and a stronger fifth.

The second inversion, in spite of the theoretical construction as a V with 4-3/6-5 suspensions, is more closely related to the root position than the first inversion. Note both the following matrices of the second inversion and root position:

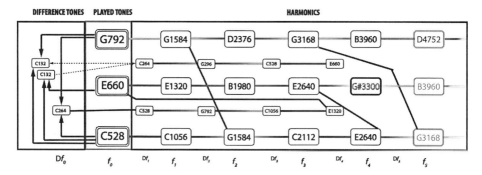

Figure 66. C triad matrix

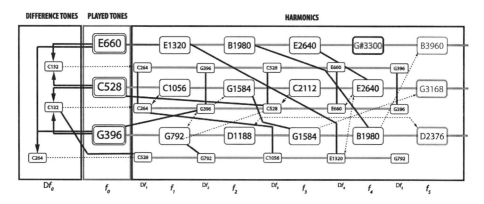

Figure 67. C triad matrix, second inversion with additional harmonic difference tones

Both root position and second inversion show difference tones of C_{132}, C_{132} and C_{264}, with corresponding oscilloscope and frequency Real Time Analyses (RTA). The difference tones produced by the first inversion are arguably weaker at C_{66}, C_{132} and G_{198}.

The above second inversion matrix also shows the additional

difference tones created by each tone in the played tones' harmonic series. These reinforce the harmonic series created by the difference tones themselves. In fact, from either the matrix construction, or by the sonograms shown below, it is difficult to tell which are causes and which are the reinforcements of these series; it is clear, however, that a lower harmonic series is generated as a result of resonating combination tones. While "generation" can be construction in terms of cause-and-effect with played or initiating tones, the overall snapshot is that of interacting tones in a matrix system.

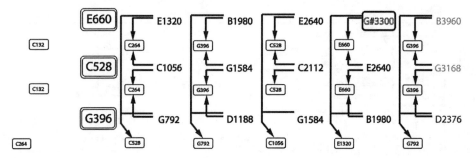

Figure 68. C triad, second inversion

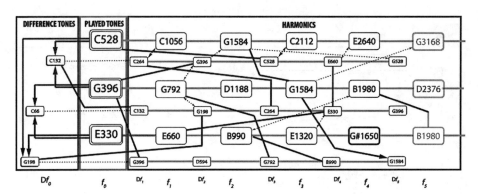

Figure 69. C triad, root position

Note the similarity in the oscilloscope display between the root and second inversion. The first inversion (Figure 70) shows destructive interference, resulting in the strengthening of a higher difference tone (G_{198}), and the corresponding amplitude drop in the root (C_{132} to C_{66}). Ultimately, it shows a readout with less definition of significant tones than the other inversions, which is an indicator of less relative consonance. A second readout from Room EQ Wizard software shows a strong presence in the second inversion of the root, in spite of or because of the phasing.

Figure 70. C triad, first inversion

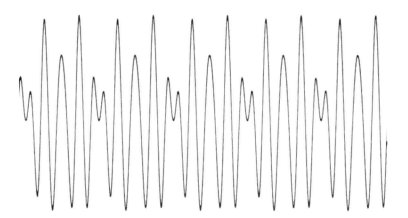

Figure 71. C triad, second inversion

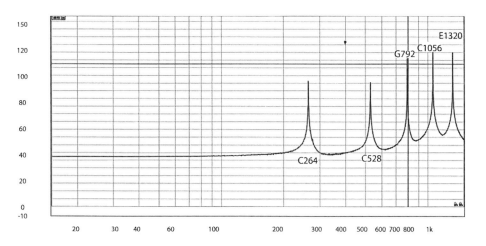

Figure 72. Screenshot of REW readout of C triad, second inversion

One will notice a close similarity to a root-position C triad in tertial (e.g., closed) voicing; difference tones are reinforced, and harmonics are both reinforced and introduced.

11

Complex Chord Systems Using Harmonic Matrices

Introduction

Chord structures are much more complicated than originally thought, as previous research into harmonics and combination tones have shown in the last chapter. The implications of peripheral tones define the relative consonance of any vertical tonal combination, differences in tuning systems that go beyond played tones, and moment-to-moment performance practice. This chapter continues to define tonal vertical sonority within the context of harmonic permutations as they apply to complex chords, (e.g., those that go beyond the octave and altered chords) and attempts to formulate a catalogue for the identification of chord consonance and classification.

Complex Chord Structure

We continue with a review of the simplest example of chord structure within the context of the above tones: the C major triad. The following diagram shows the "played tones" as those expressly presented by an oscillator in sine waves, using C as represented by the frequency, 528 Hz. These produce harmonics in various relative amplitudes, based upon the spectrum production of the initiating oscillator, such as an orchestra instrument. In the matrices, the initiating tones are restricted to sine waves, to simplify any harmonic production, and to identify any ambient resonance, if any. These are "possible" harmonics but are consistently present outside the oscillating medium, as acoustic dynamics react resonantly to the audio excitation. Lines presented to the right from each played tone and from each difference tone indicate the relationship of the tone to its respective harmonics series. Thirdly, the difference tones of the played tones' combinations are presented to the left of the played tones, and finally, their respective harmonics line up to each difference tone's right, if applicable.

In the last chapters, we examined the advantages of voicing to additionally reinforce played tones and existing harmonics.

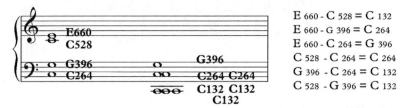

$$E_{660} - C_{528} = C_{132}$$
$$E_{660} - G_{396} = C_{264}$$
$$E_{660} - C_{264} = G_{396}$$
$$C_{528} - C_{264} = C_{264}$$
$$G_{396} - C_{264} = C_{132}$$
$$C_{528} - G_{396} = C_{132}$$

Figure 73. Reinforcement of a voiced C major triad (1-5-8-10)

Even though re-voiced, the additional C_{264} reinforces itself by phasing with the C_{528}, and adds more amplitude to the C_{132} by phasing with G_{396}. In fact, C_{264} receives two reinforcements through phasing, and C_{132} is represented three times. G_{396} is reinforced as well, produced by E_{660} and C_{264}. Tonal composers are well aware of this phenomenon, as many use only two notes to represent a full triad:

Figure 74. Resonating harmonics in tonal compositional practice

Lest this application of difference tone principles seem an exaggeration, examine the spectrogram display below. The four bright bars show the played tones as indicated by Figures 75 and 76. The depth of visual intensity corresponds to the relative amplitude. One must consider that all four tones are presented equally by the oscillators: all *played* amplitudes are the same. Thus, part of the phasing that occurs does not just present additional combination tones but phases with the existing tones as well. This is a representation completely within the computer CPU and does not take into consideration external or acoustic resonance, AD/DA processing, electrical or acoustic influences and properties, which will add more tone interaction, harmonics and phasing. The brightness of each line indicates its relative amplitude.

G_{396} is clearly attenuated, while as we've seen, C_{132} is produced and C_{264} is reinforced so strongly that the bandwidth is expanded slightly. E_{660} is also reinforced through harmonic interaction. One reason for this can be the redistribution of a set amount of applied energy as some are dampened and some are correspondingly enhanced.

While in the previous chapter we focused on the difference tone and frequencies, here we can see the relative amplitude of each played tone, difference tones and harmonics. The addition of C_{132} is significant. Phasing also increases the relative amplitude of C_{264} and E_{660}, although the latter to a smaller extent. This becomes more extreme when the overall amplitude is increased (see Appendix C).

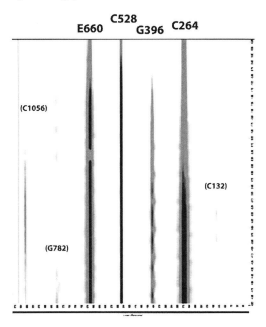

Figure 75. Phasing in a voiced C major (1-5-8-10)

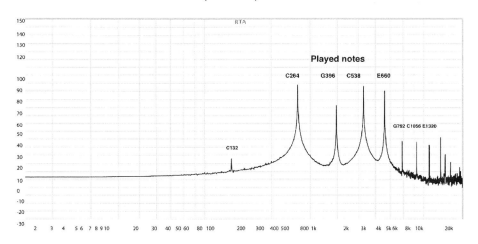

Figure 76. REW readout of a voiced C major (1-5-8-10)

Complex Chords

Major Seventh Chords

This same principle can be applied to more complex chords. There is a prevalence of the note B in the harmonics of the C triad (based on C_{528}), which has implications in additional consonant chords. The following charts show how primary (played) and secondary (harmonic) tones reinforce each other:

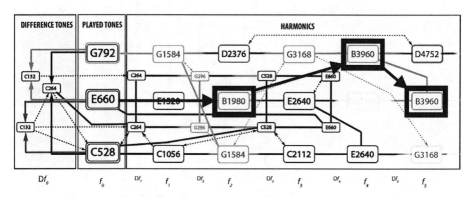

Figure 77. Maj7 tone prevalence in the C triad

One chord in particular, the major seventh chord, has a consonance that has been explained in various ways theoretically but less so from an acoustic perspective. Probably the most significant consonance within the chord intervals involves those that resonate in fifths, significantly the root and the third. The root resonates the fifth but the played and harmonically derived major third series resonates the major seventh strongly through its third harmonic.

The interval between the root and the seventh is arguably a dissonance in most tonal music of simpler harmony in spite of this and clashes with the harmonic octave of the root. This dissonance becomes even more pronounced in inversions, as the major seventh is translated into minor seconds. However, regarding just intonation, we see how even this interval provides an avenue for consonance on several levels. Schenker states that the fifth relationship is progressive but also interdependent.[1] This also shows the consonance of the major 7th and minor 7th chords as a function of the consonance of perfect fifths. It also impacts other fifth-relation extended chords, such as ninth (f_3 of the fifth) and 13th (f_3 of the ninth) and is a significant player in achieving a "blues" sound.

The following structural diagram shows the relationship of the various notes in a Cmaj7 chord, and the relative consonances (difference tones resulting from harmonics are omitted for clarity's sake):

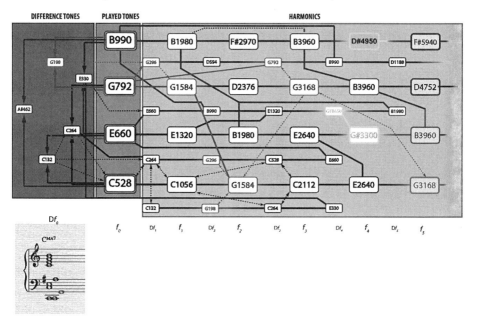

Figure 78. Cmaj7 matrix

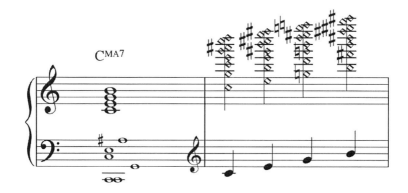

Figure 79. Cmaj7, harmonics and difference tones in notation

This particular chord structure adds two more combination tones to the root and the fifth as we have noted above. The fifth is the result, however, of the combination of the played fifth and the seventh and so is very strong. The other two combination tones are the E and the A♯. The inset grand staff shows the played tones (black) and the resulting combination tones. The chords shown outline a lower harmonic series, including tones f_1–f_8. The fundamental is missing in this extra series (f_1), as is the octave of the fifth (f_6), although f_3 is reinforced. The complete lattice shows the reinforcement of these tones, as well, through the interactions of the harmonics as we will see. It should be noted that the A$\sharp$ difference tone is also the f_7 of C_{66}. This becomes particularly important in light of voicing alternatives and continue to the comparative "lushness" in different voicings.

Once the major seventh is inverted, we notice new dynamics taking place as the B (seventh) and C (root) are placed close to each other, in a voicing most commonly associated with jazz. This voicing and others like it are equal or similar to those shown below, depending upon style, genre, usage or composer preference. The placement of the half step is contingent upon the "conflict" or dissonance desired (e.g., the higher the half-step), the more perceived conflict as the critical band frequency reaches mid-range:

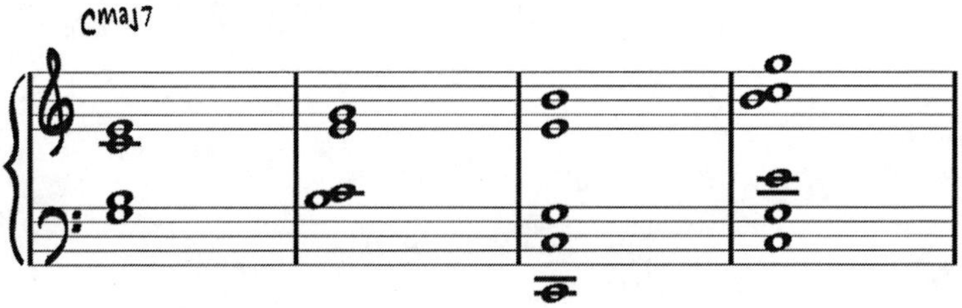

Figure 80. Jazz voicing examples of Cmaj7

Naturally, one must consider the interactivity of the tones individually, in pairs, trios, and beyond, and their relative amplitudes. On one level, the perspective is that of overall sonority in the perspective of Rameauvian theory. On another, the pre-tonal concepts of Palestrina and his contemporaries take precedent as we compare the consonance of intervals between pairs of lines. Jazz musicians, for example, listen to both: their notes' placements within their total chord sonorities, and the same notes' specific intonation with relation to another part, often the next one up or down. Therefore, the multiple ways of tuning—overall *Klang*, relation of the part to the lowest note, and part-to-part—contribute to contextual tuning, or tuning moment-by-moment.

The consideration of part-to-part tuning, as it relates to those parts next to each other, come to play in jazz especially in the tuning of whole- and half-steps. Acoustically this has impacts as it encroaches upon the ability of the ear to distinguish between tones and the point at which they do so. Howard and Angus describe at length the phenomenon of beat waves relating to tuning and the ear's ability to identify two tones at a given point of frequency (progressing through the "critical band" function of the ear, and associated phenomena).[2] Beat waves are directly related to the phasing issues we have described before, as amplitude upon amplitude are constructively or destructively added to produce period increases. Once the two tones are separated, the shifting of positive and negative pressures against each other creates an additional pulsing or "beats." The farther apart the two tones, the faster the third frequency until we have beats as fast as ±30 Hz, or one audible combination tone.

There is a point where the ear hears a "roughness" as the phasing frequency conflicts with the initial "two" tones. Once the beat wave's frequency reaches 20 Hz (20 times per second), theoretically an audible tone may be heard, generally present as a sort of rumbling, up to 30 Hz, depending upon the tonal acuity of the listener. We have demonstrated the difference tone as a result of the phasing of two tones; this shows its development and function as a beat wave phenomenon. This may be roughly diagrammed as follows:

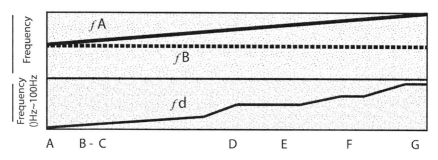

A - In tune (f_d=0Hz)
B- Slow beat waves (<2Hz
C - Medium Speed Beat Waves (2Hz-15Hz
D - Critical Band "roughness" (15Hz-30Hz)
E - Low frequency (30Hz - 40 Hz)
F - Low tone (C 33Hz)
G - Initial frequencies are far apart; Increasing audible difference tones

Figure 81. The transition of beat waves to combination tones

Jazz musicians and piano tuners among others, identify the beat wave in relation to the two initial tones and tune accordingly. A slight adjustment will have wide-ranging implications and there is a fine line for such musical application between being too close and blurring the distinction of two tones, and too far apart, where the necessary low frequency is too high. Using the matrix approach above, a Cmaj7 chord voiced 5-7-8-10 will have the following frequency implications:

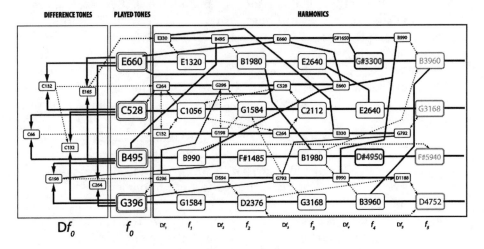

Figure 82. Cmaj7 matrix (5-7-8-10 voicing)

Figure 83. Cmaj7 (5-7-8-10 voicing) in notation

The following diagrams show a breakdown of the component reinforcement of difference tones and harmonics:

Extended Chords and the Impacts of Voicing

To take such implications to a tonal extreme, examine the following matrix showing the matrix of a Cmaj13$^{(+11)}$, a standard, extended

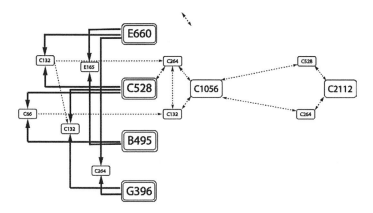

Figure 84. C components of Cmaj7 (5-7-8-10)

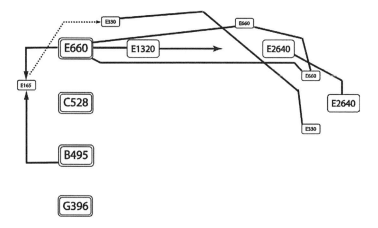

Figure 85. E components of Cmaj7 (5-7-8-10)

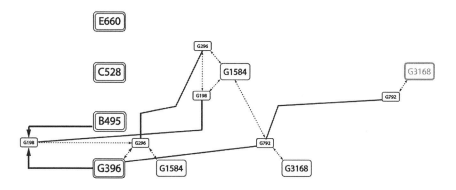

Figure 86. G components of Cmaj7 (5-7-8-10)

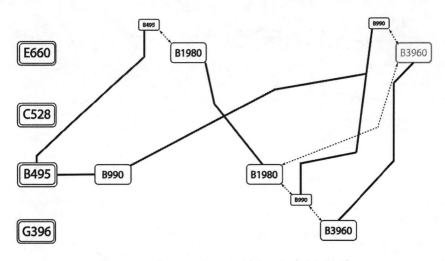

Figure 87. B components of Cmaj7 (5-7-8-10)

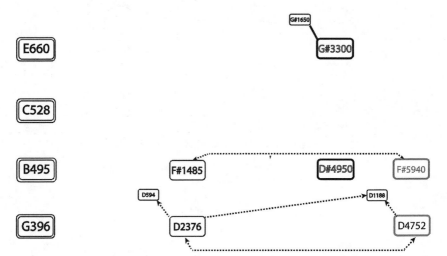

Figure 88. Non-fundamental components of Cmaj7 (5-7-8-10)

jazz chord, voiced in a traditional format and consonant, (according to the accepted jazz combo style). See Figures 89 and 90 on the next page.

A different voicing follows. Compare the matrices of the two voicing approaches. The sound says less about the reinforcement of the initial fundamental than it does about how the sound is affected by shifting the D_{594} up an octave to D_{1188} (for the sake of comparison, F$\sharp$ is kept at 1485 Hz). See Figure 91 at the bottom of the next page.

The following diagram shows these same frequencies on a

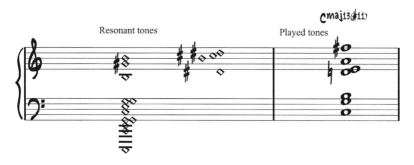

Figure 89. Cmaj$^{13(\#11)}$ voicing 1 (1-5-7-10-13-16-18)

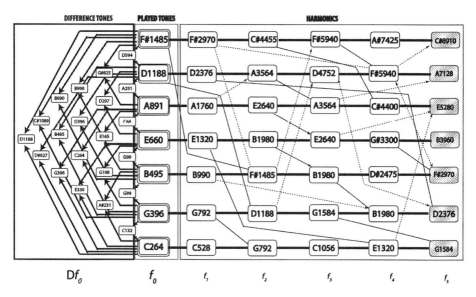

Figure 90. Matrix for Cmaj$^{13(+11)}$ voicing 1 (1-5-7-10-13-16-18)

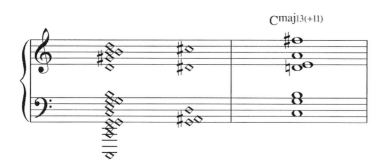

Figure 91. Cmaj$^{13(+11)}$ voicing 2 (1-5-7-9-10-13-18)

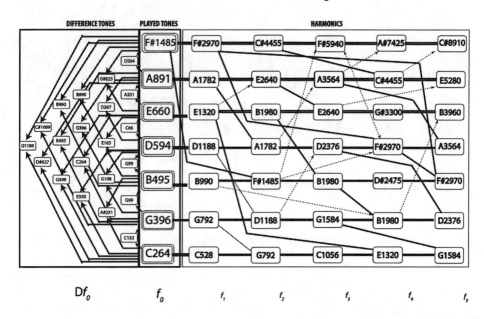

Figure 92. Matrix for Cmaj$^{13(+11)}$ voicing 2 (1-5-7-9-10-13-18)

dispersion chart. The original played tones are included and the difference tones and harmonics are indicated by pitch class and frequency. The boxes indicate the frequency categories of each pitch class. See Figure 93 on the next page.

For better comparison, note the contrasting patterns below, based on the grid. The first set represents only the difference tones as shown above; the second adds harmonic grid patterns. Observe the differences as well as the similarities in patterns. These only indicate tones that are present as a result of phasing, and not their relative amplitudes, which will also give indication of what frequency interaction is actually going on. It also does not show resulting harmonics, nor any combination tones that are the results of harmonic interactions. See Figures 94 and 95 on page 114.

Below are the same two chord structures, with basic harmonics added. See Figures 96 and 97 on page 114.

These two types of voicing show a standard way of writing this *Klang* can still maintain its sonority while reinforcing internal ideas of consonances. For example, a distinctly Schenkerian/Pythagorean approach emphasizes the consonances that rely on the relationship of the perfect fifth (f_3, with a 3:2 ratio), whose harmonic relationship was acknowledged by Helmholtz and others as audible to the average listener as we have seen. We can use each voice and its relationship to

	<100Hz		100-200Hz			200-300Hz			300-500Hz		
C class	C66		C132			C264					
C# class											
D class						D297					
D# class											
E class			E165						E330		
F class											
F# class											
G class	G99	G99	G198						G396	G396	
G# class											
A class											
A# class						A#231	A#231				
B class									B495		

500-1kHz			1kHz-2kHz			2kHz-4kHz			4kHz-10kHz		
C528	C528		C1056								
			C#1089						C#4455	C#4455	C#8910
D594			D1188			D2376					
D#627			D#1221	D1188	D1188	D#2475					
			E1320	E1320		E2640	E2640		E5280		
						F#2970	F#2970	F#2970	F#5940		
G792	G792	G792	G1584	G1584							
G#825						G#3300					
			A1782	A1782		A3564	A3564				
									A#7425		
B990	B990		B1980	B1980		B3960					

Figure 93. Cmaj$^{13(+11)}$ voicing 1

others as the basis for voicing rather than harmonic placement, much like pre-tonal composers did. Once again, we imply equal amplitude of each tone.

Taking the tones of the same chord, we find a consistent pattern using fifths, where all relationships look very much like the Schenkerian/Pythagorean structure of harmonic fifths. See Figure 98 on page 115.

We now run into two issues. First, we deal with the Pythagorean comma phenomenon if we tune to harmonically perfect fifths, where each fifth is progressively stretched beyond an equally tempered system

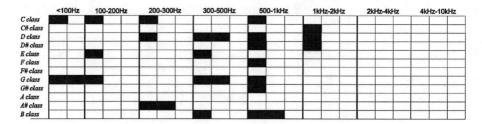

Figure 94. Cmaj¹³⁽⁺¹¹⁾ voicing 1 (difference tones)

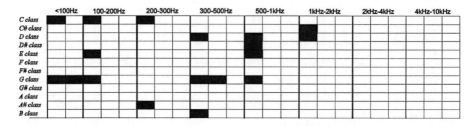

Figure 95. Cmaj¹³⁽⁺¹¹⁾ voicing 2 (difference tones)

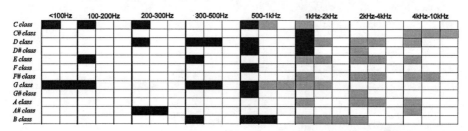

Figure 96. Cmaj¹³⁽⁺¹¹⁾ voicing 1, difference tones and harmonics

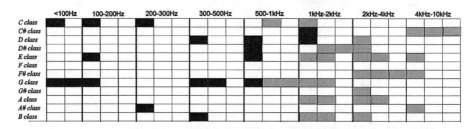

Figure 97. Cmaj¹³⁽⁺¹¹⁾ voicing 2, difference tones and harmonics

as the voicing extends to almost two octaves. However, given the tolerance that such a tuning system requires, one can take each fifth relationship and compromise with its relationship to the root (C_{264}). Secondly, each note is far enough apart from each other that the harmonic quality is compromised and individual notes begin to be heard. Since each ratio

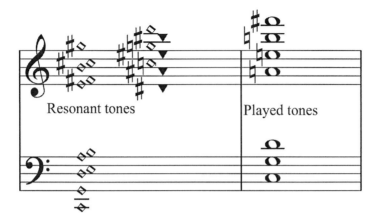

Figure 98. Cmaj$^{13(+11)}$ voiced in perfect fifths

(3:2) of the fifth is the same throughout, it makes sense that their difference tones between neighbors are also stacked in fifths, and relate to each fifth relationship, not the whole.

Another interesting note is the grouping (or lack thereof) of difference tones and the separation of interactive harmonics. As one can see, the initially produced tones simply reflect the relationships of fifths in the played tones. However, additional tones produced by relationships of ninths, thirteenths, etc., tend to cluster more in the mid-range and upper levels, reinforcing or conflicting with harmonics. Since the C fundamental is still reinforced, we have a *Klang* that resonates the same overall but is far weaker as it does not support the C harmonic series as well. In fact, the spread of persistent fifths emphasizes the "fifth" sound rather than the traditional tertial *Klang* of Cmaj$^{13(+11)}$, although technically its components are the same. Examine the example below:

Each tier conforms to its own series of perfect fifths, each true to its

Played tones	C264		G396		D594		A891		E1320		B1980		F#2970
1st Tier		C132		G198		D297		A446		E660		B990	
2nd Tier		E330		B495		F#726		C#1089		G#1650			
3rd Tier *				D#627		A#924		E#1386		C2079			
4th Tier				C1056				G1584		D2376			
5th Tier*						G#1716		D#2574					
						E#2706							

* Out of tune (sharp to ET letter designation)

Figure 99. Voicing in fifths

lowest note in its tier. However, the moment you add a low bass (C^{132}) in a jazz context, things "lock" in, as our difference tones interact with the new frequency:

Note that this time, our added difference tones reinforce in the

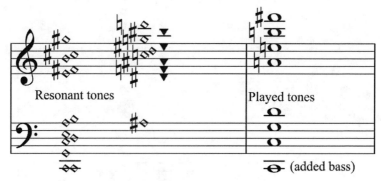

Figure 100. Harmonic implications with added bass

Played tones	C132		C264		G396		D594		A891		E1320		B1980		F#2970
1st Tier		C132	C264	C132	G198	B495	D297	F#726	A446	C#1089	E660	G#1650	B990		
2nd Tier				A#462	E330	D#627		A#924	G1584	E#1356	C2079				
3rd Tier *					F759		C1056		G1584		D2376				
4th Tier						D1188		G#1716		D#2574					
5th Tier *							A#1848		E#2838	F#2706					

* Out of tune (sharp to ET letter designation)

Figure 101. Grid with added bass

same way our simpler major seventh chords do. Now, we present our root, fifth, third and even an A♯ (f_7). It seems that not only the presence of harmonic and difference tones are important but their vertical "shape," as well. Perfect fifths stacked spread a general timbre effect throughout the middle ranges, rather than actively supporting a fundamental nearly to the point as mixed or tertian voicings. It also reinforces our general principle of proximity-to-harmony, to wit: *The closer the voicing, the greater the perception of harmony; the farther the voicing, the greater the perception of individual tones.*

At this point, we pass beyond any idea of reinforcing the root or other lower harmonics, which constitute our ideas of consonant and dissonant chord sonorities. Any tone, from f_1 above can be reinforced with comparative voicing, or octave reinforcement. Tonal changes will also reinforce harmonics, according to the spectra of the participating instruments. Complex chords have interaction that show unique patterns based upon the combination of difference tones and harmonics. The "shape" of the sonority corresponds directly with its pattern as the three types of diagrams above show, in music notation, matrix and visual patterns. The two show similarities and differences that relate to phasing issues and harmonic development patterns.

12

Manifesting Inaudible Sound

One argument against digital audio in commercial renderings is the limitations based upon the so-called CD standard. Commercially accepted as 16-bit, at 44.1 kHz, the idea was to provide a high enough "ceiling" for audio in the digital realm, and a high enough resolution with the 16-bit binary code to prevent most audible quantizing and aliasing issues. The 44.1 kHz sampling frequency effectively doubles the audible frequency applying the Nyquist theorem with some room to spare (22.05 kHz of audible frequency).[1]

The problem is the arbitrary limitation that humans can only hear from 20 Hz to 20 kHz, and in most cases of physical attrition due to age, a narrower range than that. However, many consumers and audio engineers alike have voiced concern that digital audio lacks "warmth," (one digital advocate complained that "[tape] hiss is considered warmth?").[2] Digital sound has been described by critics as "cold" and "crystalline," and "lacking in color or character."

This is one possible reason for the resurgence of vinyl records for commercial audio reproduction. As a "lossless" format to the particulate level (e.g., without digital quantization of the soundwave and a corresponding reduction of memory and frequency resolution) the atomic components of the medium allow for the highest possible resolution of the medium, far outperforming that of the CD standard as far as the accuracy of the signal goes.[3] Part of this is the idea, shown by Haeff and Knox among others, that the human perception of hearing is far more expanded than the simple accepted audible range.[4] This also implies that the perception of audible sounds is limited by the media itself, particularly air in our case.

In water, bone induction and other transfer mechanisms allow humans to hear up to 200 kHz.[5] The fact is we don't exactly know what, how and how much frequencies can impact us. Some discussions indicate that air can convey frequencies into the GHz range, thousands of times our aural perception (e.g., with our anatomical ear systems) but what this "means" to us may be far greater than we know and extend beyond what we would consider "hearing," at least with the ears and with air as the primary medium.

Considering the finite possibilities, harmonic matrices from resonances and phasing interaction are incredibly complex. Many matrices that have frequencies in the MHz range may generate difference tones—albeit at low or indistinguishable amplitude levels—in the aural range (20 Hz–20 kHz). For a very simplistic example, we take two waves, say of 21.12 kHz (C_{21120}) and 31.68 kHz (G_{31680}). Separate, they are just above the hearing range of humans but superimposed, one over the other produce a difference tone of 10.56 kHz, or E_{10560}:

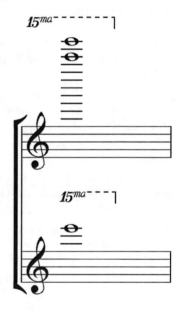

Naturally, this is unusable at worst and impractical at best (although some enterprising *avant-garde* composer might find it inspiring) but it also makes the point: somehow, some way, the listener can perceive aurally the result of the superimposition of inaudible frequencies, regardless of whether they can hear the propagated "tones" above human hearing.

One thing that is important to note is that at these ranges, suddenly our simple reduction of two tones one fifth apart resonating the bottom note is gone, as it actually resonates the third of the triad, E. Granted, at this range, a "triad" and certainly our perception of the triad is confused, especially as we cannot aurally perceive the extra-aural frequencies we began with. One may notice that the optimum resonance for chordal resonance exists roughly between C_3 and C_5, while

Figure 102. Hypersonic difference tones

the matrix to interacting frequencies and even chords act very differently once the propagating tones develop higher or lower than this range.

Let us continue with a simple triad, by filling in the E_{26400} (26.4 kHz). Our simple difference tone pattern result is:

$$31.68_{kHz} - 21.12_{kHz} = 10.25_{kHz}$$

$$26.4_{kHz} - 21.12_{kHz} = 5.28_{kHz}$$

$$31.68_{kHz} - 26.4_{kHz} = 5.28_{kHz}$$

Suddenly, we are aware that the "simple" matrices of our mid-range, not to mention audible, chords no longer apply in the same way. It should be noted that all the above notes are harmonics of a C triad played at 500_{Hz}, albeit located at a ridiculously high range. It still figures into a precise mathematical situation. However, all frequencies—played and difference tones—are octaves:

Figure 103. Hypersonic triad

$$C_{528} \times 21 = C_{21120}$$

$$E_{660} \times 21 = E_{26400}$$

$$G_{792} \times 21 = G_{31680}$$

$$E_{660} \times 4 = E_{2640}$$

$$E_{660} \times 8 = E_{5280}$$

As such, they reinforce the major players of the mid-range C triad, with special reference to the third of the triad, E.

Once again, these are just "present" tones, and we have not yet considered implications of amplitude apportionment, which will directly impact timbre, of course, and in compilation with the boosted amplitude of resonating frequencies, the reinforcement of chord tones. Part of the reason for this is the wide range of possibilities in timbre and resonating frequencies, given electronic and acoustic oscillators, effects and distortion, wave media and resonating chambers. Most importantly, this is one example of how extra-aural frequencies can impact even the audible range. We can take these, raise them by their octaves into well beyond commercial sampling frequencies and see if the interaction produces audible tones. Clearly, music notation at this point becomes impractical.

$$G_{63360} - C_{42240} = C_{21120}$$

Unfortunately, this is still above aural detection, albeit marginally. Now, consider more tonal interaction, this time from the phasing between difference tones given sufficient amplitude and resulting resonance:

$$G_{63360} - E_{52800} = E_{10560}$$

$$E_{52800} - C_{42240} = E_{10560}$$

$$G_{63360} - C_{42240} = C_{21120}$$

$$C_{21120} - E_{10560} = E_{10560}$$

Once again, there is an inordinate emphasis on the E_{10560}, with three difference tones all in the audible range.

It is important to remember that we don't consciously perceive or otherwise actively listen to extra-aural tones and their manifestations. However, it is clear that what is impacting our ears and listening system, not to mention psychoacoustics and physical impact, goes much farther than what is comparably a simplistic system as found in digital audio. There are old experiments that show how ultrasound as well as audible sound can be "heard" through bone induction.[6]

Our demonstrations above show only the most simplistic models for perception. Nor do we know what levels of amplitude are necessary for a person to get some sort of physical, not to mention psychoacoustic experience. These principles only dictate the frequencies involved, not the relative levels each tone has to begin with and what levels are the result of phasing attenuation and summation.

One thing also seems clear: the relative closeness of presented tones, the amplitude, and the "octaves" (e.g., relative frequencies) can impact the format of each matrix. This may explain the relative changes in voicing, as demonstrated in later chapters. A trained musician will hear subtle changes between different voicings, but the overall *klang* remains the same. Still, hypersonic tones somehow seem to burst through the literal "noise" of high frequency timbre and shape the *klang* of the total matrix, much as spikes occur in a graphic equalizer:

Commercial digital audio of 44.1 kHz is "lossy," in that it of necessity eliminates every frequency above 21.05 kHz. Professional systems that have the capability of 192 kHz sampling frequency or higher may capture more, however rendering and reproduction of these frequencies are still subject to the hardware, the ADDA rendering and the software management systems, not to mention the necessary reduction to 16-bit 44.1 kHz standard for commercial applications. It is clear that in commercial recordings we may still be missing a significant portion of harmonic resonance.

13

Chord Classification

Chord classification in this case can show relative points of consonants as harmonics and difference tones are reinforced, ignored or conflicted. As shown in the last chapter, choices of voicing can reinforce or ignore implications of resonance, including the perception of harmony vs. individual notes, additional harmonics and even special effects. Composers aware of these effects can make more informed choices.

Chords can be classified according to sound, *Klänge* and resonance. Since styles, voicing and other effects are only limited by the imagination, technique and innovation, classification must be done on a tertial basis for comparison sake and are best considered on a comparative basis only. The previous chapter qualified its statements by demonstrating equivocal perception based on frequency placement of chord tones (e.g., hypersonic, vs. optimal *Klang* generation in the mid-range). However, the greatest perception of tonal quality again is in the mid-range and so by placing the triad beginning at C_{528}, we can compare the overall sound and consonance of each chord.

The following chart shows the classifications for chords that are based on a C root, and are tertial in nature, according to the following criteria:

- Chord designation is per either figured bass and/or jazz chord symbols.
- Order is per order-24 (half steps over two octaves), with 0 as the base.
- Class is according to the author's classification method, based upon the number of partials present in the *Aggregate Difference Tones* (ADTs).

The ADTs refer to the difference tones actually produced by the chord. The first number consists of three immediately audible harmonic series according to Helmholtz (he claimed up to f_6 were legitimate

122

considerations), including root/fundamentals and their octaves, secondary order (fifth) and tertiary (thirds). The second column contains the number of secondary audible harmonic series such as sharped sixths, extended partials to the ninths, any number of audible and harmonically valid harmonics in the ADTs up to f_{12}. The last column in this classification has any number of chromatic, altered or anomalous ADTs that deviate from the *root's* harmonic series, such as interactions between extended harmonies that may destructively interfere with the primary series or ADTs alternative tuning anomalies.

The classification *Root Quotient* (RQ) is based upon the number of root tones present in the ADT out of the number of interactions between played tones possible. For example, a root-positioned triad will produce three interactions: R-M3, R-P5, M3-P5. The three interactions produce three roots of the total number possible of the interactions, thus the RQ in the case of a C triad is 3/3. The higher the RQ, the more harmonically consonant and fundamentally stable the chord.

The *Harmonics Quotient*, or HQ, is based upon the number of harmonics present in the ADT that correspond with those consistent with the root fundamental. A second number may be shown as the presence of harmonics in the root fundamental *or* the sub-positioned series. The higher the HQ, the more relatively consonant the chord. Two observations may be made. First, these are all developed from the perspective of the chordal root, even on cases where the inversion may be enharmonically the same in equal temperament. For example, repeated modes such as augmented chords are considered interchangeable with enharmonic respelling. However, they still have a sonority that depends upon the strength or presence of the root and its harmonics, and in just temperament of the moment, the resonance will reflect this. Therefore, the inversions or the C augmented triad will change in their classifications as they are as they are based upon the reference of the root, and possible voicing or reinforcements of it. The second inversion of a C+ chord, for example, will still reference the root, C, not G♯ or A♭, as it might in contextual perspective in equal temperament.

An additional consideration is the tuning approach the musicians will use. A jazz musician, used to half steps as a measure for complex chord tuning, may choose to see an augmented fifth as an aberration from an existing perfect fifth harmonic but tune it as an equally tempered minor second conflict. A classically trained musician may tune it based upon the nearest true third or upon the root, depending on the context and tonality of the piece. For the sake of chord classification and as we are concerned with the vertical resonance, rather than

Chord (Figure)	Order (inversion)	Notation	Class	RQ	HQ
Major triad C	0,4,7 (Root)		300-0-00	3/3 100%	3/3
C/E	0,3,8 (1st)		210-0-00	2/3 100%	3/3
C/G	0,5,9 (2nd)		300-0-00	3/3 100%	3/3
Minor Triad Cmin	0,3,7 (Root)		100-0-20	1/3 33%	3/3
Cmin/Eb	0,4,9 (1st)		100-0-20	1/3 33%	3/3
Cmin/G	0,5,8 (2nd)		100-0-20	1/3 33%	3/3
Dim Triad C°	0,3,6 (Root)		000-0-21	0/3 0%	1/3

Above, opposite and following two pages: **Table 4: Chord classification**

alterations, we will consider the latter. In this example, the chord C_{528}-E_{660}-$G\sharp_{825}$ (based on true harmonic thirds with a root reference to C) will elicit a 33 percent RQ with C reinforced on RQ C_{132} only (others at E_{165} and D_{297}) while E_{660}-$G\sharp_{825}$-C_{1056} will be classified with a 33 percent RQ, as both produce one classifiable root tone based on the C's presentation of

Chord	Order (inversion)	Notation	Class	RQ	HQ
(C°/Eb)	0,3,9 (1st)		000-1-11	0/3 0%	1/3
(C°/Gb)	0,6,9 (2nd)		100-1-10	1/3 33%	2/3
Augmented Triad	0,4,8 (Root)		101-1-00	1/3 33%	3/3
C+/E	0,4,8 (1st/enh Root)		101-0-10	2/3 33%	3/3
C+/G#	0,4,8 (2nd/enh Root		100-0-11	2/3 33%	3/3
Cmaj7	0,4,7,11 (Root)		311-1-00	3/6 50%	6/6
Cmaj7/E	0,3,7,8 (1st)		321-0-00	3/6 50%	6/6
Cmaj7/G	0,4,5,9 (2nd)		411-0-00	4/6 66%	6/6

Chord	Order (inversion)	Notation	Class	RQ	HQ
Cmaj^7/B	0,1,5,8 (3rd)		401-1-00	4/6 66%	5/6
Cmin^7	0,3,7,10 (Root)		100-0-50	1/6 16.5%	1/6 6/6
Cmi^7/Eb	0,4,7,9 (1st)		100-0-50	1/6 16.5%	1/6 6/6
Cmi^7/G	0,3,5,8 (2nd)		100-0-41	1/6 16.5%	1/6 6/6
Cmi^7/Bb	0,2,5,9 (3rd)		200-0-40	2/6 33%	2/6 6/6
C^7	0,4,7,10 (Root)		300-1-20	3/6 50%	4/6 (66%) 6/6 (100%)
C^7/E	0,3,6,8 (1st)		210-1-20	3/6 50%	4/6 (66%) 6/6 (100%)
C^7/G	0,3,5,9 (2nd)		300-0-21	3/6 50%	3/6 (50%) 5/6 (83%)

Chord	Order (inversion)	Notation	Class	RQ	HQ
C^7/Bb	0,2,6,9 (3rd)		300-0-21	3/6 50%	3/6 (50%) 5/6 (83%)
Cmaj$^{13(+11)}$	0,4,7,11,14,18,21		442-2-45	4/21	12/21 (57%) 16/21 (76%)
Cmaj$^{13(+11)}$ Jazz voicing	0,7,11,16,21,26,30		431-2-35	4/21	10/21 (48%) 13/21 (62%)

C_{528}, E_{165} and G_{396}. However, the tuning of each chord, within the context of the style and the reference points of the player, may also produce slightly different matrices, depending upon the amount. Atonality may be "equally" tempered, given its aim of complete keylessness and will tune equally, while a tonal piece tuned in just intonation will allow the resonance of each chord.

14

The Minor Triad

Once we establish harmonic resonance as a basis for chord classification, we can see how the perspective with which we listen to each sonority changes. The major triad and its derivatives attribute their relative consonances to the harmonic series and the more dissonant chords, such as augmented or diminished display conflicts against the harmonic series. However, the minor triad has attributes consistent with a dissonant *Klang* as it nominally conflicts with the harmonic series (minor third versus major third) but has been culturally and practically considered a consonance since at least the late Baroque period. Various explanations exist, ranging from its origination as an aberration of the major triad to a "natural"—if not truly resonant—formation from the so-called "undertone" series.

The former relies on a cultural perspective readjusting the ear to tolerate the half step difference between the two chords, a more detailed version of the similar principle applied in the tolerances expected within the equal tempered system. It may also be attributable to the laws governing the concept of the blues tonality and its use of quarter-tone tolerances as intentional aberrations to more consonant sonorities. The development and subsequent elimination of the Picardy third discounts this, as perspectives on what constitutes "consonance" changed through the last millennium. To be considered a consonance, a *Klang* loses its categorization as a dissonance except in perspective. In other words, a dissonance may be considered thus in light of its conformity to an exterior standard but then cannot be thought of as a consonance by that same standard. Therefore, if our criteria for dissonance that needs to be resolved relies on conformity to the harmonic series, then this standard may not be used to also justify the minor triad as a consonance.

The undertone series, first proposed by Hugo Riemann in the 19th century, has been revived as a method of composition, theoretical approaches and even justifying harmonic perspectives, especially the minor triad. A recent proposal by Jose Sotórrio has shown some tonal promise based on his experiments with guitar tunings and string manipulation.[1] However, while beneficial in terms of melodic perspective, compositional approach, and even harmonic development, the undertone series is deficient when it comes to resonating sonorities. Many of the attempts to harmonically justify it are weak, at best. Even the difference tone concept does not adhere to the traditionally presented undertone series in their strict senses, as will be shown.

Both theoretical and spectral analysis methods used above and in the previous chapters show a different perspective on the consonance of the minor triad. In the classification table, we see the following:

Minor Triad Emin	0,3,7 (Root)		100-0-20	1/3 33%	3/3

Table 5: Minor triad

The low ADT numbers belie the triad's consideration as a consonance, until we look at the contributing factor from a difference tone perspective. The matrix for the minor triad is:

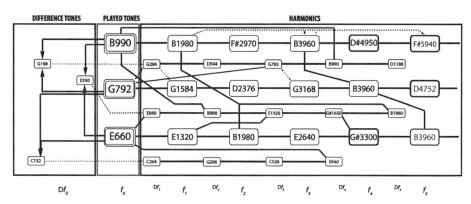

Figure 104. Matrix of E minor triad

The difference tones for an E minor triad include:

$$B_{990} - E_{660} = E_{330} \text{ (the one root tone in the ADT series)}$$
$$B_{990} - G_{792} = G_{198}$$
$$G_{792} - E_{660} = C_{132}$$

This results as the following notation, in effect. See Figure 105 on the next page.

Taken into consideration the harmonics of the chord and its

difference tones, the much more consonant and justifiable Cmaj7 chord becomes clear. The classification of the Cmaj7 chord shows:

Figure 105. The minor triad with difference tones

Cmaj7	0,4,7,11 (Root)		311-1-00	3/6 50%	6/6

Table 6: Cmaj7 classification

It is also shown on the *iSpectrum* application spectrograph waterfall. The brightest lines are those actually played (E_{660}, G_{792}, B_{990}). Notice the presence of C_{132} and C_{264} when only the E minor triad is played (within the box) and the redistribution of amplitude as other notes are added:

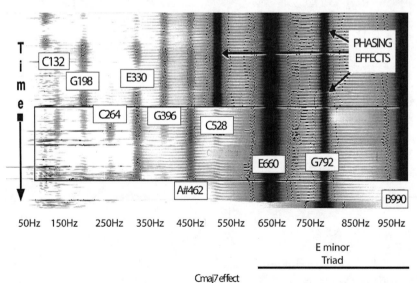

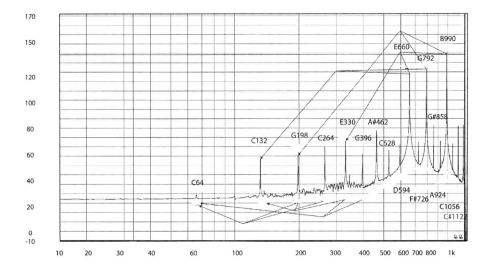

Figure 107. *Room EQ Wizard* **readout of E minor triad**

There is theoretical allusion to this principle, if in differing contexts, from Rameau's justification of extended chords within a textual context to Piston's insistence on the relationships of the vii° chord as a functional V°9 chord. This is an acoustic proof that the perspective of sub-position is a viable principle of tertian function and that certain chords can be derived from a diatonic third below the actual played bass that goes beyond the composition justification of the vii° or vii°7.[2]

Opposite, bottom: **Figure 106.** *iSpectrum* **readout of E minor and Cmaj7 chords**

15

Shifting Harmonic Imagery

Given the concepts of sub-progressions and harmonic progression, the spectra of harmonic matrices constantly shift, itself a progression without voices or sometimes even chords. The *Kläng* is the focus itself as the color changes based on the adjusting matrix from moment to moment. On occasion, it only needs a single note to change, whether on a linear, melodic basis against a textural background, or through triadic "transformation."

In the above example of a pedal-tone, note how the upper voices, while aligned as melodic patterns also provide a shifting landscape from matrix to matrix.

Transformation theory holds that triadic change can be radically affected by the stepwise change of the triads' single notes. A musical example would be the common chord and common tone modulations in theoretical aspect, where the commonality provides a "new" image, if different perspective on consonance. In this chapter, we focus on the shifting matrices that even simple transformations impel.

In our earlier example, we saw multiple directions in which a single triad can go, by changing one or two notes by linear half and whole steps. One example changed a C major to a C minor by lowering the third to produce a completely difference *Klang* and its accompanying matrix from the first chord. A stepwise motion of G to an A changes a C triad to an A triad, and the shift will provide a completely different sonority:

Figure 108. Transformation of triads, difference tones and harmonics

The more notes that are not common, the more extreme the matrix shift, except when all shift in the same direction, effectively transposing the same *Klang*.

Figure 109. C-F# and the corresponding matrix in notation

Even in these two examples, we move from one chord to another. But a single tone will generate a new perspective on matrices, as shown in the notation below. Here we move simply from a G chord, resolving—in Rameau and Piston's generation—through the passing of an F, or the seventh of the G chord, producing a dominant effect and tension needing resolution:

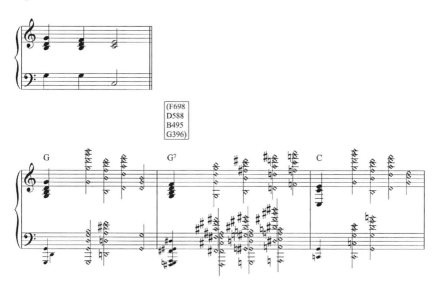

Figure 110. Comparable dissonance with a dominant 7th chord

We find that our pleasant world of "consonant" becomes suddenly much more complicated. Note the complex of the difference tones and their corresponding harmonics in the chord generated by the simple moving of the fifth scale degree through the passing tone of the fourth scale degree to resolve to a C triad.

One perspective would be, were we to take a snapshot of it, a *transitory klang*, one that may be considered neither consonant nor dissonance but is transitory. Nonetheless, it is a valid color increasing a momentary tension, particularly since the mind has two anchors based on time: the first chord and the second chord. Regardless of relative consonance, which in itself is depend upon context, style and perspective, the mind hears and has accepted the tonality of both chords.

This actually lends credence to the early tonal reluctance to give any dominant seventh chord status as a stationary sonority, much less consonant. However, as a non-harmonic tone, it works very well, allowing a color in the harmonic matrix to create a momentary tension between (in this case) to two demonstrably consonant chords. Any non-harmonic increases the harmonic dissonance of the entire momentary *klang*, to be resolved upon the resolution of the following harmonic (in the Baroque term "harmonic") that follows. It provides a *klang* in its own right that may be considered progressive only in light of its function between to sub-progressive chords. Every moment that the frequency changes, the matrix itself changes as the phasing results in new frequencies, each its own matrix. These may be radical or gradual depending upon the amount of change.

Naturally, we may complicate to a great degree the matrices of each chord and each non-harmonic tone on a simple diatonic or even chromatic level. A matrix analysis of an intentionally atonal piece would be very complex but interesting as one identifies shifting matrices within the colors of such a piece. Microtonal music such as blues and jazz will reveal even more complex matrices as shifts include strident difference tones that the mind has a difficult time "forgiving," even in its expansive perspective on equalized and other close tunings. One interesting jazz example refers to the sliding notes in Gershwin's *Rhapsody in Blue* or *American in Paris*.[21] In the opening case of the Rhapsody, it is solo with no texture to phase with but other sliding factors in the same pieces are against a tapestry, as it were, of harmonic matrix progressions. Below, we use a simple version of the progression commonly known in jazz and classical music as a "turnaround," as described in an earlier chapter. It includes non-harmonic tones, root and an inversion. The matrices will graphically demonstrate the following chord progression, in C major.

ii   vi   ii   V7   I

Emin—Amin—Dmin—Gdominant—C

Figure 111. The diatonic turnaround

This works analogously for any key: the musical relationship between the chords within this sub-progression will remain the same.

Next is shown the progression of matrices based on the harmonic interaction of each of the chords in the above series. The resulting matrix is based on quantification of actual frequencies. It does not represent complete accuracy, of course, and the chords are only presented in transformed inversions of triads: voicing, including the addition of a supporting "fundamental" bass, provides additional, unique matrices.

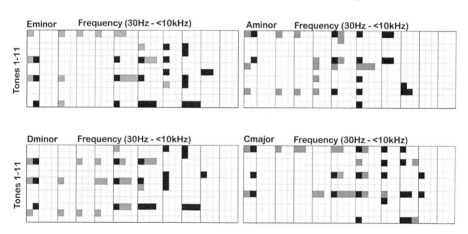

Figure 112. Matrix patterns of the jazz turnaround

There are several things to note. First, the patterns change as the chord changes, demonstrating the harmonic interactions and the difference tones. Second, while the patterns change, there are common tones between the chords that are reinforced and interacted. Not only are the relationships common but the notes themselves are as well. This speaks to the third implication: that there are multiple common interactions within one key, due to components being shared within a tonal context.

An analogy may be made here of a line of progressive Venn

diagrams, whose commonality blends as it shifts from one circle into another like a common chord modulation "shares" chords between two keys. This is not unlike film editing, whereby a scene shifts to another scene through varying degrees and methods ranging from common elements, to foreign transitionary elements, to sudden changes or "cuts." The collection of colors and textures shift and change, through blends from scene to scene, going from one cohesive unit, through a no-man's land, as it were, into another.

Finally, Figure 116 shows how it might look based on the grey scale scheme in a kaleidoscopic pattern that demonstrates by analogy the shift from pattern to pattern. The initial and final patterns are clearly cruciform, or "consonant" in our analogy. Note how a single element ("non-harmonic tone") introduced to the initial cross pattern causes it to shift, producing a brand new pattern, one that may resemble elements of the initial cruciform but slightly distorted. Pattern #3 shifts more away from the cruciform pattern to one dominated by "X's," and so on. Each pattern is valued individually as a *Klang* even if transitory to the next or eventually to the final pattern.

Each pattern thus progresses to the next, until through a series of matrices or patterns, we arrive at another cruciform ("consonant") pattern. This is not unlike Schenker's perspective on the *Uhrlinie*, wherein the most complicated chord and melodic patterns can be reduced progressively. Each chord (or note) may be either a major player in the progression, or a minor decoration used for transition.

Figure 113. Visual pattern shifting

16

Hyperextended Chords

This book proposes that chords may be extended into the third and fourth octaves of the tertial system, here afterwards referred to as "hyperextended" chords. The apology for this lies in the harmonic series and the related principle that as two notes are separated farther, the more consonant their relationship is.

One composer, Messiaen, wrote a short treatise explaining his method of composition, demonstrating at the request of admirers and responding to the public's misperceptions his technique of harmony, melody and general composition. One approach is worth mentioning here. He approached one cluster of chords from a harmonics perspective, and derived both notes and voicing from the resonance inherent in a single note. In his *Techniques of My Musical Language*, he discusses the derivation of a chord using a cluster with the intervals of the ninth, raised eleventh, raised twelfth and major seventh using functions of the harmonic series. One interesting observation is his use of these chords without the supporting fundamental and triad. He writes them as a cluster by itself, and thus the relationships seem to rely more on the internal intervallic relationships than his actual reasoning of resonance derivation.[1] For our purposes, it is also interesting to note that he did not derive new approaches in chordal construction from this in a tertial sense but merely maintained the cluster voicing and did not justify each individual note.

This clash of a perfect fourth interval produces additional harmonics, as well. Again, the voicing is an interesting approach but retains the same as in his example derived from the harmonic series. We see a chord resonating with the harmonic series' found in both G and D, these bass notes being low enough to provide the (arguably) audible tones of both series. In this case, the actual fundamentals are provided as well as expressed noted reflecting each series.

The hyperextended tones proposed by this paper include the raised fifteenth (major fifteenth), raised nineteenth (♯19) and raised twenty-third ($\sharp$23). The raised seventeenth ($\sharp$17) is non-existent in non-microtonal music, as it corresponds on the keyboard to the perfect fourth, or its octave, the perfect eleventh, both of which are arguably the most dissonant interval in a tertial context. Theoretically, it may be included if voiced properly with relation to the fundamental and especially if included in a microtonal construct so as to relate to the harmonic, f_{21} but there are octave considerations here that may not work sonically in other applications, at least in equally tempered tonal music. The raised twenty-one ($\sharp$21) is exactly the same harmonic as the multiple octave of the fundamental (f_{16}) and therefore is not considered a separate added tertial interval in practical applications of this paper.

Also included in the examples below is the raised eleventh ($\sharp$11), for although fairly low in the harmonic series and the tertial system (it is in the commonly understood "extended" area, that is, the second octave of the tertial approach), it is nonetheless non-diatonic and in function and sound corresponds well to the effect of the hyperextended chords, especially the raised fifteenth. Its consonance with other hyperextended chords (perfect fifths) will go a long way in discerning their relative consonances with relation to the chord's sonority.

Hyperextended Tones—Definitions

+15 or "major" 15 (minor second from the fundamental plus two octaves; Harmonic f_{17}):

Figure 114. +15 chord

+19 or "major" 19 (augmented fifth plus two octaves: Harmonic f_{19}) (see Figure 115 at top of next page)

+23 or "major" 23 (raised ninth, plus two octaves) (see Figure 116 on next page).

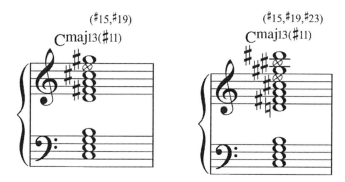

Left: **Figure 115. +19 chord.** *Right:* **Figure 116. +23 chord**

The consonance of hyper-extended chords is directly related to their positions on the harmonic series and their application with regard to voicing and range. In the figures below, those with noteheads marked "x" are the major fifteenth, major nineteenth and major twenty-third tones in our discussion. The notes listed are not the *actual pitches*, which in some cases actually do not correspond exactly to our twelve-tone, equal temperament notation system. However, since such notation is acceptable, although "out of tune," we can make the close approximation and rely on performer intonation or other designation to more accurately portray such, when necessary. In the figure below, the hyper-extended chord appear with the notehead, "x."

Figure 117. Hyperextended tones within the harmonic series (C$_{132}$ fundamental)

The Major Fifteenth: A Discussion

A major fifteenth is *not* a double octave in a tertial construction, for it is not heard as the natural doubling of frequency (as a "natural" octave would,) but as an *additional* subdivision of the vibrating material.[2] A double octave (f_4) is a ratio of 4:1. The third octave (f_8) is 8:1. The fourth octave (f_{16}) is 16:1. A major fifteenth in the harmonic series would be 17:1 with relation to the fundamental (it is the 17th harmonic where the fundamental is designated f_1. Thus, major fifteenth is designated f_{17}). As such, it is not a derivation of the octave but a consonant tone introduced in its own right.

It is also not a *stretched* octave, that is, the intentional extending of the normal octave by several cents to produce an intonation discrepancy in the harmonics of the fundamental's octaves. An example of this phenomenon is in the construction and sound of steel drums, the gamelon and other ethnic instruments.

This is considered a "major" fifteenth as an interval, because it is nonetheless not one of the "simple" intervals to the fundamental (perfect unison, perfect octave, perfect fifth or the less consonant perfect fourth). A "perfect" designation would imply one of these relationships. Its relationship with the previous tertial interval (major thirteenth, or) is also a major, not minor third. Why not just "fifteenth" without the raising designation of a sharp? Because any other label would imply key affiliation whereas this is a relationship to the fundamental, *not* the key, except in a very roundabout way. This is applicable to the major nineteenth and major twenty-third as well.

According to some sources,[3] the half step first appears in conventional Western notation and composition at the harmonics f_{11} and f_{10} with a similar ratio of 11:10. However, this harmonic is 51 cents too low to be considered in tune with the literal half step (even given alternate tunings at the same ratio). A second approach to the problem of the half step is the ratio of the harmonics at 16:15. According to the table in the Tonalsoft encyclopedia, the distance is 11.7 cents "off" of the 100-cent division and is outside the detectable deviation of 5 cents to the human ear.[4]

Finally, the ratio between f_{16} and f_{17} harmonics is not only conducive to our major fifteenth but also is the "truest" aspect of the half step interval. The half step at f_{16} and f_{17} is closer in "tune" (deviation of only +4.96 cents according to *Groves*.[5] In either case the difference is too small to be psychoacoustically important) and is a better justification for the half step. We may thus justify our major fifteenth (C to C# when C is f_1) both from a half step evolution as well as a harmonics or resonance perspective.

The Major Nineteenth Tone

Is a "♯19" tone considered an augmented fifth derivation? No, because it is not an alteration of/against the harmonic series' third harmonic of the perfect fifth and functions strictly as a naturally occurring consonance (see above regarding altered tones). As a "nineteenth," it is a higher harmonic (f_{25}), albeit it very faint with regards to the fundamental. With the Schenker perspective, only the first four tones are actually heard or considered while the others contribute to timbre only. However, as we've seen, Messiaen derived his harmonic thesis from the extension of the audible harmonic series to f_{17}[6].

In our consideration, building upon Messiaen's tonal thesis (although he derived tones from resonance, he also applied them in an equally tempered environment), we must consider both the harmonic implications as well as those consistent with equal temperament. Our major nineteenth is four octaves plus 772.63 cents from the fundamental (the perfect fifth is one octave plus 701.96 cents). Equal temperament perfect fifth is 700 cents plus one octave from the fundamental, which is 1.96 cents flat from the naturally occurring third harmonic (701.96 cents plus one octave from the fundamental). f_{24}, the perfect fifth closest to our major nineteenth, is four octaves, plus 701.96 cents, so the deviation is equivalent to above. The major nineteenth, or f_{25}, is 772.63 cents off the fourth octave of the fundamental.[7]

Therefore, the equally tempered fifth is only -2 cents off of the naturally occurring harmonic (f_{24}). f_{25} is 70.67 higher than the *naturally* occurring perfect fifth, or 29.73 cents from being exactly one-half step away. Although Messiaen justified it in his *accord de resonance*, this intonation difference will clash quite a bit to the ear and is questionable in its bid to be considered a consonance within the context of a resonant tertial chord.

As a dissonance, it holds its own if only in a rehashed dressing of the altered thirteenth chord. The benefit of such a chord comes from the tension produced between it and the real, or implied perfect fifth. This tension comes from the superposition of the minor ninth over the perfect fifth from the fundamental, producing the same—if slightly less irritating—dissonance as a minor second. There are several examples where the composer uses a minor ninth on a consistent basis to provide some semblance of comparative consonance within the limits set by himself.[8] This perspective uses the half step dissonance as a source of consonance: not the implied consonance of the harmonic series, which is still out of tune with the equally tempered #nineteenth.

This still calls into question the use of the term major nineteenth as a new chord tone. Its placement in the tertial construct implies some consonance or other justification. We will take into consideration Messiaen's perspective and justify the tempered major nineteenth based upon dissonance as well as upon the harmonic series.

The Major Twenty-Third Tone: Discussion

A "major twenty-third" tone is related to the "augmented ninth" tone, being its octave. Therefore, if we justify the second harmonically, we justify the first. The augmented ninth is the f_{20} harmonic. Its relationship to the fundamental is four octaves plus 297.51 cents. The naturally occurring minor third's octave (f_{19} is 297.51 cents above the fundamental's third octave) is 88.8 cents higher than f_{18}, or the major second.[9] The equal tempered chord brings in a new element, considering the several ways theorists have justified the minor triad in light of the major triad's "natural" existence.

Schenker's theory propounded the justification of the major triad as a natural reinforcement of the harmonic series, while the minor triad is an aberration of the major. We throw in another twist when we consider the equal temperament system tends to "communize" the system: everything is forced to be equally out of tune (except the octave) but at least all are equal! Specifically, this has implications for us in this way:

1. The major third, in equal temperament, 14 cents sharp
2. The minor third (#9 down one octave) is 2 cents sharp

For a listing of the various relationships, regarding the major and minor thirds, and the major twenty-third, refer to the following chart[10]:

natural maj3	386.31	Derived min3	315.64
ET Deviation	**13.69**	ET Deviation	**-15.64**
Tempered Maj3	400	Tempered min3	300
natural min3	286.31	natural maj3	386.31
Tempered min3	300	"natural" min3	286.31
Deviation	**13.69**	one-half step	**-100**
Derived min3	315.64	#9 (f19)	297.51
#9 (f19)	297.51	maj9 (f18)	203.91
Deviation	**-18.13**	Add 1/2 step	+100
		Deviation	**6.4**
Tempered min3	300	natural min3	286.31
#9 (f19)	297.51	#9 (f19)	297.51
Deviation	**-2.49**	deviation	**+11.2**

Table 7: Tuning relationships of hyperextended tones

The deviations of the naturally occurring augmented ninth to accepted minor third derivations are as follows:

- The derived minor third (e.g., as derived by the difference between the frequencies of f_5-f_4) is -18.13 cents flat to its equally tempered counterpart
- With relation to the naturally occurring maj9 (f_{18}), the augmented ninth is 6.4 cents flat
- With relation to the tempered minor third, the augmented ninth is 2.49 cents flat
- With relation to the natural minor, the augmented ninth is 11.2 cents sharp[11]

The augmented ninth (and again, by inference, its consonant octave, the major twenty-third), is considered by most theorists, including jazz theorists, to be an "altered" tone, that is, the intentional alteration of a consonant, diatonic tone, to be used against the major third for the dissonance of a minor ninth (minor second), and to enhance the inherent dissonance of the tritone existing between the major third and minor seventh interval (dominant effect and function) by producing an additional tritone between the perfect fifth and the minor ninth.

The augmented ninth tone is also used as the superimposition of minor third against an existing major third to simulate psychoacoustically the microtonal tendency of the blues scale. We will examine this in detail below as an artificial method to produce a specific, ethnic effect or style. It is not a functional consonance in equal temperament but is well worth examining in detail on its own merits.

Theoretical Precedence and Other Historical Indicators

The traditional and non-traditional uses of extended chords are well documented in both theory and example throughout the late nineteenth and twentieth centuries. As composers began to explore harmony beyond traditional uses, extended chords came into their own as vertical sonorities, rather than as incidental chords based on the coincidence of harmony and contrapuntal writing. How and why they are used is an interesting study, which ranges from dissonant to consonant, functional to non-functional, and even tonal to post- and a-tonal.

Composers began to explore harmonies non-functionally, that is, for their harmonic effects rather than through traditional principles of tension and resolution. For example, Ravel's *Pavane*[12] uses parallel dominant seventh chords without resolving them. Other pieces reflected ethnic and other influences such as the blue tonality of American jazz and the pentatonic-derived fourths and fifths of American folk. Tonal clusters, chords built on fourths and fifths, polytonality and other perspectives came into vogue in tonal music as the century progressed. Atonality, twelve-tone row and other attempts at non-functional tonality introduced a new aspect with regard to sonority.

In the area of "resolution" within a tonal context are the uses of these chords as "altered tones," usually found in authentic and related cadences, and as approach tones within a chord or progression. A second area relates to those which access a new perspective in harmonic consonance or non-resolution. However, "consonant" is a relative term and in this case we will examine and discard uses that are so harmonically advanced that "consonance" has no real meaning, are non-tertial in approach, imitative of micro-tonal or ethnic perspectives (such as the blues), or atonal in effect and intent.

The phenomenon of the hyperextended chords is to be considered beyond the vast majority of the uses that seem prevalent. Its validity remains in the area of using sonority for its relatively consonant sake and disregarding the potential of each of these intervals for dissonance in both tonal contexts that need resolution and other harmonic contexts that need none.

17

The Approach Tone
and Chord

The approach tone or chord is a concept in resolution, as it may be defined as a chord that approaches a target note or chord from above or below. The reason why this technique works has as much to do with linear resolution as to the nature and relationships of the chords' *Klänge* themselves. Often used as a substitute for the dominant in classical theory and jazz practice, the enharmonic sound is well known respectively as a Neapolitan sixth or ♭II. However, in addition to its progressive uses, the superimposition of an approach chord simultaneously over its target can provide both a harmonic tension and even an odd sort of consonant sonority that depends upon the context and the culture, such as in Spanish flamenco and derived styles.

Substituting and Substituting Extended Chords

When substituting extended chords, the same principle is similar to the rule regarding common-note modulations: the higher percentage of notes that are common between the two chords, the more consonant or more related the substitution. The relation of common tones is also important when determining function, lest the use of the color tones in the extended chords deter from the actual resolution of the *Klang*. The *Klang's* resolution must not be confused with the resolution of individual notes within each chord.

By using sub-positioning, we can identify function and relationship by adding tones a third lower to an existing triad.[1] In Figure 118, Bmin is merely the top three notes of Gmaj7, or to put it another way, Gmaj7 is a Bmin with a G added to the bottom. It is true that the chords contain three common notes (B, D and F♯ make up 75 percent of Gmaj7 and 100 percent of Bmin) but the chords themselves are of different characters and often of function. To properly assess this, consider the comparative consonance of the chords involved. Bmin contains three notes only. The Gmaj7 contains the G triad but adds a major seventh on top. The consonance of the *Klang* decreases as notes are added in any case, although the consonance of the inner intervals remains the same regardless of the intervals produced by the added notes. The addition of new notes adds harmonics that may interfere and compliment those in the original chord. Therefore, Gmaj7 with its four notes and major seventh interval has a different consonance than Bmin, which has a minor *Klang*.

Figure 118. Sub-positioning the B minor triad

Figure 119 shows another example in this major/minor relationship. $C\sharp$min[7] contains all of an E triad, or $C\sharp$min[7] may be thought of as an E triad with an added $C\sharp$ on the bottom. $C\sharp$min[7] is comparably more dissonant than E by virtue of having one more note, although a substitution works well here as in a Rameavian deceptive cadence. Sub-positioning implies a diatonic descent, which maintains consonant chords: e.g., no dominants or diminished chords. Including these more dissonant chords would entirely change the function, dissonance, and context of the chord within the turnaround. Maintaining the diatonic approach by adding a major third below $C\sharp$ turns the sonority into an Amaj,[9] which is more dissonant to the original substitution with five notes, although it would be considered a consonant chord in its own right and in most contexts.

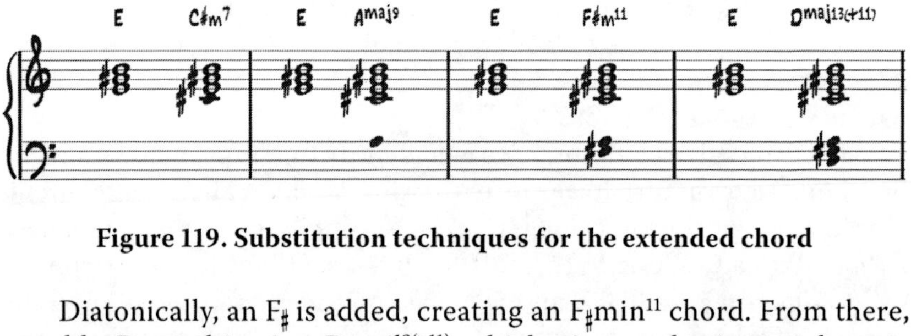

Figure 119. Substitution techniques for the extended chord

Diatonically, an $F\sharp$ is added, creating an $F\sharp$min[11] chord. From there, we add a D, resulting in a Dmaj[13(+11)], which a jazz enthusiast might consider entirely consonant. At the least, it is comparable the most dissonant chord in the series.

It is possible to actually think of Dmaj$^{13(+11)}$ as a substitution for an E major triad, since all three notes of the original chord are contained in it. However, referring to the original principle of relative consonance emphasizes the determination of function by comparing the number common notes. Although an E triad contains 100 percent of the notes involved in the original chord, only 43 percent of Dmaj$^{13(\#11)}$ is made up of notes involved in the E chord. Therefore, this is a weaker harmonic substitution for E major than Amaj^9 (60 percent) or C$_\sharp$min^7 (75 percent). Function and context are another thing entirely.

Substitutions therefore may be made based on one note, such as the melody. Common-note modulations may be considered related to this. The composer needs to keep in mind the chord progressions involved to allow harmonic development, as well as the percentage of common notes (in the above example of Dmaj$^{13[\#11]}$, the percentage of substitution based on a single note results in a common-tone percentage of 14.3 percent, from a ratio of 3 original notes to 7 total, a very weak substitution by this measurement). A second concern is the selection of tones in or out of the diatonic key. One must also consider the context of the chords within the progression, and intent, style, or culture of the piece. In Figure 120, substituting a "flat" oriented key such as F for a sharp key can imply changing keys entirely, and while very interesting in an advanced tonality, it has less applicability in a consonant tonal context.

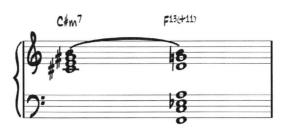

Figure 120. Extended substitutions out of progressive context

Inversions and Rewriting Substitutions

Enharmonic spelling and rewriting chords as inversions may help substitutions by reconsidering which notes are function, color, or root tones. These techniques may also help redefine linear function by observing the labeling scale degrees. While we examined its *Klang* earlier, a compositional example changes an "add 6" chord into a "min7" chord by inverting the voicing. For example, a chord spelled D, F, A, and

C may be considered a Dmin7 chord, or an $F^{(add6)}$ chord in third inversion (Figure 4).[2]

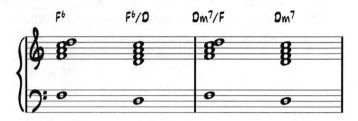

Figure 121. Comparing the functions and inversions of the D, F, A, C *Klang*

Similarly, a diminished seventh *Klang* maybe viewed enharmonically (Figure 121) by seeing $G\sharp^{\circ 7}$ (which is vii°7 of Amin) as an enharmonic first inversion of $E\sharp^{\circ 7}$ (which is vii°7 in F♯min) allows for a different function to be used. In this case, the same enharmonic pitches allow for a smooth resolution into either the key of A minor or F♯ minor and using a similar *Klang* for two contextual purposes (see the classification for these chords).

Figure 122. Comparing context and inversion in diminished chords

The V^{alt} to ♭II Substitution

The most important extended substitution as far as this book is concerned is associated with authentic cadence predecessors: the V^7, vii°, and related altered chords that are dominant in function. The most dissonant V^7 chord is altered (e.g., $^{-/+5}$ and $^{-/+9}$), and by respelling the notes in the chord, a new approach is developed that can be used in a number of ways. Figure 123 shows the possible combinations when the designation "alt" is found in jazz and popular chord symbols.

Enharmonic manipulation respells all the notes in an "alt" chord, in our example, according to the following schematic (see also Figure 124).

G remains
B becomes C♭ in the new chord

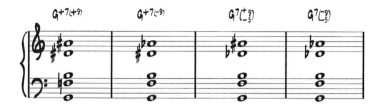

Figure 123. Altered dominant chords

D♭ remains the same
D♯ becomes E♭
F remains the same
A♭ remains the same
A♯ becomes B♭

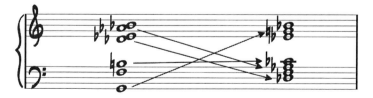

Figure 124. Enharmonic respelling of the altered dominant chord

Changing the "inversion" of this altered G7 chord produces the following results:

E♭ to the top
G to the top leaves C♭ in the bass
B♭ to the top
C♭ to the top leaves D♭ in the bass

Figure 125 shows this chord stacked in thirds resulting in a $D_\flat^{13(+11)}$ chord or a ♭II in C major. None of the pitch classes have been changed, just the spelling.

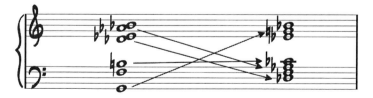

Figure 125. Enharmonic respelling the Galt[7] chord

An extended ♭II is not a substitution for an altered V7 but is the exact same thing in a different inversion. Although the order of intervals and their relationships to the fundamental bass provides different sounds and harmonics, the *Klang* essentially remains the same. Part of this results from the key role of the function tones of each chord.

The enharmonic pitches B (C♭) and F are the chord scale degrees 3̂ and 7̂ in the G^alt chord and chord scale degrees 7̂ and 3̂ in the D♭alt chord: the same tritone, merely inverted. According to common practice voice-leading rules, tritones are best resolved by half steps in an ensuing chord. In the C major scale, these same notes (F and B) are scale degrees 4̂ and 7̂ of the key, resolving melodically to scale degrees 3̂ and 8̂ (Figure 10-9). Because of the existence of these tritones that resolve to E and C (1̂ and 3̂, respectively) in the key of C major, D♭13^(+11) (♭II) and Galt (V^alt) are interchangeable as authentic cadence chords.

D♭ chords (♭II) may be considered less consonant as a chord in relationship to C only because it is not diatonic to C major (I) and introduces dissonance by the fact that dominant chords in any position are by nature dissonant. In addition, the notes D♭ and A♭ resolve to C and G (1̂ and 5̂) as half-step intervals, providing maximum tension and resolution (Figure 126).

Figure 126. The common tritone

Eliminating altered and color tones, in that order, can reduce this dissonance. D♭7 still contains the 4–7 tritone that needs to be resolved but it does not now have the ^(+11) (G), or the 13 (B♭), which can increase dissonance (Figure 127). Therefore, D♭7 by itself makes a fine substitution for V7 in the key of C major.

Figure 127. A ♭II of any consonance can provide an effective resolution

The Approach Chord

Even less dissonant as a chord but still dissonant as a half step resolution to Cmaj7 is D♭maj7 or just D♭. Either chord is successively more consonant than related extended dominant chords correspondingly resulting in weaker resolution and may still be used as a substitution for V[7].

Referring to modulations, a fully chromatic chord modulation involves moving all chord tones by half steps. Linear or melodic resolutions are also most effective when resolving by half steps. All D♭ chords we have seen above taking the place of Galt demonstrate another perspective on this. Any chord may be preceded by its own ♭II chord or approached from above chromatically. For this reason, such ♭II chords are called "approach" chords, and they are effective as an enhancement of all kinds of chord progressions and modulation problems. By inserting approach chords into a cadence, a much more interesting progression is produced that can prolong simple cadential tonalities. As with all techniques, one must remember to consider the style in which one is writing. In jazz circles, this is commonly referred to as "tritone substitution,"[3] and it is a common element in the ii-V7-I pattern common in jazz chord progressions, as shown in Figure 128.

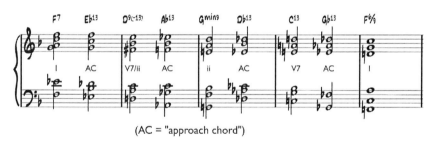

(AC = "approach chord")

Figure 128. The approach chord in a popular music tag

What the jazz community has known and used in this relationship for decades, music theorists began to apply more recently to twentieth-century analysis. Alexander Scriabin was known for it interesting harmonic approach that did not ignore the harmonic series as did many of his time, but used it hyperbolically. In Figure 129a, the "mystic" chord shows the combination of voicing in fourths but altering to reflect elements of the harmonic series. In 129b, it has been revoiced to reflect the common jazz chord, C13[(+11)]. Because the voicing sympathizes with the harmonic series, it is more consonant (refer to Chapter 11).

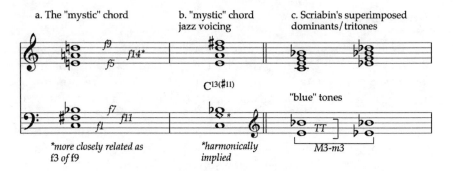

Figure 129. Examples of Scriabin's uses of the "mystic" chord and superimposed dominants

In addition, Scriabin uses several manifestations of the tritone substitution as a method of composition and harmonic complexity. Jonathan Powell cites Dernova's arrangement of Scriabin's "complementary dominant chords separated by a tritone." Continuing:

> This relationship forms the essence of the tritone link, in which the two chords, called departure and derived dominants, "are like brother and sister having related but equal and independent functions within a ... family of harmony" [Dernova, 1968].

In his analysis he states: "These pairs of chords, when arranged in an interlocking series, each pair a tone or minor 3rd higher than the last, form the harmonic backbone of many of Scriabin's late works."[4]

This aspect of Scriabin's work is particularly interesting in that these are considered by Powell to be both consonances (in that they don't really resolve) and yet contain tension at the same time.[5] The interesting thing about the tritone and minor third relationships is they form clear "blue" tones when superimposed over each other as dominant chords, providing the necessary tension in the thirds and seventh to simulate microtonality.

Scriabin's tritone relationship shows progressive and vertical justification for this order of substitution. In Powell's, the relationship also displays the inherent interchangeability similar to Messiaen's modes. This interchangeability also can influence the vertical sonority by approaching a given moment based on vertical sonority as well as progression, regardless of the level of inherent dissonance or context of the piece.

The fact that the developing tritone substitution structurally forms the basis for this relationship supports both the idea that an approach chord, or ♭II, relationship to a target chord functions in two different but related ways (Figure 130):

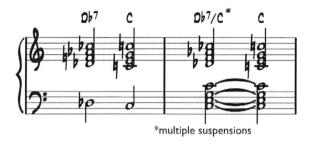

*multiple suspensions

Figure 130. Chromatic approach chords in context

In measure 1 of Figure 130, the D♭ functions as an alternative to a dominant seventh chord, as discussed above. In the second measure, the effect is laterally similar while engaging the ear in a highly tenuous sonority on the first beat of the measure. Out of context, this sonority provides a unique *Klang* completely out of the normal tonality, and each half step or minor ninth interval creates a tension seeking imminent resolution.

A third context is the voicing or selection of the D♭ chord with vertical relationship to the fundamental C (Figure 131).

Figure 131. The D♭/C *Klang* within a C harmonic series

Such a superimposition requires a number of manipulations to consider the sonority "consonant." The tension produced by overt harmonics as well as those implied creates additional harmonics, which the ear's components cannot physically reconcile. The D♭, F, and A♭ have to be voiced so high in the chord that the harmonics of the fundamental chord components are not heard beyond the sense of timbre and are not adequately reinforced. For this reason, the hyperextended tones justified in this book are limited to those that can be supported by the harmonic series alone—the D♭ and A♭ in this case—which occur low enough to be considered (refer to Messiaen's resonant chords). According to

Helmholtz, Messiaen, Howard and Angus and others, "audible" harmonics are themselves very subjective as education, musicality, and even physical and psychoacoustics play a part. The F does not occur until the next octave, which is distant from the fundamental. Even Messiaen admitted that anything above the fourth octave of resonance fades into timbral coloring heard by all, and even to those who are trained to hear them, audible notes cease to exist at all.[6]

Both the D♭ and the A♭ also fit easily into the series of fifths justified by our use of Schenker's approach. The F again does not occur until some time later (Figure 132):

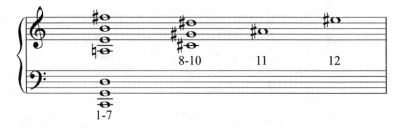

Figure 132. A3 (P4) does not occur until the twelfth permutation

Thus, as a consonant chord, the D♭/C *Klang* in its entirety does not exist in most tonal situations, although elements of the chord may be effective.

The enhanced dominant, its substitutions, and the tension in the *Klang* and the context increase the potential for effective resolution in advanced tonalities. One of the styles that most effectively uses this technique is jazz, whose consonant harmonies often extend into the second octave.

18

Jazz Analysis and Context Using Hyperextended Tones

Altered tones are often applied when the composer wishes to enhance an already unstable dominant chord. In jazz, the sounds of the dominant chord transcend the conventional Rameavian theory that such a chord is "dissonant" and therefore an unstable chord to be resolved. If a resolved, relatively consonant chord in jazz has a dominant-sounding—but not functioning—*Klang*, the composer must produce a comparably more dissonant chord that needs resolution to our more consonant, dominant-sounding I. One cannot resolve a dominant *Klang* to an equally dominant *Klang* with the same effect as in conventional notions of resolution.

By definition, an altered chord begins as a dominant or a tritone substitution of its related dominant (♭II) and usually resolves conventionally to its corresponding I. To produce an effective resolution to a I that has a dominant *Klang*, the dominant is enhanced chromatically, resulting in internal intervals of minor seconds and ninths.

This method appears especially in the areas of bebop, cool, and other late swing periods of the forties and beyond, where the tonality is more complicated than in popular or earlier styles. Progressive jazz, with its habitually extended harmonies, developed altered chords a matter of course and even extended their purposes to consonant ideas. The consonant use of altered chords was perpetuated by the chromatic improvisations of the soloists or the improvised accompaniment of the piano and guitar. Often, the ♭II/V^{ALT} substitution allowed alterations of the ♭II itself to enhance an approach chord resolution in both classical and jazz styles. In the following example (Figure 133), chromatic enhancements create relative, not static, resolution (spellings are with respect to the *Klang* of each chord, not for purposes of voice leading).

The tension-producing chord or chords in jazz that are intended for

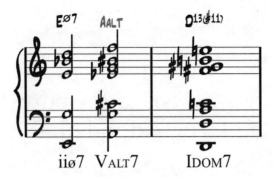

Figure 133. The altered chord in a jazz context

eventual resolution may include expressed tones and/or implied tones. The tension-producing chord contains tones that are actually played and thus provides a direct volume and subsequent harmonic relation between it and any tone close to it. This includes either half- or whole-step relationships, often regardless of octave. The implied-tone chord does not rely on expressly played tones but upon the relationships between tones implied by expressed tones and their resulting harmonic series.

The acoustic reason for this is found in the example of the $G7^{(b9, \natural 13)}$ chord (Figure 134). In this case, the expressed tones are the root (G) and the fifth (D). Both are *root* tones as defined above. The tension-enhancing tones are the A♭ and E♭, which bring out the half-step dissonance found in Western music. This expressed-tone chord shows how the root tones are reinforced to bring out the half steps.

Figure 134. Expressed dissonances

An "implied" tone in a tension-producing chord may be found in the common augmented chord. The G+ (V+ in C major) in Figure 135 is made up of comparably consonant intervals; the chord contains stacked major thirds. Even the aggregate augmented fifth is merely an enharmonic minor sixth and may be regarded as a somewhat consonant interval. The chord is nonetheless highly unstable and requires resolution of some sort in tonal music. The root tone, "G," sounds a series of harmonics, whose effect cannot be disregarded. The third harmonic (after the fundamental) is the fifth, D, which sounds reasonably strong regardless of timbre. This "implied" fifth strains against the expressed augmented fifth, again producing the instability of a half-step interval. The resolution in this case is not necessarily to another chord and may be merely the releasing of the augmented fifth to the (now-expressed) perfect fifth.

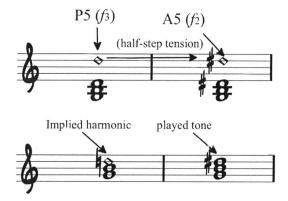

Figure 135. Half step between implied and expressed A5 harmonics

V-I Resolutions

Resolutions of the V-I relationship may be enhanced by the addition of half steps to either the tension-producing chord or the linear relationship. The $\hat{7}$- $\hat{8}$ and $\hat{4}$ - $\hat{3}$ relationships were mentioned above as the primary mode of linear resolution in the V-I progression. Others may be added, as in Figure 136.

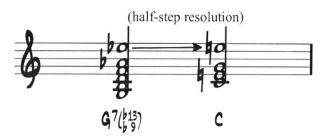

Figure 136. Linear resolutions (V-I)

All these cases have dual purposes: harmonic and melodic. The chromatic tones create dissonance within the tension-producing chord and resolve melodically by half steps to the ensuing chord tones. This also works in relevant substitutions:

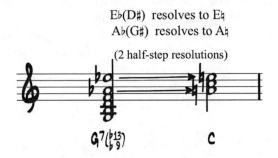

Figure 137. Linear resolutions with substitutions

The Approach Chord in a Jazz Context

A *fully* chromatic chord modulation involves moving all chord tones by half steps. Linear or melodic resolutions are also most effective when resolving by half steps. The D♭ chord taking the place of G^alt demonstrates another perspective on this as well. By inserting approach chords into a tag, one produces a much more interesting progression than a simple series of V7-I.

Chords may also be approached chromatically from below, but these are significantly weaker and are not often used, except as special effects. Approach chords from below are weaker due to the multiple reinforcing of a single leading tone in parallel movement and a movement between similar chord dissonances (e.g., no distinct tension-resolution model). A movement with contrary motion both reinforces the leading tone-tonic resolutions and resolves the tension-resolution relationship more completely. The approach chord from below is often found in rock where "scooping" to the target chord is done on the guitar,

Figure 138. Approach chords from below

particularly in those styles that have "rockabilly" or Southern rock roots. These scooping chords are often analyzed as "neighboring" chords[1] (Figure 138).

19

Approach Chords Applied in Improvisation

Improvisers apply approach tone principles in the following ways:

* Approach tones to chord or melodic tones.
* Arpeggiated approach chords over a static progression.
* Arpeggiated approach chords over a moving progression.
* Consonant tones providing extra "color" (as melodic and harmonic "hyperextended" tones).

As approach tones to chord or melodic tones, chromatic notes can enhance an otherwise bland melody. In Romantic music, we see chromatic ornamentation written by Chopin, for example, used in a fashion over the basic contour of a melody. In jazz improvisation, the same can be true, and the melodic line contains chromaticism for providing momentary tension-and-release moments within the overall contour.

In a Rameauvian context, this may be an "extended" non-harmonic tone as a type of "chromatic neighbor" (CNT). Each chromatic approach tone in Figure 139 can be used in traditional but chromatic, "non-harmonic" ways, such as neighbor tones (measure 3), appoggiatura (measures 5, 10–11), and passing tones (measures 8 and 9). Even in a Schenkerian context, chromatics may be extended until resolution occurs, even measures later.

Arpeggiated approach chords can be applied in a similar way but the aggregate tonality of the arpeggiation prolongs the chromatic relative tension and enhances the resolution when it occurs. It also approximates the overall sonority that a simultaneously played A♭/G *Klang* will produce (Figure 140).

Such a technique best occurs when there is a solid anchor around which to arpeggiate the improvisation. This is common when a fourth

Opposite, bottom: **Figure 140. Arpeggiated approach tones in improvisation**

Figure 139. Single approach tones as momentary resolution

type of "non-harmonic" situation happens in the pedal-tone. The first movement of the second concerto for piano contains such an anchor as shown in Figure 141. The rhythm section provides a tempo, rhythm, ostinato, and harmonic foundation (C minor) during the cadenza: a "pedal tone" as it were, in each field. A tonal anchor provides a way to leave the security of tonality without confusing the ear as long as it is referred to either on continuous or momentary bases. The piano improvises, returning to the tonic during this short version but exploiting the Phrygian tonality as the following diagram shows.

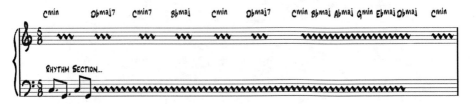

Figure 141. Diagram of the harmonic progression in the cadenza (Ballard, Jack. *Concerto for Piano, Orchestra, and Jazz Continuo, no. 2* (Portland, OR: Kiwibird Music, 1994). Used by permission.

The advantage of such an anchor arrangement is the departure from an established tonality and its eventual return in spite of whatever dissonances may occur during the departure. In this case, the chords return to the predominant C minor and the initial theme.

Even though it is more dissonant without such an anchor, arpeggiated approach chords *can* work over a moving chord progression. In this case, the arpeggiation still acts as an unresolved non-harmonic approach chord but merely prolongs the tension before resolving it (see Figure 142).

Hyperextended tones provide extra color to an otherwise ordinary diatonic melody and can give an extra lushness to a resolution (see Figure 143).

In measure 1, the D is a raised eleventh appoggiatura leading to the fifth of the chord. This acts as a momentary leading tone to the chord tone (its position as the fifth of the chord is immaterial in this approach). Another leading tone is found in measure 5 as a D leading to an extended chord tone (E♭). In these cases, the aspect of resolving half-step tension is clear. However, other chromatic tones (F♯ and F§) act as *unresolved* approach tones (to the G and G♭, respectively), as does the augmented fifteenth in measure 8 (A§). These provide an extra prominence to the chord without sounding completely dissonant, transitory, or tension-producing.

Figure 142. Arpeggiated approach chords over a moving progression

Figure 143. Approach tones color the melody

20

The Blue Tonality
and the Augmented
Twenty-Third

In a previous chapter, we explored the idea of a "non-functional" dominant in the context of using enhanced dissonance to improve resolution in style that have inherently complex "consonant" chords. The limitations of the Western gamut, a microtonal system, instrumental limitations and advantages, and context combined to develop the system characteristic of modern blues.

The "blues" developed in American music with the interaction of African and European cultures from the seventeenth through twentieth centuries and arguably is still developing. One characteristic of the blues is its unique method of utilizing the microtones with respect to the equally tempered tones of the twelve-tone system. The aggregate sound results in a tonality that awkwardly balances between the major and minor tonalities.

Significantly, the primary tone that defines a blues sound is somewhere between the minor and major thirds of our Western system (refer to Figure 144). The second tone is arguably between the minor and major sevenths but it is possible that the lowered seventh favored by blues and jazz musicians is either developed from an attempt to fool the ear into the microtonal area between major and minor scales, or a microtonal compromise between the lowered seventh and major sixth to adhere to the microtonal harmonic, H^7. The least important tone in the blues scale but still significant, is the microtone between the diminished and perfect fifths.

The half-step approach in Western music opposes minimizing tuning as a function or reason for hyperextension. The *relationship* defines the intonation issue. Hindemith touched on this when wrestling with the issue of the minor triad. Elizabeth Godley and Roger F.T. Bullivant

Figure 144. The blues scale

assert that "the minor triad in Hindemith's view is a 'clouded' version of the major triad ... but why the almost negligible distance between the major and minor thirds should have such extraordinary psychological significance remains a mystery."[1] The perspective on minor and on the even more "negligible" blue tone depends upon the ear and brain's relationships with an existing environment or culture (such as a major tonality, not to mention usage). This relative hearing accounts for much of Godley's and Bullivant's concern.

Very often, the context extends beyond culture or compositional approach. A blues relationship is clear when in melodic context with the tonic, dominant, and related scaled degrees of 1 and 5, which are melodically stable, or consonant tones of the scale. Without this reference and without the comparison to these scale degrees, as well as the major scale, a "blue" tonality becomes indistinguishable from a borrowed chord, altered minors (harmonic) or even superimposed major/minor contexts:

Figure 145. Blues in context

An excellent example of a blue tone and the "impossible" reconciliation the ear must accomplish is found in Solomon Burke's recording of "None of Us Are Free," as performed with the Five Blind Boys from Alabama.[2] The song has an overall minor sound, with some modal highlights. As the song finishes, the concluding chord settles on a blue-sounding major triad, with the middle voice's very slow vibrato or ornamentation settling somewhere between the major and minor thirds. In a minor key, the effect of this "brighter" blue triad is not unlike the Picardy third technique of the Baroque period, yet in relationship to the tonic chord, emits a strong blues impression.

Practical Notation

The only way to attain a "bluesy" sound in an equal-tempered twelve-tone system is to play the nearest equally tempered notes one against another. Generally, this presents the minor tonality superimposed over a major environment: the minor third against the major third, the minor seventh against the major, and occasionally the diminished fifth against the perfect (Figure 146).

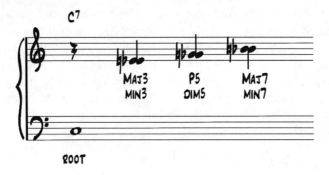

Figure 146. Blue notes as imitated on the piano

A second, more common way imitates this method with the harmonic conflict of the tritone in the major third and minor seventh, resulting in a dominant seventh-sounding chord. This tritone interval is in direct conflict with our earlier assertion regarding perfect fifth consonance on a vertical basis. Whereas we can justify a major seventh chord because of the resonating perfect fifth of the third (B and E in a Cmaj7 chord), the tritone in the dominant seventh provides the half-step tension necessary in either the third or the seventh to approximate the quarter-tone blue tonality. The function of this dominant sound is therefore completely different, being harmonic and not progressive.

The blue tonality is found in both post-tonal classical and popular styles. An examination within the context of hyperextended chords shows these styles develop different purposes and effects and hyperextended chord writing generates the deliberate alteration of existing harmonic tones and consonance within triadic perspectives.

Figure 147. The blue note implied in the dominant seventh sound

Moreover, the comparably low voicing of the blue third (and other notes) decries the purpose of harmonic resonance that a hyperextended context relies upon. Similar to Hindemith's perspective on the minor (as an aberration of the major triad resonance), the blue note requires the tension between the expressly played major and minor notes for the effect to actually occur. This includes the raised ninth in the dominant seventh chord of classic funk, jazz, and rock tunes whose placement directly lies against the octave of the major third, as in Figure 148.

Figure 148. The 7$^{(\sharp 9)}$ chord

Harmonic Considerations

Probably the most common use of hyperextended tones in jazz resolution contexts is found when the intentional writing of such chromatic tones fights against the prevailing diatonic sonority. One characteristic of the blues is its unique tonality of utilizing the microtones between the equally tempered tones of the twelve-tone system, attempting to fool the ear into "hearing" the actual microtonal system.

A chord common in funk and jazz styles is the dominant seventh with an altered ninth, which demonstrates the difference between a "blue" effect using major and minor thirds, and a marginally more consonant 7$^{(\sharp 9)}$ voicing emphasizing the augmented ninth. The predominant sound of the song is that of the blues tonality: such consonance is representative. This *Klang* relies on the voicing to enhance both the blues and better consonance.

An augmented ninth approach allows the harmonics of the fundamental to be reinforced, not opposed, rather than voicing the minor third against the major third. With the major-minor third voicing, the half-step dissonance is very strong. However, the major seventh of the

Figure 149. D7$^{(+9)}$ funk chord

augmented ninth voicing merely reinforces harmonics at that octave that already exist. This is especially true when an initial voicing includes a deep fundamental bass that reinforces its octave harmonics in the optimum chord perception range between 300 Hz to 1 kHz. In jazz, this might be shown with a string or electric bass two or more octaves beneath the chording instrument.

Figure 150. Comparing voicing in the blues context

Such a low fundamental brings the natural audible harmonics within the middle frequencies where listeners are more likely to identify the *Klang* most effectively.

Consonant Tones: Melodic Application

Hyperextended chords may be used in melodic construction as compatible, if not consonant, tones. Melodies can be transitional, as in non-harmonic chromatic tones. This is demonstrated above,

Opposite: **Figure 151. Jazz example**

as successful improvisation is merely spontaneous and intentional composition.

The harmonic elements of the underlying chords in jazz must be considered as well. This relies on the melodic line but also on the

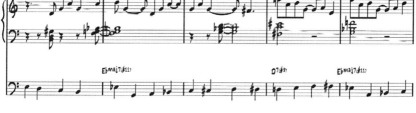

aggregate effect of the melody in partnership with the chords. In the previous example (Figure 151), the superimposition is shown of a quartal melody over a comparably static chord progression.

The boxes indicate the hyperextended tones with relation to the prevailing harmony. What may be most interesting is the series of tension-and-release based on the hyperextended tones, in spite of (or because of) the inherent tension in the chromatic chord progression. The melody is arguably F mixolydian (the occasional B♭ and E♭, especially at the end support this interpretation), and it is possible that the chord progression is the dissonance that needs resolution into the F tonality of the melody.

The first four measures contain an aggregate quartal harmony based on D^4. These are normally very dissonant with relation to a basic "E" major chord (or in jazz, even the consonant non-dominant E7 chord) and would be analyzed as an aggregate pedal chord resolving as the third and fourth measures' chord resolves to an Fmaj7. This may be identified as bitonality in classical analysis, recalling Ives' style. Even here it may be analyzed as hyperextended tonality, albeit in a dissonant, not consonant context.

One of the basic tenets of analysis encourages the theorist to look at the beginning and ending for points of relative resolution in a tonal piece. This piece begins and clearly ends on an $E^{+7(\#9)}$, and there are several points of resolution at the end, as demonstrated in Figure 152.

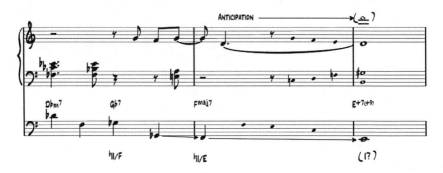

Figure 152. Ending, with triad analysis

On initial analysis, the ending shows a simple $\hat{5}$ - $\hat{1}$ in the melody. A second observation shows the descending chromatic chord progression, containing two successive ♭II-I pairs. Both approaches support a consonant "resolution" in measure 20. The Fmaj7 sounds conclusive given the ♭II preceding it (the G♭ is even dominant in sound *and* function, which lends credence to the first resolution), and the A-D in the melody merely sounds like a jazz ornamentation. The brilliance of the composition is shown in the successive movement to E+7$^{(\#9)}$, a dissonant chord in itself but perfectly consonant given the context of the song, the beginning chord (the same), and the compatibility of the sustained melody (minor seventh). This ♭II-I resolution establishes the E+7$^{(\#9)}$ as a chord that is resolved *to*, not one that needs resolution. As such, it may be argued that the $^{+5}$ and $^{+9}$ may be voiced as shown in Figure 156 as hyperextended tones (augmented nineteenth and augmented twenty-third, respectively), and is, given the standard practice of piano and guitar voicing in relation to the fundamental bass. However, it is to be understood that this "more consonant" voicing also relies on the principle of separation of lines where the harmonic interaction is not nearly so strong and individual tones are more distinct.

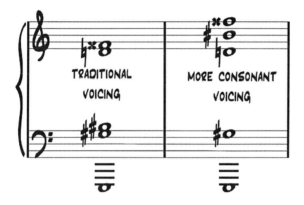

Figure 153. Consonance in an E+7$^{(+9)}$ chord

The extension of harmonies and the use of chromaticism within both tension and resolution contexts progressed as the tonality of jazz became in turn more acceptable to the public, composers, and improvisers. As such, hyperextended tones become useful as both dissonant and consonant *Klänge*, and such an approach to analysis requires reconsideration as to the context of chromatic tones with relation to primarily diatonic chords. It should come as no surprise to see that the best examples of this tonality in the symphonic and chamber worlds recall the jazz and blues sounds.

21

The Enigmatic Spanish Phrygian: A Contextual Case Study

Introduction

One case that focuses on unusual uses of these interactive harmonies, with cultural, popular and classical crossover, is that of music from southern Spain, noticeably associated with the Andalusian area. This area was strongly influenced by the tidal conflict between Arabian invasion and subsequent European responses, bringing culture from both sides into a unique progeny. A comparison of the instruments and the contributions to our Western Rameauvian music theory gives several perspectives of what constitutes consonance, dissonance with its corresponding resolutions, and harmonic interactions.

From ethnomusicologist Henry Farmer through the guitarist Paco de Lucía, there have been few dissenting opinions declaring the Moroccan invaders of the eighth century had a direct influence on the music of Spain over the next seven hundred years. One of the most significant fights in early ethnomusicology involved long papers and even books written by Kathleen Schlesinger and Farmer over the question of how much influence the Arabs actually wielded over Western musical approaches. Most scholars agree this has never been settled. The question is, what was this influence and what influenced the "influencers," so to speak? Indications seem to be that they were at least influenced by, if they did not actually assume the complete knowledge of, the Grecian thought on music from the ancient philosophers and mathematicians, as well as passing on the Arabic perspective on mathematics and music to the European growth of modern music theory.

Sources

The most dependable manuscripts on music and theory are dated from no earlier than the eighth century itself, and as Islam has always turned a suspicious eye towards music as a possible avenue of licentiousness, the pre–Islamic pagan and other sources lend themselves to a significant position regarding the philosophies of the Arabs.

Amnon Shiloah, one of the leading experts in Middle Eastern music at the Hebrew University of Jerusalem, sees these influences as significant:

> [Ancient Oriental civilizations] vanished with the advent of Islam, [and] has left traces of a sophisticated modal system, probably of the same nature as that which later evolved in the Muslim realm. Most of the information concerning Sassanid court music and its system has reached us indirectly, through Arab literature. But even though the information may be corrupt and mutilated, we cannot be mistaken about the existence of an organized modal system [in pre–Islam][1]

Others see Grecian influences in the writings of Al-Farabi and other significant Arab theorists. If nothing else, the consistency in philosophy, the approaches to empirical data and experimentation, the historical cross-pollination from trade and politics, and the references to musical relationships indicate that the "pagan" Greeks may have directly impacted the Arab musical approach.

Part of the issue is the mystery of the so-called "Spanish Phrygian." This scale is an approach unique to the Iberian Peninsula, specifically associated with the Andalusian culture. There are several "problems" with the scale in its unique deviation from Rameauvian and church music theory. Most important, the harmonic perspective is impossible to reconcile by ordinary means. This chapter will attempt to bring forth a hypothesis justifying the harmonic sound and the historical background and bring into context its position that justifies the A15 as noted in the previous chapter.

Many papers on this topic wrestle with the issue of historical accuracy. Shiloah states that problems erupt from "vagueness of definitions, inconsistency in the use of a fluid terminology, and the likelihood of mistakes made by copyists who did not always understand what they were copying."[2] Related to this are the issues of language and language alphabet, then seeing this (even if interpreted properly) through the lens of the culture, then finally interpreting it according to the culture as it existed at the period of writing. A non-musical example is in the adamant instruction in Islam of the need to read the Koran in Arabic for complete understanding. Finally, the filter of musical interpretation and expression, and the inherent bias of the primary writer come into play. As a result, many "primary" sources are truly "secondary" and must be considered suspect. New conclusions may be drawn from existing data.

Context

The Moorish occupation of southern Spain in the eighth century produced an uncannily tolerant society. For the next seven hundred-odd years, Andalusia was a true melting pot of Muslim, Christian and Jewish cultures, sworn enemies throughout most of the rest of the Mediterranean area. This tolerance provided an interaction in the arts and sciences to the benefit of each. It is in this "Andalusian" culture—for no longer could it truly be called any combination of the above, given its homogeneity—that classic "give-and-take" in the disciplines produced ideas that were the brainchildren of two or more parents. It is in this area that Spanish theorists began to challenge the conventions of Boethius and Guido of Arezzo and reconsider the interactions of the tetrachord systems hitherto established.

The Arabian school of scientists included several who investigated the modal approach to music theory. Al-Farabi was the foremost with very clear and concise approaches to melodic and linear harmonic perspective. Ibsen, while discussing Wright's commentary on the modal system, mentions two others: "Safi al Din Abd al Mu'min al Urmawi, the so-called 'founder'; of the 'Systematist School.' ... contributed two important works *Kitab al Adwar* and *Risalah al Sharafiyyah* [and] Qutb al Din al Shirazi (1236–1311)."[3]

The period in which these are written is within the established time period of Islam's maximum influence, to the present day. The influence of Arabian music theory spread throughout northern Africa and was in turn influenced by others.

Spheres of Influence

From the early Greeks through Boethius to the Arabs, the concept of "order" being a relational part of music and integrally involved with the "harmony" of the universe was well accepted in both European and Arabian schools. Farmer makes it clear that this concept was very much a part of the Iberian peninsula and "had already found acceptance among the Western Arabs of Al-Andalus or Spain, with this rather interesting addition, that the colour scheme found expression in the strings.... How all these ideas were developed in the west, we see in a work entitled the *Ma'rifal al-naghamat al-thaman...*"[4]

He continues by taking issue with Wright regarding an idea that North Africa and Spain were somehow isolated from the rest of Arabian science, in that the "Andalusian modal system of the *Maghrib* seems to have developed features of its own."[5] It is clear that the element of geography and cultural metamorphosing must be considered in light of the unique elements that Spain developed over that significant seven hundred-odd years.

The Arabs also were influenced by other aspects of the Mediterranean area. The all-encompassing Pax Romana from the time of ancient Greece through the Dark Ages propelled Hellenistic philosophy and culture through its possessions. It is difficult to believe that the Arabian culture and sciences would remain untouched by such philosophies, not to mention celestial, logical, artistic and empirical approaches, no matter how aloof they held themselves. The reverse is also true: as advanced as the thinking within Arabic music theory was, and as "enthusiastic" as Islamic proselytizing could be, it is equally difficult to imagine that others could not be influenced or appreciate the approaches of the Arabs.

The peoples of Andalusia, North Africa, Turkey, Iran, Afghanistan, Central Asia and even Northern India "shared important ideas on music theory, anecdotal materials about music and musicians, the importance of the vocal tradition, the legitimacy-of-music discussion, concerns for maintaining the purity of Qur-anic chant...."[6]

Shiloah discusses one theorist who influenced others:

> abu'l Farajj al-Isfahani (d. 967) in his Kitab al-aghani (The Book of Songs) ... [had a] profound impact of Persian art music and, to a lesser degree, that of Byzantine music ... we cannot determine the extent of the influence of the Persian modal system but it undoubtedly played an important role in the establishment of the new musical art, which developed both from pre–Islamic Arabic music and from the important contributions of the nations converted to Islam.[7]

Each mentioned scholar—Middle Eastern and Western—was unequivocal in the fact that influences were somehow felt throughout all of Western and Middle Eastern societies. Only Farmer seems to adhere to the dogma that practically anything good found in Western music theory came from the Arabs. Others are more generous in asserting that "the door swings both ways." If the Arabs influenced other cultures, there is no question that ideas were brought into their cultures from others, through their own conquests of others or assimilation through trade (note the development and geography of *lingua franca* in Arabian, English, and Swahili, for an example of cultural assimilation and adoption).

Tillyard comments further:

> I put forward the view some years ago that the so-called eight modes of the modern Greek or Chrysanthine system were based on Arabo-Persian scales, borrowed through the Turks. A full confirmation of this opinion is supplied by some phonographic experiments of Pére Thibaut, who found that the modes as sung by a Greek Archimandrite corresponded minutely to some of the Arabian varieties ... we may still assume that Byzantine melodies have survived, though not untouched by Oriental influence, in contemporary Greek Church music. A purer tradition may probably be found among the Graeco-Albanian colonies in Sicily.[8]

Farmer's assertion at least agrees with such cross-pollination, stating that instrumentalists and theory went hand-in-hand with the political, literary and intellectual elements of each culture.[9]

One thing that seems to fly in the face of this utopia of free idea exchange is the emphatic legalism of the growing new religion of Islam. As Islam and related cultures developed, it looked with askance upon the "forbidden pleasure" of music. It saw music as an art that could use its influences to affect a person's mind in the same manner of a drug, even to the point of rendering him prostrate or even killing him. Certain elements were clearly forbidden, while others were (depending upon the interpretation, culture and geographical influences) tolerated.

If music is a "forbidden pleasure" to many Muslims, how is it that the instrumental contact, not to mention the theory, survived from the time of Muhammad until the tenth century or later, when European theorists began to take it seriously? It is possible that music as a division of Mathematics, as with the Greeks, was acceptable as it dealt with the emotionless concrete science, whereas the actual operation that elicited sensuosity (and therefore transgressions against Allah) was not. Thence, how did the modes survive and how did they so drastically influence the execution styles of the Spanish and western Europe?

Arabian Music, Instruments, Tuning and Modes

Instruments

For many ethnomusicologists and theorists, the legacy formed by old and current culturally based instruments provides a concrete format from which to derive theoretical implications. While manuscripts may be considered "concrete" in nature, the symbols, colloquialisms and contexts inherent in such MSS are subjective to the experience and interpretation of the researcher, and the context of the culture in which it was written.

Instruments do not change. Once it is created—even on a single, unique basis in culture, materials or construction—it exists and the ideas, methods and rules of the builder remain intact as long as the instrument itself does. For this reason, the instrument is a primary source of current ethnic and historical data regarding the tuning, modes and scales and possibly the harmonic implications of the music in question.

A primary instrument of the ancient Arabs (pre–Islam and early Islamic periods) for theory perspectives was the *'ud.* This is the Arabian version of the "lute" with several strings running over a neck or soundboard. Several things are to be taken into consideration. First, the *'ud's* strings were fretted and as such give a dependable basis on what "tuning" means within an instrumental context. Second, a "lute" as we might know it is generally thought of as being a chordal "accompaniment" as more than one string are actively or passively played. Every scholar of Arabian music of the time indicates the complete absence of intentional harmony or chordal perspective in Arabian music and the concept is that of consistent melodic support. "Whether a musician had his song accompanied by one or fifty instruments, nothing save the melody was performed, for as the author of the *Kitab al-aghani* says, everyone 'played as one....' Harmony, in our sense of the word, was unknown. Its place [of importance] was taken by rhythm (*iqa*')."[10]

However, this cannot mean that there is *no* perception of harmony. Several treatises hint at, if not actually indicate, a concept of drone, and the very fact that the *'ud* has a resonator with more than one string must indicate some sort of sympathetic vibration. How this is used, perceived or tolerated is not known for certain.

Jerome of Moravia mentioned the *rubeba* as being significant in the middle ages. The *rubeba* is indicated as a European instrument, although Christopher Page comments on its analogy to the *'ud* if not actually denoting this instrument:

> The source of this word itself is clearly Arabic *rabab* which today, in various forms, denotes a host of stringed instruments all of the Arabic-speaking world ... this instrument is bi-chordic (a relatively rare phenomenon in medieval Europe), and is tuned to a fifth.... This Moroccan instrument was widely distributed in the middle ages [*sic*].[11]

Tuning

Tuning is probably the biggest issue in considering the Spanish Phrygian scale. It is well known that the Arabic scales are literally twice as complicated as our Western scales. Where the Western octave is generally divided into twelve parts (and this has changed over the centuries), Arabian octaves are generally accepted as having been divided into twenty-four, usually equal, parts. This also is assumed to have changed somewhat in the last thirteen centuries. Collangettes argues ... "the modern scale is not a tempered scale that derives its progression from 24√2; it is the old scale of the thirteenth century to which have been added several small intervals."[12]

The various applications of tunings in Arabian and North African music are often subject to the voice. Instrumental music is derivative and supports vocal work, especially in those farther removed geographically from the Middle East, proper. Tunings on accompanying stringed instruments began on upper strings and generally related in fourths, producing various tetrachords. These in turn depended upon the culture and application of the music and/or instrument. Two *general* scales seemed to be a pentatonic derivative and a chromatic modification of this pentatonic scale, although modes more analogous to Grecian and medieval Church modes are also evident. When these actually developed and which came first are part of the question.

Touma's *La musique arabe*: "while the earlier system was of purely Arabic origin, the later one 'relied on a form derived from the Pythagorean system—origin of the actual Turkish and Persian tonal systems.' It was by departing from the purely Arabic tonal system 'that the modern Arab theorists proceeded to the division of the octave into approximately twenty-four equal intervals.'"[13]

Farmer's work with Al-Farabi developed a scale based upon the division of a string into forty parts. How these parts are developed is also part of the question, for while the Church modes of Western music may be derived from an octave's dodecatonic division, they are unique. There is a multitude of modes and their variations in Arabic music that often are analogous to these modes. These may be interchanged, added, merged according to the performer/composer.

In either case, derivative modes are significantly part of the Arab mien. Again, the *'ud* is an instrument of choice for the Arab theorist, much as the keyboard is the instrumental reference for Western theorists of the last five centuries. Wright says, "Arab writers of this period generally discussed intervals and scales in terms of notes produced on the lute."[14] His extensive cataloging of Arabian modes reflects the tunings of the *'ud,* which was in fourths. He believed the available notes on the *'ud* was reduced to two, conjunct tetrachords, much in the same way modes in the West developed from the tenth centuries. The fact that "conjunct tetrachords" were significant approaches to music theory in both Islamic and Christian worlds indicate some sort of cross-pollination, as the approach would probably never have developed along parallel lines, given the divisions of the octaves between the two cultures.

In this context, the octave has a special consideration. The Arabs recognized that the octave was not merely another note as did many in the European pre-tonal collective but corresponded in tone to the fundamental. A scholar in Arab music theory will notice when it occurred but during the time that Arabian music most effectively influenced Spain, the octave was an accepted phenomenon much as we know it today. The octave is called the "reply" and modes have names in the seven-degree scale, which possibly corresponded (in usage, if not in literal tonality) our modes, much as the original Church modes have.

Modes

Several things confuse the issue. We have mentioned the "possibilities" of "notes" as indicated on the *'ud* and other stringed instruments ranged from twenty-four to forty divisions of a single string. "Modes" as defined by several authorities, could mix, match and merge selectively from these available "notes" or lute fingering positions.

There are indications that the term "modes" may be misleading, although for our purposes, matching them allegorically or literally to Rameauvian theory may be of value. It is easiest to think of "modes" as ways to indicate a special starting point or perspective in a scale from which they could write new melodies, not unlike alternate tuning on a guitar that can generate unconventional sounds. It is possible that "modes" to an Arabian was more similar to the Indian *raga,* in that it was an established "melody" whose notes could be selected and assembled (much in the same way a jazz musician may use a ii-V-I progression or a blues pattern in various keys to "write" or perform a new song or as a basis for improvisation).[15] This is likely what is meant by the "conjunction" of modes as stated by several writers. "In addition, according to Safi al-din, some other modes were used in practice that did not receive proper names, and these are designated by a general name: *murakkabat* (singular: *murakkab*)—compound modes. This implies the possibility of multiple combinations."[16] Is it possible that the two scales, Ionian (major) and Phrygian implied in the "Spanish Phrygian" are derived from the combination of the practice of these "combination" scales and/

or the addition of a Spanish/Arab version of a Picardy third? Permutations of scales are numerous and they probably varied according to song, region and style: basically by analogy all of the issue we deal with in both classical and folk/traditional music.

Yunus al-Katib (d. c. 760) and Al-Khalil (d. 791) in *Kitab alnagham*,[17] presented eight modes and Khusrau Parwiz (590–628),[18] twelve but Wright claimed

> the normal octave was heptatonic…. As it is certain that the normal range was a full octave (at least) and that therefore the octave note was a part of the gamut which all calculation would have to take into account, it follows that the normal number of notes to the octave was seven. The eight notes of statement must then be held to include the octave note.[19]

This is consistent with Western theory in which the octave is held to be the "eighth" note. Ironically, the "eight" and "twelve" modal concepts coincide with the discussion over the same modal interpretations in sixteenth century Europe. It does not seem surprising, then, that one of these modes coincided with the so-called "Phrygian" mode of sixteenth century (and earlier) thought. In fact, Collangettes, Wright and Farmer give comprehensive listings of the various modes found in Arabian music. One of the most interesting and applicable modes regarding the Spanish Phrygian is listed by Collangettes as *Sabbaba fi majra al-wusta* with the following Western designation:

| E | F | G | A | B | C | D | (E) | i | II | III | iv | vo | VI | vii | (i) |
| 1 | ↓2 | ↓3 | 4 | 5 | ↓6 | ↓7 | (1) | min | MAJ | MAJ | min | dim | MAJ | min | (min) |

Figure 154. E Phrygian and associated chords (Wright, "Ibn al-Munajjim," 32. Note: this is in relation to the major as found in the original article)

This mode is clearly Phrygian of the Church modes, according to Wright's above interpretation and the corroboration by other scholars. This is also subject to their interpretation of the tunings (twenty-four or forty, as the case may be) as they relate to our Western approach to the octave's divisions.[20]

Andalusian Music and Tonality

Flamenco Music Elements

"The specifically Andalusian character of flamenco is clear in its Arab-influenced modal melodies and melismatic vocal style, and in its combination, or juxtaposition, of European common-practice I-IV-V harmonies with progressions and chords that have evolved from modal originals (most notably, the familiar progression Am-G-F-E, in E Phrygian/major)."[21]

The "dual tonicity" of Am-G-F-E is commonly heard by the Westerner as i-VII-VI-V but by the Andalusian as iv-III-II-I. This works only if Phrygian mode is accepted as the basis for the melody. Even in Western European theory, the paradigm shifts the ear to the Aeolian mode (relative minor), especially with the E major (as per above reference, with no sharps or flats) serving as an awkward V. With the guitar (and early *vihuelas*) intentionally performing a chordally based accompaniment to the (usually) vocal lead, we bring in two new dimensions, as well.

An examination of the Phrygian mode reveals an anomaly in the field of modal composition: namely, that the *final* is E (in the key of C)[22] when considered melodically. With the guitar (or chording instrument) introduced, the resulting *final* should be E minor. However, in classic Andalusian, including *flamenco* and its related styles, the *final* chord is E major. This flies in the face of traditional modal approach, be it Western or Arab.

Manuel brings in the Arabian element. There is no question that the Arabs influenced the melodies inherent in the Andalusian style: Moorish conquerors could not help leaving some legacy on the Iberian peninsula in seven hundred years of occupation. Harmonically, he says, Andalusian music revolves around modes, specifically what is often referred to as the "Spanish Phrygian." This tonality does not derive from the more familiar Grecian or Church modes (which are different in themselves) but from a "re-tempered" version of two Arabic modes (*maqāms*) from the Arabian: *Bayātī* and *Hijāz*. These modes may be summarized as follows:

Bayātī: E F# G A B C D c D C B A G F# E
Hijāz: E F G# A B C# D c D C# B A G# F E[23]

Manuel seems to think that the shift in chordal tonality comes from a combination of the above two modes. However, given that position, it seems that he is saying that one can jump from one to the other at will. One can say the same about "borrowed" chords from the minor or the arbitrary use of pan-chromaticism or pan-diatonicism. In both cases, the harmonic element is ignored by the composer and the subjective approach often does not rely on an accepted cultural "system" but on a system designated by the composer at will.

Second, it is important to remember that Arabian music of the time and other North African cultures rely on the melody, usually vocal in emphasis. Harmony as defined by Western theory was not considered an intentional part of a composition or performance. There are some interesting anomalies even here. Throughout Arab theory writings, one comes across interesting terms relating to the melodic tunings of the 'ud and other instruments. Intervallic—not scalar—relationships are emphasized. For example, the third has three designations based upon the tunings of the third: that is major, minor and so-called "neutral." These tunings may be significant, in that they are mentioned in the first place. However, even these designations may be merely a way to designate any arbitrary interval, with no real special meaning inherent in their use as an example. While Wright has been criticized for trying to fashion apparent scales in his own image (see Ibsen's reviews), he, Farmer and Manuel seem to agree on the overt present of the phrygian mode as significant tonality within the Arabian system.

Shiloah refers to Ishaq al-Mawsili (إسحاق الموصلي d. 850) whose "modal theory became known as the theory of *asabi*" and is related to the frets of the 'ud. He says:

> In the indications that introduce *The Book of Songs*, the relevant string is given, together with the finger (*isba*) corresponding to the main degree of the modal scale; the course (*majra*) then designates one of the three kinds of thirds, the major, minor, or neutral (possibly first introduced by Zalzal, Ishaq al-Mawsili's uncle and teacher). "...This system allowed for twelve fundamental modes."[24]

There was one interesting comment by Wright that indicates a slightly different perspective on the harmonic element of Arabian music:

> All of [Safi al-din's] calculations and demonstrations were based on the division of a monochord, or referred to the five strings of the 'ud, an approach already used by all of his predecessors. [He described] the octave as the sum of two conjunct tetrachords plus an interval of a tone; or a combination of a tetrachord plus a pentachord.[25]

Significantly, we are looking at referential tunings, tunings based upon the concept of relative pitch (e.g., one to another), or *harmony*. When we look at the concept of "thirds" as indicated in scalar relationships, we also see "thirds" as related to a fundamental pitch, or string in this case. The 'ud was tuned in fourths as is most of the guitar. These relationships are significant in the fact that they correspond vertically, as well as harmonically.

Philosophy and Its Implications

One ancient manuscript refers to the "harmony" of the celestial spheres (and other physical principles) being directly analogous, if not related to, musical principles. This same passage in *The Epistle on Music of the Ikhwan Al-Safa* (from the related *Encyclopedia:* إخوان الصفا رسائل) also enigmatically refers to the relationship of "beats" within rhythms, and the relating cooperation between these elements:

> 18. Another said: Since the substance of the soul is of the same nature as that of harmonic numbers and corresponds to them, when the beats of the rhythms presented by the musician are measured, when in these rhythms the periods of beats and silences are proportionate, human nature takes delight in them, the spirit rejoices and the soul experiences happiness. All this is because of the resemblance, the relation and the kinship which exist between the soul and musical harmony. It is the same when the soul marvels at the beauty of countenances and the ornament of natural things; for the beauty of natural beings arises from the harmony of their constitutions and the beauty with which their various parts are composed together.[26]

While the term "harmony" is interpreted by scholars to mean mere "music," the emphasis is still on the continuous relationships between elements, events or objects, including possibly the vertical interaction and matrices heretofore mentioned in previous chapters. Such consistency may be inferred to mean "harmony," this time in the musical sense: that is, continuous interaction between melodic or tonal elements of different types (including octave relationships). Later, Stanza #21 mentions the

> harmony of the beats emitted by the musician's strings, the proportion that exists between them, the delight procured by their strings, the proportion that exists between them, the delight procured by their notes, inform the individual soul that the spheres and heavenly bodies produce in their movements notes that are proportionate, harmonious and exquisite.[27]

Once more, the idea of "relationship" is reiterated. The usual interpretation of "beats" in both passages is that of "rhythm," or elements of rhythm. However, the immediately following passage—"the proportion that exists between them"—throws in an interesting twist. It is difficult to believe that multiple strings might exist on a single instrument, be it 'ud, guitar or lute, without an opportunity made of interaction. Beats may also include the modern understanding of consistent phasing between frequencies, more evidently in the pulsing that is cause through the application of microtonal tuning approaches. Similar to the intended effects of a Partch instrumental performance, such "beats" may be an intentional aesthetic effect.

In all of the above examples from the *Epistles*, an emphasis is made of continuous cooperation. The "spheres and heavenly bodies" do not "take turns" in their celestial motions. In the spirit of the epistle, and the culture of the time, the emphasis is on concurrent, cooperative movement, a *matrix* if you will, very much like C.S. Lewis' concept of an interdependent cosmic "dance."[28] This philosophy is clear from the Pythagoreans to the present day. Shiloah comments in footnote #68 of the *Epistle*:

> The harmonic numbers or the numbers of harmony are certainly 6, 8, 9, 12 for the harmonic proportion is found in the relation of these numbers. In addition, the theory of the soul-number is very old, and goes back to the Pythagoreans. It perhaps refers to the analogy between the perfect consonants expressed by the relation 2:1, 3:2, 4:3 and the three parts of the soul.

It is interesting that he should refer to the harmonic ratio as a mathematical part of musical philosophy. While some commentators may still emphasize the melodic relationship of the ratios only within the context of the monochord, it is unlikely that multiply stringed instruments, such as the *'ud*, the *vihuela* or the guitar are strictly melodic in nature.

However, even if indicators of passive, if not active, harmony in Arab theory are discounted, there is another possibility to justify harmonic perspective in Spanish music.

The Picardy Third

About the time that Spanish music matured, theorists on the Iberian Peninsula also began to question the concepts of harmony and relationships as accepted in both Western and Arab worlds. The idea that music could have an intentional, vertical aspect, as opposed to an incidental or accidental relationship, began to develop in the sixteenth century.

This is also the time that the *vihuelistas*, the early "guitar" players, developed the form often called "theme-and-variations," and related to the ensuing Baroque styles, such as Domenico Scarlatti. The approach of "lead melody and [guitar] accompaniment" is a significant part of flamenco style and likely had its formal application in composition at about this time. When one considers the influences of Western music and theory on recently emancipated or conquered Spain (as the case may be), it is difficult to get a definitive feel for how much Spanish theory, and classical and folk music styles were influenced and by what. With a harmonic dimension that Andalusian music is now developing (and that is beyond question) ideas from Europe certainly were acceptable.

The practice of the Picardy third developed in the 1500s as a compositional and possible *musica ficta* for the resolution of songs in minor tonalities. The sound is that of a stable, relatively "comforting" consonance at the end of a minor sound. Since one approach considered the "minor" tonality an "aberration" or deviation from a more consonant, satisfying major tonality, the minor becomes a comparably dissonant chord to resolve "to" and results in this "brightening" or harmonic release that corresponds to the harmonic series. When one considers the progression of harmonic acceptance from the octave organum of the eleventh century to the "resolved" chords of progressive jazz, there may be something to the idea that harmony may be perceptively related to the series.[29]

This is likely, given the progression of tuning as it also began to develop in the sixteenth century. In this context, a "satisfying" resolution to a major triad is not just acceptable but expected within the context of the 1500s performance practice. It is thus quite possible that a "minor" Phrygian mode, will be the initial scale or reference point for the melody. This would not normally change. However, if we introduce triads as a supporting chordal structure—not even necessarily polyphonically but more in light of the emerging thorough bass accompaniment—a major triad is not an aberration a modal system but a consonant resolution in a minor context:

Figure 155. Spanish Phrygian chord progression

While not conclusive, the evidence seems to indicate that an arbitrary selection of notes from a foreign collection of modes, with equally alien tuning is somewhat of a stretch. When music is considered harmonically, the absence, presence and control of relative beat waves and other harmonic consonance indicators point to the harmonic series as a basis for sonority. This is an acoustic phenomenon, and the perception of such is a human condition. It ultimately does not matter whether the human in question is Chinese, Native American, Western, Spanish or Arabian. In each culture, the relative acceptance or rejection of harmonic modes (in a "vertical" consideration) is something to consider when determining the relative consonance or dissonance of elements within the culture's music.

The major triad, in the context of the harmonic series as well as the Spanish harmonic culture, is the most consonant collection of three different non-octave notes. It would not be surprising to learn that the *musica ficta* of the *flamenco* accompanists knew this and adapted the Phrygian mode in such a way as to reflect this, minor sound notwithstanding. Considering that the Picardy third as manifested is primarily a European phenomenon (as far as we know), and that the Spanish theorists, at least, were directly influenced by both Arab and Western thinking, it would not be surprising to learn that the performing musicians of the same centuries adapted their music to reflect sounds and innovations brought south to them from Europe.

Progressions, Approach Tones and Harmonic Issues

Sub-Positioned Harmonies

As may be expected, there is a great deal of interaction between any of the parts in this particular study: harmony, context, melody and culture. The Andalusian culture is particularly fitted for a case study in harmonic considerations, as it uniquely deals with its influences on Western and non–Western theory, alternative tunings with concrete sources in established instruments, and a culture that prizes mathematics but alternately loves and distances itself from passionate music expression. Its harmonic context has formed and changed slowly over centuries and solidified both perspectives as shown in North African and Spanish cultures.

Several things to bring out concern the ability to listen in context: for this reason we will identify the uniquely "Spanish" sound in the next chapter concerning classical music. The composers of national music, in this case those of Latinate countries, depend on both the source in folk music and classical music to identify, emulate and codify elements of the culture.

Below is a melody similar to some of Arabic cultures of present day. I had the chance to work with some musicians of Lebanon and the area and was surprised to see that one particular song had a melody that redefined the underlying chords. Again, the codification of Arabian music into Western notation and equally tempered tuning actually enhance the dynamics in the harmony and that implied by the melody (see Figure 156 on the next page).

One thing to notice is the persistent consonance contributing to the B♭maj7/D sound. Although the underlying chord is a D minor, the aggregate B♭ in the melody strongly supports a B♭maj7, without the tension of an augmented fifth sound (with the major 3rd). As noted earlier,

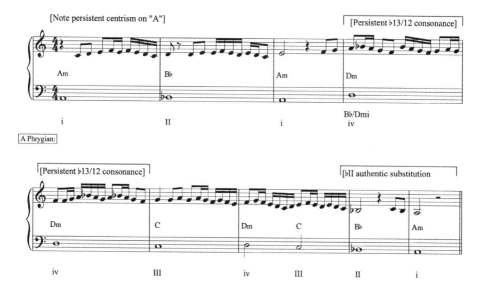

Figure 156. Lebanese melody with persistent ♭13/12 consonance (mm.4-5)

the first inversion of a major triad is harmonically a consonant manifestation of a triad; moreover, as we demonstrated, the minor (Dmin in this case) is consonant by the sub-position of a low B♭, resonating from difference tones but this is emphasized through the persistent playing and reinforcing of octave harmonics of B♭. So this has a completely different purpose and set of consonance than other harmonic and hyperextended tone.

Sub-Progression Perspectives

Perspective on consonance in a chord progression, not to mention harmonic structure, changes based on culture and context, as we have seen. One principle is commonly seen in the "blues" progression, in which all harmonic content emphasizes the dominant seventh sound but not function. In the following example, we see how the fourth bar of F^7 does not change harmonically but context dictates its function as a secondary dominant as it moves into the IV chord. Ironically, we do not see this as a function until we hear the IV chord but in retrospect, we identify it as a strong authentic secondary dominant resolution (see Figure 157 on next page).

To review the perspective of Spanish-Arabian culture and the chord progression: the Spanish Phrygian also is an odd case for two reasons. One regards the sub-progression stated above: Ami-G-F-E. Again,

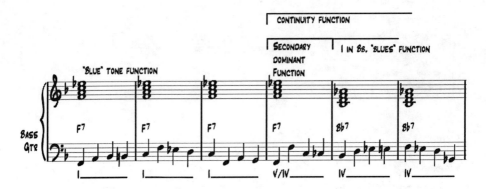

Figure 157. Perspective change based on continuity and progression

in Western ears, this is heard as a i-VII-VI-V, culminating in a half cadence and resolving to "i," or A minor. In an Andalusian (and by extension, related Moroccan and North African cultures who were inversely influenced) context, the E is seen as a resolution to I, using the Phrygian sound to place relationships and the *musica ficta* of the Picardy third as a resolution to I. The example below shows how this perspective changes based on context. Note again how principles of continuity dictate the perception of harmony.

From mm. 1–8 in the selection above, we see the classic "Spanish Phrygian" progression, again common in both Arabic and Spanish sources. However, it plays as a classic Phrygian since the ending is only an open fifth chord, implying a minor if anything at all. However, the context of this minor "becomes" a strong "Spanish Phrygian" tonic as the "A" section of the main theme progresses to a resolution on the VI chord (substitution for the IV). So, approaching a minor I underlies a Phrygian; the continuity principle fuses the Spanish hearing with more traditional Western listening, as it progresses as a functional V/IV that resolves. The perception afterward reinforces the idea that it is a dominant functioning major, resolving in the following section.

Opposite: **Figure 158. "Mvt. 3, 'El Corazon'"** *Symphony No. 5* **(Spanish)** **(Ballard, Jack.** *Symphony No. 5 [Spanish].* **Alliance, OH: Kiwibird Music [ASCAP], 2016. Used by permission)**

22

Concert Music Analysis

There are applications of hyperextended consonance in concert music, as one may expect, and within the genre there are degrees of tension and resolution, based upon the level of relative sonority. In the simplest music, resolutions may be as simple as V-I, using only triads and their relative positions to provide the effect of resolution.[1] More complex music requires more complex harmonies for resolution, if indeed resolution is something to be encountered or desired in an advanced tonal environment. As such, examples must lie somewhere in between: harmony complex enough to require the addition of chromatic alterations to be truly effective but simple enough to allow such resolution to actually have an impact on the listener.

One interesting example of approach tones and chords is found in Maurice Ravel's piano piece *Jeux d'eau* in measures 13–15 (Figure 159). The harmonic rhythm suggests the tonality of an augmented fifteenth consonance, as there is enough time on it to allow its eventual acceptance to the ear. Still, it does eventually seem to resolve in measure 15.

The eventual resolution is linearly to the C♯–G♯ and is belied by the bass's motion to A. The C♯ is tonally predominant as a bass in measures 13 and 14, and these two measures build this tension. From a harmonic perspective, the clashes between the D and C♯ and the A to G♯ have the

Figure 159. Maurice Ravel, *Jeux d'eau* (mm. 13–15) (Maurice Ravel, Piano Masterpieces of Maurice Ravel (New York: Dover, 1986)

190

same effect as the jazz voicing of a seventh or extended chord, providing a color in response to the bass's C♯. This brings other issues into the mix: how important is the bass and its corresponding harmonics to resolution in the upper voices? Alternatively, it may be possible to resolve only in the upper voices while discounting the action and possible resolution in the bass. Finally, given the perception of consonance and time, consonance must be accepted at some point in the need to resolve and in the resolution itself.

Referring to Riemann's perspective on relativity, it is possible for the ear to become so completely oriented to a sustained sonority of any kind that any deviation from that sonority becomes a dissonance. In fact, this may be the underlying psychoacoustic principle behind "minimalism," and this principle can happen in reverse. That is, dissonance becomes relatively consonant the longer one listens to it. Hindemith's *Sonate für Flöte und Klavier* introduces and sustains sonorities normally considered "advanced" regarding tonal resolution.[2] The last chord ends on a stark major triad. This triad, being the "chord of Nature," should be the resolution and should give the ear a contextual ending but with the ear's acclimation to Hindemith's advanced tonality, it rings against the ear as a completely unexpected—and almost dissonant in context—*Klang*.

Blue Tonality in Classical Music

In the early twentieth century, Darius Milhaud, Igor Stravinsky, George Gershwin, and other composers resisted society's schism between classical and popular composers. Although others had breached the "popular" music anathema, notably through the use of European folk songs, classical America still stung from its status as the "bastard child" of the concert music establishment in Europe, resisting this degradation of fine art. Nonetheless, composers experimenting with new tonality discovered an appealing sonority in the blues effect and wrote accordingly.

After gaining notoriety in classical music by the premiere of his *Rhapsody in Blue*, Gershwin continued to dabble in the blues, other Afro-American and Celtic-American folk music, and popular music sources. In *American in Paris*, a chord is held for some time, establishing that sonority as a consonance and not as an irritation that needs resolution within the context of his harmonic environment (Figure 160).

This is also clear in a linear perspective in the second of his Preludes (Figure 161) where the tonality is not presented in a vertical sense

Figure 160. *American in Paris*, m. 31 (George Gershwin, *An American in Paris* (Secaucus, NJ: Warner Bros. Publications, 1987)

but in an ever-shifting atmosphere where the major-minor perspective perpetuates the illusion of blue microtonality.

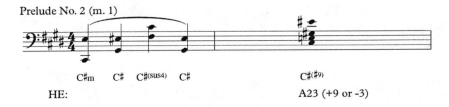

Figure 161. George Gershwin, *Prelude* No. 2, m. 1 (George Gershwin, *Preludes for Piano* [New York: New World Music Corporation, 1927])

Atonal and Non-tertian Approaches

Because of the context in which the following chords are found, they may be considered within the scope of our discussion. However, two things must be considered before jumping to the conclusion that the *Klänge* are relatively consonant.

Intention, as far as it goes, must be considered first. The method of composition and arrival at these chords has much to do with how these chords were written (which is arguable) and are perceived (which is subjective). As the composer works through the piece, the result is often coincidental and not according to the idea of true resonance or consonance within our definition of harmonic or sympathetic resonance. This leads to the second criterion, which is context itself. As we have seen, much of what constitutes "resolution" is directly dependent upon the relationship of tension-to-release on a melodic or progressive basis, not upon the inherent dissonance within each chord.[3] While a C7$^{(\#9)}$ chord may be considered dissonant in late Romantic or even some Impressionist movements, within a jazz or blues context it may be a comparably comfortable consonance within that tonal system. As discussed earlier, to effectively resolve to this particular level of comparable consonance, something yet more dissonant than a V^7 is needed.

Several of the tonal and non-tonal systems below allow for the presence of minor second and minor ninth intervals to be considered consonant by comparison. Several have merely a continuation of dissonance and do not rely at all upon "resolution," at least within a tonal perspective. Others rely on their chord systems and constructs to provide merely an "effect," without regard to consonance or resolution at all.

This perspective deals with the *Klang*. Many of these chords are also incidental and result from the apparently coincidental workings of primary and secondary melodic lines. Analyzing any hyperextended chords within this context must be approached in the same vein as proving Schoenberg was tonal in his atonal works, even by Schoenberg's definition of "tonal." Therefore, purpose and intent combine with melodic perception to show the workings of such chords, or the absence of such workings.

Quartal and Quintal Systems

One approach to harmonic construction develops through non-tertian means. By stacking chords in perfect fourths or fifths, we see a construction of harmony in quartal or quintal intervals, respectively. While these chords may be analyzed within a tertian context, their voicings include notes that will leave function tones out or contradict them (such as an eleventh directly competing with the major third). Conversely, many tertian chords can be voiced so the effect is that of quartal or quintal chords, as Figure 162 shows.

In some early twentieth-century writing, chords are voiced explicitly in fourths or fifths to produce that particular sonority. Darius Milhaud ends the first movement ("Tranquille") of his *Sonate pour flute, hautbois, clarinet en si bémol et piano*[4] with a melodic setting of quartal chords superimposed over a quintal effect (see Figure 163).

The first harmonic effect is reduced to tertian terms in the bottom staff. The resulting tertian reduction is untenable as a tertian interpretation, since many alterations are necessary. The second chord has a clear, consonant sound and is not voiced in fourths or fifths. It has a bit of the

C5
Cmaj13(♯11)
C4
Cmi11(+5,-9)?

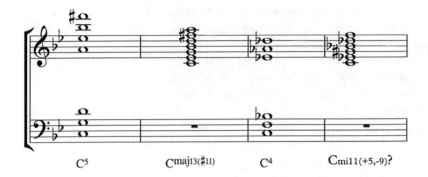

Figure 162. Tertian analysis of quintal and quartal voicing

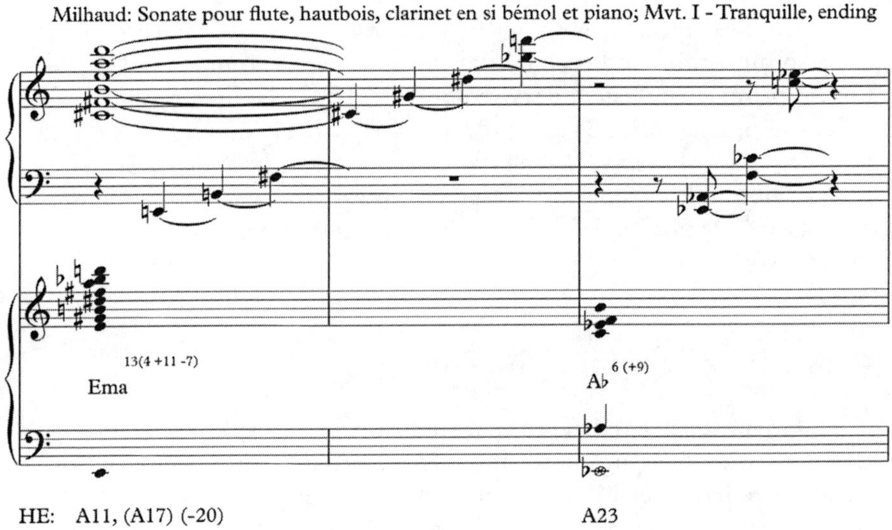

Milhaud: Sonate pour flute, hautbois, clarinet en si bémol et piano; Mvt. I - Tranquille, ending
Ema 13(4 +11 -7)
A♭ 6 (+9)
HE: A11, (A17) (-20)
A23

Figure 163. Quartal and quintal effects in *Sonate pour flute*

"blue" effect, with the major and minor thirds fighting for ascendancy. There is an interesting sound in the inversion of the third and enharmonic minor third, the minor ninth giving an extreme sonic edge to the chord while maintaining that major/minor conflict. This compares to the usual more sonorous effect in blues writing of inverting the major and minor thirds so that the interval is that of an enharmonic major seventh instead of a minor ninth, a much more consonant tone. The distance can justify the inclusion of both thirds against the voicing of the root (A♭).

Polychordal Approaches

Several composers in the early twentieth century approached harmony from a bitonal or polytonal perspective, combining comparably consonant tonalities—even mere triads—to form complex chords. This superimposition did several things. First, it produced new chords and treatments in voicing and harmony. These new chords were extended and hyperextended, analyzable from the fact that the resultant harmonic effect produced a unique sonority as a composite, rather than the sound of two or more separate chords. Second, chords from earlier compositional approaches that extended beyond the eleventh could be analyzed from a polychordal perspective, as one or more triads stacked upon another triad. Finally, it provided opportunities for parallel lines within the context of a macrolinear contrasting counterpoint.

Milhaud and Charles Ives demonstrated the technique of superimposing two chords of extreme consonance over each other to produce an aggregate harmony. In Milhaud's *Serenades orchestra*, Op. 62 (Figure 164) we see an excellent example of two contrasting lines, each containing parallel triads producing a more complex harmony. The chord analysis in this figure does not refer to inversions according to accepted jazz notation but each letter represents a triad.

Milhaud, *Serenades Orchestra*, Op. 62, reh. no. 4

	D/G	C#/A	C/B	B/C	B♭/D___	A/E	A♭/F
HE:	A19	A15, A19	(A17)	A11, A23	A19, A23	A19, A23	(A17)	A23

Figure 164. Darius Milhaud, *Serenades Orchestra*, Op. 62, reh. No. 4 (Darius Milhaud, *Serenades Orchestra*, Op 62 [Munich: MPH, 2003], 72)

In this example, descending triads are superimposed against rising triads in the bass. The aggregate effect is as follows:

- Several chord lines result in contrasting motion.
- The progression moves from consonant chord to dissonance to resolution.

- The vertical effect is incidental rather than intended, although the disparate voicing lends itself to harmonic/resonant consonance.
- These overarching chords are a break in the rhythmic feel of the piece, and as such also contrast harmonically with linear movements, which horizontally outline various distinct consonant keys.

Much of the rest of the piece is harmonically sparse, even in sections of rhythmic pause. The effect is that of traditional counterpoint but even here it is harmonically lean. There are many doublings in octaves in all parts; string writing in the whole piece is usually sparse, these measures being an exception. The above chord structure gives an amazing point of contrast within the environment of the rest of the piece.

Written and Intended Consonant Chords

Finally, composers wrote in the occasional technique that intends for these tones to be included or emphasized in and as consonant chords. To guess at one's intention, the criteria we must use are as follows:

- There must be an amount of sustain or repetition, establishing the sonority of the chord beyond question.
- The *Klang* cannot resolve to another chord but must be a resolution from another, more dissonant chord.
- The *Klang* cannot be an ornamenting chord, such as a neighboring or passing chord.
- The *Klang* cannot be incidental to contrapuntal influences.
- The *Klang* must be consonant within the context of the harmonic structure of the piece.
- The harmonic structure and context of the piece must be intentionally tonal, however complex the tonality may be.
- Centric pieces are subjective to the perspective of the analyst and/or listener. As such, they may be included.

An interesting example is found in the guitar-driven drones of Spanish music, and their orchestral derivatives. In the so-called "Spanish Phrygian," the sustained pedal tones show a dissonant chord with the minor ninth. In a relatively tonal piece of the twentieth century, it would sound as a transcription error except for the context. Another conclusion is that it was intentionally dissonant (see Figure 165).

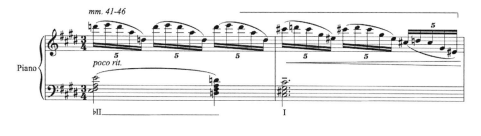

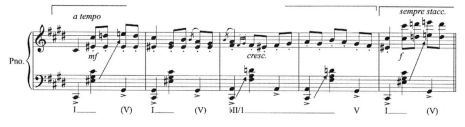

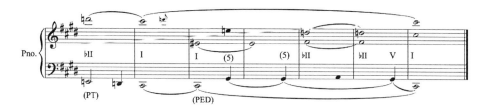

Figure 165. Ernesto Lecuona, "Malagueña" *Andalucia* **(Ernesto Lecuona. "Malaguena,"** *Andalucia for Piano Solo.* **Published by Edward B. Marks Music)**

This sample fits into all the criteria above, especially in the interesting way that this hyperextended chord acts as a resolution. Although the initial chord in measure 438 is B major, the C is prevalent in the melody. This melodic line begins on a C and ends on a G. Contrasting this is a bass, which begins on a B and ends on a C. Chordally, the bass acts as a tonal passage as the following analysis shows:

♭III–♭II–I–V–I–VI–♭II–(V)–I (etc.)

The melody is also consistent with a "blue" tonality or possibly a mixolydian tonality derived from the Spanish Phrygian model. The Spanish context and its accompanying culture would imply the latter (see Figure 166).

In this case, this juxtaposition of the C as a melody over a B major triad advances a strong augmented fifteenth chord. The question is

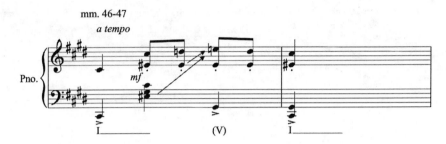

Figure 166. Melody line from "Malagueña" *Andalucia* (m. 440)

whether it is dissonant or consonant. Subsequent phrases in this piece support the idea that it is consonant, for the half cadence shown above is resolved by the I chord in the next phrase (see Figure 167):

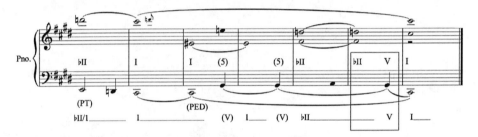

Figure 167. Roman numeral analysis, "Malagueña" *Andalucia* (m. 41-46)

The clear V-I progression (♭II, or D/C, or C♯sus$^{[+5,-9]}$, is a substitution for V7) gives a strong resolution to a C♯ major chord, justifying its use as an example of the augmented fifteenth (♯8 plus one octave or A15). Melodically, we have a reinforcement of this V-I progression in the continuity half cadence of G♯ resolving to a C♯. As both parts individually support a I-V-I progression, their juxtaposition strengthens rather than weakens this analysis.

For further illustrations of classical music applications, refer to Appendix C. The examples, which are organized by context will show the diversity of hyperextended tone analysis. It is surprising how much advanced tonality may be easily seen as consonant *Klänge*, notwithstanding the organization, context, voicing, or chromaticism in which they occur.

23

Light Correlations: Conjecture

In the final chapter of this book on the interactions of harmonics, I wish to make clear that this is conjecture only based on the implications of the work so far. There are many well qualified scientists whose perspectives may discount this as an option even by analogy. That said, several things need to be said for the unbiased reader in music, physics or astronomy. First, consider these are ideas that were reached through "logical conclusion," and are qualified with the realization that air, liquid and light media are not necessarily perfectly comparable much less exact when considering wave theory.

Second, after reading dozens of peer-reviewed journals on astrophysics and some of the subjects of this chapter, I have found little, if any, material that rejects these ideas out of hand. That said, while I can understand most of the mathematics involved and can even work out a few implications, that field is best left for those best qualified to empirically and progressively—rather than by inference or analogy—conjecture. As well, many articles on astronomy use terms that make statements such as: "there are indications that…," "near, if not actually at the same number as…," and "it is so, according to these authors, however, I believe that…" and so on. Therefore, conjecture is, if not openly welcomed, at least tolerated as much in the field of astrophysics as it is in music theory.

Third, I am well aware that the properties of light clearly have some odd kinks that do not correlate exactly or even in some places analogously with audio. For one thing, the results of any combination waves do not necessarily have anything to do with identifiable "harmonics" or certainly none that we could perceive as being analogous to "music." Any surmise in this area deals much more with the philosophy of Kierkegaard and string theory than the concrete reduction of Newton and Einstein, even in the arts. The wide range, not to mention nature, of the electromagnetic spectrum, for example, cannot relate except possibly by ratio or exponent with that of acoustics in air and thus the impracticality of a direct relationship is impractical if not impossible. However, we may be able to see seismic (acoustic movement or wave action of any kind in or made of a medium) actions that relate to our principles of phasing and relationships as material is being actuated particle to particle, as it were. In music, the *Klang* is the same to human and musical perception, whether C_{264} or C_{528} but the analogy does not at least perceptibly follow through to be the same in electromagnetism (although this might be an interesting area of exploration). These will be made clear as these ideas are explained.

Finally, as a colleague in chemistry reminded me, it is often those outside the field itself that have the understanding to see ideas challenging the paradigm of those whose proficiencies are immersed in it. As Will Rogers famously stated, "There is nothing so stupid as an educated man, if you get him off the thing he was educated in," and it is hoped that my naïve approach to another's expertise sparks some interest and generate supporting research.[1]

It seems that since much of astrophysics is "philosophy" that proceeds to physics and thence to engineering, then much—necessarily and to their credit—comes from a healthy attitude of the "what if we...?" world. My friends who are literally world-renowned in nuclear physics, chemistry and medicine are as much philosophers and artists as they are scientists and mathematicians. It is from such esoteric people that scientific advancements are often made.

Light to Sound Correlation

There have been some ideas put forth from an artistic, religious or mystic philosophical ground of equating sound frequency with equivalent light frequency. Of course, there is also the well-known phenomenon of synesthesia: that odd ability (or affliction) of seeing colors when one hears music is one manifestation of the neurosis that has a person sensing a different media upon the stimulation by another.[2,3] But, as with our perception of harmony, harmonics, phasing and difference tones, the jury is still out regarding how much is physics, psychoacoustics, neurological aberration, or sheer "talent." Not unlike so-called "perfect pitch," synesthesia may or may not be learned as well as innate and likely has little or nothing to do with the physical properties therein.[4]

One approach in this line equates actual frequency in acoustics with the same number of Hertz in electromagnetic waves (EMW). As per our discussion above, this is dangerous ground as the philosophy takes little into consideration the physical properties of quantum issues. It considers only global and possibly spiritual elements that extend beyond the "material" (for lack of a better word): chakra, celestial analogy, principles of numerology, etc.

Based on the direct correlation of frequency in light as fHz $\times$ 40 octaves = fTHz or fHz $\times 2^{40}$ for visible light purposes, the approach established each tone within a 12-tone system, irrespective of octaves.[5] Thus, the frequency of C^{528}_{Hz} simply translated to f^{528}_{THz} in this system is the visible light familiar as a shade of "green," regardless of whether we present as 528_{THz}, 132_{THz}, 264_{THz} or 1056_{THz} all being reduced to f^{528}_{THz} regardless for visibility purposes. Limiting it to these frequencies does not work for our purposes, as the simple assignment of tones within an octave and attempting to use it in a chord or even 1-on-1 combination simply results in an oversaturation of black pigment or white light as they do not seem to phase harmonically. However, even in this case, the nodes of the waves themselves line up at binary intervals as well, an interesting perspective worth exploring.

To do this properly would require all octaves of C (in this case) are translated literally, so that 132_{Hz} correlates to 132_{THz} and thus we are in the realm of invisible electromagnetic waves (in this case somewhere well below infrared). This can work for our purposes as the matrices in this case can spike in different areas without oversaturating and creating "noise," or "white" light. One example we will see below is the spiking of wavelengths in spectrographs from stars.

Phasing in Electromagnetic Waves (EMW)

The question remains whether phasing in EMW is viable to our applications, by superimposing two waves of equal but delayed, frequency (AM "chorusing" in EMW, as it were) or superimposing differing wavelengths (FM with the addition of a modulating wave of a different frequency to a carrier wave).

The implications of this relate to what is "observable" in astronomy, for the fact remains that the only information we obtain about any object or activity in the universe is through observation through vision, measuring instruments or both electronically and AI enhanced. Our instruments are able to measure far more than with the naked eye, so we can "see" more than ancient man and measure it more accurately. Nonetheless, it still measures only what we receive, whether photons or neutrinos. We may be able to infer principles based on changes through time, amplitude and frequency spectrum but ultimately relies upon only what actually reaches us, which is only energy in the form of various electromagnetic waves, particles and related energy.

Even spectrography, useful for measuring elements in light by breaking the information down into its various frequency components, identify the wavelengths with the greatest emissions energy. Wavelength numbers are inversely proportional to frequencies (e.g., the smaller the wavelength, the higher the frequency) given the same velocity, and thus are related through the same formula with the substitution of the speed of the wave through media (c=the speed of light, instead of the speed of sound), in meters per second[6]:

$$\lambda = \frac{c}{f}$$

A star's spectrograph showing the amount and existences of elemental components will have an absorption drop in different frequencies based upon the elements present that absorb specific wavelengths, and inversely corresponding frequencies based upon amount of energy emitted in specific wavelengths.

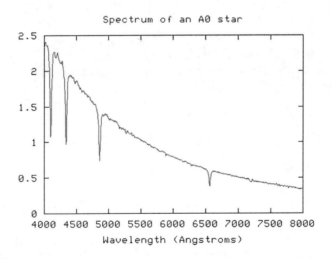

Figure 168. Spectrum of a type A0 star

Since the smaller the wavelength, the higher the frequency, the frequencies would be in reverse order from the wavelength (lowest to highest from left to right).[7] The absorption spectrograph above has a corresponding emission spectrograph, with spikes and corresponding frequencies of the data shown above, as rendered below:

$\lambda = 4050\text{Å} \qquad f = 7.40 \times 10^{16}$

$\lambda = 4450\text{Å} \qquad f = 6.74 \times 10^{16}$

$\lambda = 4800\text{Å} \qquad f = 6.24 \times 10^{16}$

$\lambda = 6550\text{Å} \qquad f = 4.58 \times 10^{16}$

We can infer phasing from these basic frequencies (without consideration for any resonance, additional absorption, reflection or interference, which is an additional concern) as:

$$74.0_{PHZ} - 67.4_{PHZ} = 6.6_{PHZ}$$

$$74.0_{PHZ} - 62.4_{PHZ} = 11.6_{PHZ}$$

$$74.0_{PHZ} - 45.8_{PHZ} = 28.2_{PHZ}$$

$$67.4_{PHZ} - 62.4_{PHZ} = 5.0_{PHZ}$$

$$67.4_{PHZ} - 45.8_{PHZ} = 21.6_{PHZ}$$

$$62.4_{PHZ} - 45.8_{PHZ} = 16.6_{PHZ}$$

This provides six additional spikes according to the above frequencies through phasing, much as our harmonic "spikes" add to an existing chord through their interactions. One may notice that the reverse image of a star's spectrograph shows a resemblance to the REW harmonic readout shown in previous chapters and Appendix C. If EWM emissions can be broken down into component frequencies and if they can be phased through their interactions, then the principles in harmonic interaction, resonance, combination wavelengths and phasing can all be applied to visible light, recognizing that there are limitations in the physics, media, and material, not to mention outside influences that science has not even observed much less solved.

Combination Wavelengths Outside of Colors Can Manifest as Visible Light

Is it possible for any EMW emission to initially emit as non-visible light, then manifest as visible? What if what we actually see is the *result* of EMW phasing and not the actual emission of originating visible light? Much in the same way that two hypersonic waves can phase and resonate, producing a low difference tone in the audible range, we can theoretically produce a visible light through the phasing of two extra-visible EMW wavelengths. If a full matrix is physically possible, it will produce even more possibilities.

Imagine an object with two similar wavelengths in the x-ray vicinity (EHz, or 10^{18}) whose difference equate to a combination wave through phasing of 580_{THz}, or

$$(3 \times 10^{18} Hz) - (2.99999942 \times 10^{18} Hz) = 580 \times 10^{12} Hz$$

$580 \times 10^{12}{}_{Hz}$ puts us into approximately the frequency of "green" color of visible light. So in this hypothesis, the initial output of energy by this imaginary object in space has never included a "visible" light— the output EMW that is actually emitted is strictly too high, providing an energy better able to permeate media—but the phasing interaction of the two produces a combination wave that is within the visible spectrum. It is quite possible that the so-called visible objects we "see" are the resulting light from phasing, not the initiating energy source, producing EWM in those frequencies.

This may give new ideas regarding inconsistencies in observations of some astral objects, such as quasars and black holes. If, for example, visible light emitted from a star, gas or other object is completely absorbed by whatever media it passes through but the differing wavelengths of EMW—assuming a necessary amount of inherent energy and unfilterable frequencies—as the sufficient characteristics to pass, whether or not it initiates resonance within any mass it encounters— then it continues to phase and produce light visible to us even after complete absorption of the original emitted visible light.

Pulsing Effects of Binary Stars

Another possibility involves the pulsing of so-called pulsars and binary stars. Again, if we consider that the effect we see is strictly the arrival of EMW, then is it possible that our inference of rotation of these objects is at present strictly based on pulsing? Is it possible to actually "see" the rotation by measuring a pulsar's sweep in the extremely small arc that our distance affords (arc in degrees, given the distances in light years)?[8] The problem with parallax measuring is that the time it takes to get from one side to another (six months, or one parsec) may be less than the "sweep" of a pulsar that is measured in seconds or less. What we see may not be the actual sweep of a rotating beacon but just a series' flash. In this case, all we are seeing is a consistent pulsing: extremely regulated up to a point. What about inconsistencies from local gravitational sources, such as the case with neighboring stars or even large gravitational objects such as superplanets or even comets or a companion star?

Likewise, we can question the appearance of the consistent pulsing of a binary star. Some say this pulsing is due to rotation between the companion stars causing the eclipsing action of one star over the other, providing a consistent attenuation of the light emitting from both: two are directly visible, increasing light, then one eclipses the other, reducing the light output from both.

Considering that binary stars have a rotation whose observations are based on "eclipsing," how is it possible for us to see that without being on the plane of orbit, or at least within an angle that allows at least some eclipsing of the other star? What if we were to observe binary stars from above, or at an angle greater than that allowed for a certain amount of eclipsing? See Figure 169.

This hypothesizes that a binary star may be seen as pulsing because of beat waves by two stars that produce light in almost exactly the same frequency spectrum, a phenomenon possibly resulting from a common source at creation. In Figure 169A below, the observer is at the planar level. It is assumed that the stars are revolving. Like a pair of dancers rotating around each other, we lose sight of each once per rotation, with transitions to and from each to full visibility as each changes position. The observer also notices a consistent pulse of light, as each eclipses the other's emission as it revolves and the total light output is attenuated periodically. In 169B below, the angle of rotation is "off" from that of the observer. There is eclipsing but only a portion of the light is actually attenuated, since the plane of orbit is oblique to the observer.

In the final example, 169C, the observer is at $90°$ of the plane of the orbit. Like watching our dancers from above, there is a rotation, but we see both for every phase of orbit. The light from each star combine and there is no eclipsing of either.

If both stars are "twins," created by a splitting of a single entity, then

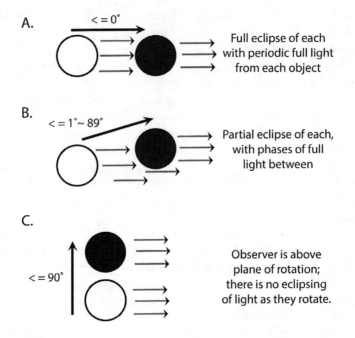

A. $< = 0°$
Full eclipse of each with periodic full light from each object

B. $< = 1° ~ 89°$
Partial eclipse of each, with phases of full light between

C. $< = 90°$
Observer is above plane of rotation; there is no eclipsing of light as they rotate.

Figure 169. Comparative angles of observation of a binary star system

the formation of light could be at the same time with the same characteristics. Any change in spectral frequency might create a phasing effect. Since our timeline is so small, any such change in the phasing might be undetectable without thousands or millions of years of comparative observation. Phasing variables: is it possible that these and pulsars show consistent pulsing, not because of the periodic release of energy/EMW/ light but because of "beat waves?" This is not to say there is no rotation, just that our observation is complicated by EMW interference and the angle at which we observe as well as actual rotation.

Sonic "Noise" vs. White Light

Strictly in the realm of philosophy, one might ask what is "the" frequency of white light? As a combination of frequencies, random or combined, emitted or phased, we have something analogous of "noise" in the sonic area. "White" noise, that is, random frequencies in the entire range, can produce specific frequencies by passing them through filters (analogous to acoustic "equalizers" or frequency filters). In the same way, one can elicit specific frequencies of light by using a "beamsplitter," laser effect or simply observe the absorption of light waves and corresponding reflection(s) from a pigmented surface. White noise is the randomizing of all frequencies, by addition or amplitude variation, so is white light "random?"

What does this imply? We have determined that "noise" is not based on only that within our hearing and acoustic resonance but expands technically into ultrahigh frequencies. Is it possible that the randomizing of EMW frequencies include implications in the non-visible spectrum, just as there are ultra- and sub-sonic ramifications? We just happen to hear above the lowest frequency—that is our range in audio—but have perception in a very small segment of EM, in the visible light range.

A "cast" of white light would be colored according to amplitude. If there is more of a single frequency in the visible spectrum there would appear to our eyes a color. Thus, a white light with a higher energy at a frequency of 530_{THz} would give a reddish cast to the "white" light. Note the use of Fourier analysis in light applications. You can get an EMW "square" wave through the judicial adding of multiple sine wave harmonics $(\exp[j\omega 0t])$; very rarely do you ever get naturally occurring monochromatic light without exterior manipulation or elemental spectrography.

Resonating Cavities in Light and Seismic Applications

Objects emitting EM outside visible light but phasing or combining to create combination tones that happen to work within the frequencies of visible light range. However, a "white" light, that is, one that has a random number of EMW frequencies and amplitudes, can elicit focused frequencies, much as noise can elicit single sine waves. One way to do this is in the area of resonance. Light-resonating objects maintain and project EMW and heat but can be captured in media and resonated based on the size of the resonating cavity.

One example is that of an "optical chamber," where the light actually acts as a standing wave within the criteria of the resonant frequency, much like a sound wave resonates in a room. So, an object or a chamber can resonate acoustically and luminously, producing resonant harmonics in the quantum realm in the same way a flute produces tones that focus on a single fundamental and its harmonics. When one considers that a room or other containment vessel can resonate multiple frequencies that are based on the relationship of the room size with the wavelength, it opens up the possibilities of all sorts of resonating bodies, ranging from dust particles to larger objects.

Another example refers to that area of solar and nuclear environment where atoms are stripped of their electrons and result in plasma. In this case, the light wave and the plasma "volume" wavelength are compatible or an EMW emission of random or structured frequencies contains the same frequency that might be propagated. EM waves in plasma are transverse with some longitudinal waves, when considered in seismic (e.g., acoustic within the plasma and thus larger than the light wave level) considerations.

This chapter conjectures that the sun and other stars may consist of trillions of plasma chambers, confined by magnetism into little "blocks" with uniformity determined by gravity and magnetism. What comes into question is the "boundary" of each block that may contain a resonating medium and how static it is, given the dynamics of internal supporting solar forces. For an acoustics example, one may refer to a trumpet or flute, which is a solid boundary (the metal) containing the resonating column of air, based on the open/closed ends, or the boundary of each length of column. The inverse may be said of idiophones with a homogenous medium, such as the metal of a bar of a vibraphone. In this case, the medium itself is the boundary to air and as such is still a vibrating medium, whose homogeneity, boundary, size and mass all impact the seismology and frequency resonance. The same may be said of plasma volume. It appears to be more along the lines of an idiophone, whose boundary is the medium itself, rather than a container with another medium as the defining border or shell.

A plasma chamber may increase light resonance as a resonating chamber and like an acoustic chamber or resonating idiomatic mass, suppresses some frequencies while enhancing the fundamental frequency. Tests have shown the seismology of such a unit but it seems possible that it may also produce harmonics in a light form, complete with harmonic phasing.[9]

Would varying states keep an aggregate "noise" while propagating resonant frequencies? There is a variety of plasma shapes, each of which may affect (e.g., enhance or "spoil") the likelihood of propagating resonance frequencies. It is clear that some plasma shapes are more stable than others at different temperatures. However, if each plasma cavity varies in shape but retains stability and size, resonance may change frequencies but stay within tolerance. This idea of "tolerance" can explain the "white" visible light emitted from stars, and yet allow the spectral and other "color" shift.

Think of a choral ensemble by analogy: each singer is slightly off from a companion but can be "tuned" within a certain amount of tolerance, to produce uniform tones. It is literally "the music of the spheres." What if stars are made of resonating "packets" of plasma that propagate visible light in specific but variable frequencies? What are other possible collective resonators for light in the universe?

Glossary

(as applied in this book)

ADDA—"Analog-digital-digital-analog" converter, referring to the processing from recording to digital (computer) storage, initially in non-codec formats: SDII, AIFF, WAV, etc.

Additive (or "constructive") phasing—A phenomenon of phasing in which waves that are both positive or both negative add to momentary amplitudes. Complex waves can emphasize various frequencies (e.g., $+a + +a = +2a$, $-b + -b = -2b$).

Additive synthesis—Superimposing random or chosen waves to induce additive and destructive phasing principles in varying degrees to produce new tones and effects.

Altered tones—Chromatically changed 5th and 9th tones in a dominant chord.

Approach tone/chord—tones and chords ornamenting a consonant or "target" tone or chord by approaching from a step above or below.

Chord Classification—Classifying chord system that determines relative consonance and comparative harmonic impact (see *klang*) based on elements of its internal interactive matrix.

Cognitive anticipation—A type of continuity principle in which syllogistic analysis of the situation determines events following. See "perceiving-the-present prediction."

Color tone—Tones of any chord that adds *Klang* but does not change the overall sound or function; includes 9, 11 and 13 in a tertian system.

Consonance—Melody or chords that conform to a relative harmonic series, or considered "pleasant sounding" according to culture or subjection.

Context—The placement and relevancy of a note, frequency or amplitude within similar elements in a time-based environment.

Continuity—A method of using rhythmic, melodic, harmonic and syllogistic components in a contextual framework to anticipate resolution or continuous subsequent elements.

Destructive interference/destructive phasing—A phenomenon in which the superimposition of two or more *opposite* waves cancel momentary amplitudes. Complex waves can cancel entire related frequencies of each other (e.g., $-a + +a = 0, +b + -b = 0$).

Difference tones—Tones produced by the phasing of two or more presented tones, where the beat waves produced exceed the audible lowest frequency of ± 30 kHz.

Dissonance—Non-conforming to contextual harmonic resonance, dependent upon context; relative consonance.

Dyad—In a tertian harmonic system, the combination of two intervals of thirds superimposed, the higher over the lower, to produce a single triad.

Electromagnetic—Waves of the magnetic field of varying frequencies; "EMW" include visible light waves, x-ray, gamma, radio waves, etc.

Envelope—The action of time-based amplitude of selected frequencies or the whole signal in a millisecond time frame acoustically or electronically dependent upon the elements of energy, mass, springiness and resulting resonance. Made of four elements—attack, decay, sustain and release.

Environment principles—The concept that human nature tends to subrogate environmental sensory input when it remains static.

Freeware—Software application that is free to download and use without restrictions; may be "open source" or edited as desired by the user.

Function tone—Scale degrees 3 and 7 in a chord as measured from the root that determine the *klang* or harmonic sonority/function of the chord.

Functional vs. non-functional chord—Within context, the use and progressive function of a chord as determined by its relative dissonance within a consonant environment or vice versa; also refers to the characteristic of the unique sonority that allows a chord to function within context.

Harmonic ratios—Whole numbered relationships of frequencies and inversely their resonating bodies' counterparts that naturally occur according to wave propagation within the medium: 1:1 (fundamental: whole string), 1:2 (f_1 x 2: half string), 1;3 (f_1 x 3: third string), etc.

Harmonic resonance/harmonics—The harmonic frequencies as produced by initial, acoustic or environmental acoustic interactions; generally adhering to the harmonic series as determined by amplitude and characteristics of the harmonic spectrum.

Harmonic separation—The principle indicating the harmonic result of the distance relationship of simultaneous melodic lines to each other. The closer, the more harmonic interaction; the farther, the more lines are distinct and therefore melodious.

Harmonic spectrum—The frequencies and amplitudes of resonating harmonics, often displayed on a chart (see "waterfall," "spectrogram") indicating time, amplitude and Hertz of each frequency. Unique to each acoustic resonator.

Hyperextended—In tertian harmony, a way of justifying consonance for chords that contain harmonic tones not accounted for in traditional consonant 2-octave tertian chords, such as 19, #15, #17, #23, #25.

Klang, klänge (German)—Sonority, sonic effect, harmonic sound, the aural impact of a harmonic matrix of resonating frequencies from two or more presented tones.

Manifestation (audio)—In this context, the audible presence (under 20 kHz) produced by the phasing interaction of two hypersonic (>22 kHz) tones.

Matrix—The aggregate collection of difference tones and harmonic produced by the interaction of two played and resonant tones.

Matrix transformation; triadic transformation; klang transformation—The principle of changing harmonic matrices due to the result of triadic and other harmonic transformation.

Missing fundamental—The psychoacoustic effect where the brain hears the harmonic matrix produced by tones matching the harmonic series (minus the fundamental) and artificially "hears" the unpresented fundamental.

Monochord—Common term for any single stringed instrument. Important for its modeling the harmonic series using string divisions by whole numbered ratios (thought to assist demonstrations by Greek and Arabic philosophers and music theorists/mathematicians).

Perceiving-the-present prediction—The principle that the mind assesses a situation and calculates the probability of future action to a high degree. See Changizi, Mark.

Perfect chord (Rameau)—A triad that resonates with the naturally occurring harmonic series.

Phasing—the interaction of two or more waves and the combination of amplitudes in time, producing new frequencies beside the originating tones.

Pink noise—A method of random frequency generation used for identifying ambient resonance of an instrument, room or other resonating cavity.

Placement theory—The concept that perception of sound is based upon the association of frequency with its corresponding place on the basilar membrane.

Progressive fifths—The principle by Pythagoras and promoted Schenker that all twelve tones can be produced through a series of progressive perfect fifths that resonate from the preceding fifth.

Resolution—The "final" resting or consonant chord or melody that previous dissonance is leading to. Often referred to as tension-release principle.

Resonating chamber—Any chamber whose inclusive medium is susceptible to seismic wave action and whose dimensions allow for resonating matrices.

Root tone—The root of a tertian chord, with the audible perfect 5th.

Separation—The technique of isolating melodic and harmonic parts by frequency, time and volume.

Shareware—Software that requires a minimum payment after an initial trial period.

Spectrogram—A graphic display identifying frequency, amplitude and time.

Sub-position or "supposition"—the principle of a chord having an unpresented functional bass one third of the played chord to facilitate chord function and movement.

Syllogistic continuity—Using logic, story progression or other subconscious process to determine future events in a musical or other progressive, time-line medium.

Temporal theory—The concept that hearing is based upon the period, or timing of firing neurons rather than the placement on the basilar membrane.

Tertian—Chord structures based on the "stacking" of major and minor thirds in various order.

Transformation theory—Changing triads in a progressive context by one or two notes to move smoothly, but often radically into new triads or keys.

Tuning—Ways of functionally tuning instruments and theoretical structures, adjusting note relationships on a minute basis. This impacts the listener in various ways or to facilitate movement or key change; just, mean-tone and equal temperament are examples.

Undertone series—A systematic theory originally proposed by Hugo Riemann in which new tones produced are due to a system of tones inverse from the natural harmonic series, descending in whole numbers rather than ascending.

Waterfall—A common way to display frequency components of a sound, series of sound or aggregate audio, often rendered as horizontal-time, vertical-frequency and brightness-amplitude.

Appendix A: Graphs

	f_1 harmonics	Partial 1	2	3	4	5	6	7	8
Series on C¹	0	12	19	24	28	31	33.5	36	38
Series on C²	12	24	31	36	40	43	45.5	48	50
Series on G²	19	31	38	43	47	50	52.5	55	57
Series on C³	24	36	43	48	52	55	57.5	60	62
Series on E³	28	40	47	52	56	59	61.5	64	66
Series on G³	31	43	50	55	59	62	64.5	67	69
Series on A+³	33.5	45.5	52.5	57.5	61.5	64.5	67	69.5	71.5
Series on C⁴	36	48	55	60	64	67	69.5	72	74
Series on D⁴	38	50	57	62	66	69	71.5	74	76

Table 8: Relative pitches based on C₁ series' components

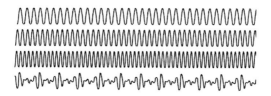

Figure 170. Screenshot of P5, P8 and M3, with "missing" fundamental

Appendix B:
Additional Musical Figures

Blue Tonality in Classical Music

Figure 171. Darius Milhaud, *La création du monde* **(mm. 4-5 after reh. 40) (Darius Milhaud,** *La création du monde* **[Paris: M. Eschig, 1929])**

Figure 172. George Gershwin, *Preludes for Piano,* **no. 2 (m. 1) (Gershwin,** *Preludes for Piano,* **1924)**

Figure 173. George Gershwin, *Preludes for Piano,* no. 2 (mm. 31-34) (Gershwin, 1924)

Blue Tonality in Progressive Harmony and Non-Tonal Work

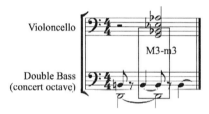

Figure 174. Arnold Schoenberg, "Summer Morning by a Lake," *Five Pieces for Orchestra* (Milhaud, *Creation du monde*)

Approach Tones in Classical/Jazz Context

Figure 175. Jack Ballard, "Bop" for string quartet (Ballard, *Bop* for String Quartet [Alliance, Kiwibird Music (ASCAP), 2007]. Used by permission.)

Hyperextended Chords in Advanced Tonality

Figure 176. Darius Milhaud, *Saudades do Brasil*, "Botafogo" (mm. 3-6) (Milhaud, *Saudades do Brasil: Suite de Dances*, "Botafogo" Op. 67 (Paris: E. Demets, 1921)

Figure 177. de Falle, *El Amor Brujo*, "Danza ritual de fuego" mm 25-28 after reh. 25 (da Falle, *El Amor Brujo*, "Danza ritual de fuego" (London: printed by Bradford and Dickens Drayton House.)

Opposite, bottom: Figure 180. Vaughan Williams, *A London Symphony* (mm. 38-39) (Ralph Vaughan Williams, Symphonies, no 2, G Major: A London Symphony [London: Stainer & Bell, 1920], 193)

Use of Consonant Sonority in a Soft Dynamic Situation

Figure 178. Ives, *Hymn* (Largo Cantabile) for String Orchestra (mm. 26-29) (Charles Ives, *Hymn (Largo Cantabile), for String Orchestra*, 1904)

#15 as the Resolution at the End of a Soft Section

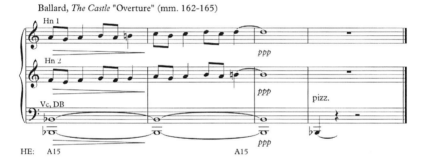

Figure 179. Ballard, Jr., *The Castle*, mvt. 1, "Overture" (mm. 162-165) (Ballard, Jack. *The Castle* [Dissertation. Kent State University, 2008]. music: Alliance, Kiwibird Music [ASCAP], 2007. Used by permission.)

Use of #19 Tone(s) in a Non-Resolution Context

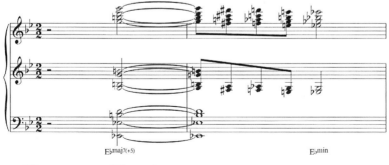

Vaughan Williams, *A London Symphony* (mvt 1, mm. 288-290, 300-302)

HE: A19

Figure 181. Vaughan Williams, *A London Symphony* (mvt. 1, mm. 288-290) (Vaughan Williams, 1920)

Rachmaninoff, Piano Concerto No. 2, Op. 18 (reh. 12)

HE: A19

Figure 182. Rachmaninoff, Piano Concerto No. 2, Op. 18 (reh. 12) (Sergei Rachmaninoff, The Complete Works for Piano and Orchestra: Second and Third Symphonies, Symphonic Dances [1901; reprint, Melville, NY: Belwin-Mills, 1973])

#23 in a Non-Blues, Advanced Tonal Situation

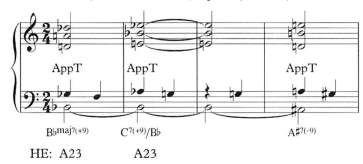

Bartók, *Bluebeard's Castle*, Op. 11 (reh. 138)

AppT AppT AppT

B♭maj7(+9)   C7(+9)/B♭   A♯7(-9)

HE: A23   A23

Figure 183. Bartók, Béla, *Bluebeard's Castle*, Op. 11 (reh. 138) (Béla Bartók, Wilhelm Ziegler, and Béla Balázs, *Bluebeard's Castle: Op. 11*, 1921; reprint [Mineola, NY: Dover, 2001])

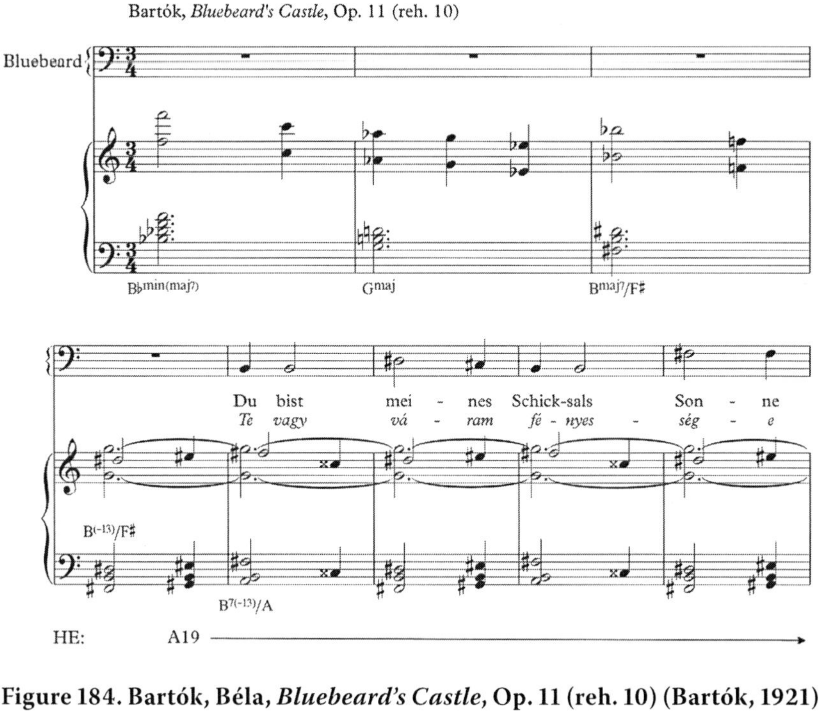

Bartók, *Bluebeard's Castle*, Op. 11 (reh. 10)

Bluebeard

B♭min(maj7)   Gmaj   Bmaj7/F♯

Du bist   mei - nes Schick-sals   Son - ne
Te vagy   vá - ram fé - nyes -   ség - e

B(-13)/F♯

B7(-13)/A

HE: A19

Figure 184. Bartók, Béla, *Bluebeard's Castle*, Op. 11 (reh. 10) (Bartók, 1921)

Appendix C:
Methodology and Systems

Beginning with the initial hypothesis, the process began by taking conventional chords and identifying the frequencies inherent. Through the music theoretical numerical assignments based on mod-12, and mod-24 systems, the approach confirmed basic structural relationships from both mathematical and theoretical perspectives. Thus, the premises were reinforced in works by Forte, Riemann, Rameau, Zarlino, and their contemporaries and by accepted tonal practice. This also gave an accepted starting point for structural deduction and reconstruction in other areas.

By working through the mathematical and musical structures, the organization was confirmed in those fields as well as those in physics that support relationships through the theoretical number, given the "forgiveness" aspect as in Chapter 5. Tuning issues were of less concern than the relationships of tones within each cluster or chord to each other and thus how they impacted each other in sonority and progressions. Since sympathetic resonances were dependent aurally and structurally upon each other, it was decided to work with tones generated from the just tuning system, particularly as musicians spontaneously tune the relevant tertial chords accordingly in performance situations. One aspect concerned the development of new structural designs based upon musically progressive relationships while others led in directions of vertical sonority.

Structural Approach (Summary)

The perspective taken on the structure combined several assumptions and facts. First, the interaction of two or more tones playing simultaneously produce through phasing additional, combination tones. In a triad, this produces a total of three difference tones whose frequencies can be calculated as described earlier. Second, this interaction can produce harmonics developed from the difference tones, in ideal environments. Third, the harmonic structures may be produced through the ordered system of additional overtones, which produce additional combinatorial interactions, producing more overtones, and so on. Finally, it was assumed that, while tests would of necessity be started with so-called "simple" tones, or sine waves, the truth of the matter was that either room or instrumental characteristics and other resonances would produce a certain number of additional audible harmonics. As per Helmholtz' assertion but tempering it with more recent theorists, these structures will reflect harmonics up to f_{20} (where the fundamental tone is designated as f_1 and emphasize those audible up to f_8).

As described in detail earlier, the resulting lattices showed the relationships and subsequent compatibility within the individual *Klang*. In addition, they set up systems that catalog sonority, allowing chord types to be categorized according to relative consonant and type and based upon the presentation of audible and secondary difference tones.

Using Sine Waves and Spectrograph Software

Spectrogram Programs

While this is not intended to be a review of available free- or shareware, it is helpful to outline the benefits of selected, somewhat representative software used to evaluate and compare the effectiveness of the results. Each of the following programs are Macintosh platforms (OSX 10.5 or above, with some limitations in upgrade), and available for download from Internet sources and include free-, share-, and commercial ware. While others are available, they were not selected for a variety of reasons. Several are old enough to be incompatible with the most current operating systems or platforms or have not been updated to the extent that they are sonically or practically relevant to this project. Others were not detailed, aspects and readouts were not adjustable, or did not run fast enough to reflect accurate assessment of the spectra recorded. The applied programs were detailed enough, and included calibration, real-time analysis, systems and acoustics analysis, and adjustable parameters.

Spek is an example of the simple real-time spectrogram freeware programs available for OSX-based systems, although it is problematic or non-functional with system 10.7 to 10.12. Its parameters are not adjustable but gives a time-based, color readout of any standard-format, non-compressed audio file. While valuable to show overall pictures of the frequency range and the implications of timbre within the context of chordal *Klang* on a real-time basis, its range encompassed all of human hearing (20 Hz–20 kHz), and the desired readout of 15 Hz–1500 Hz was too small to identify detail within that range. Its advantage was open source display with visual time-based generation. Many software programs were similar to this. Some of the readouts failed to show difference tones due to lack of resolution or programming but showed otherwise unexplained phasing issues.

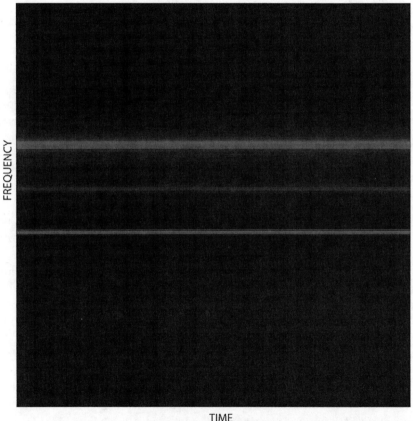

TIME

Figure 185. AudioXplorer showing additive phasing in a C major triad

For example, Figure 185 shows the three tones that were calibrated to play at 92 dB at the computer's built-in microphone, through AudioXplorer, a freeware whose advantages were the comparatively pixel-free generation of tones, with brightness relating to amplitude. This generation also reflected the tendency for wider bands of frequency related to amplitude. All three tones were generated through Apple's Logic Pro software and had equal amplitude at output. The brightest or loudest tone is G_{792}, the dullest is E_{660} and the lowest tone is C_{528}. Clearly, there is an element of destructive and constructive phasing occurring at some point in the system. The picture also shows no difference tones below the generated frequencies.

However, the oscilloscope function of the software *iSpectrum* shows measurable pulses from the simultaneous generation of the three tones[1] shown:

iSpectrum, the supporting software shown in Figure 186, is similar to

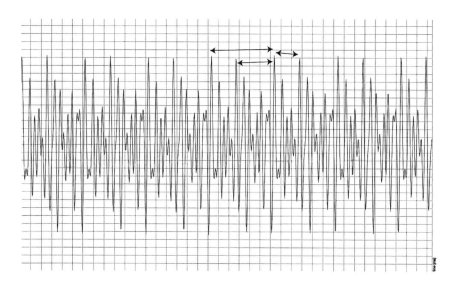

Figure 186. Unplayed but audible periodic soundwaves

the other two, with two elements, a window that acts as a real-time oscilloscope, and a "waterfall" display, that reads out frequencies in intensity of color on a real time basis. An example of this lay in the first indications of phase cancellation in played tones as a result of secondary harmonics. Its drawbacks include a tendency to display visual anomalies that may result from audio, software, hardware or even display sources. The display indicates frequency from which inferences may be made and is useful for general comparisons but is not specific enough for proofs. It was most valued as an initial indicator and a visual evaluator for general, real-time readouts. It identified differences between real time addition and subtraction of tones for basic, visual assessment, without needing to do a file-to-file comparison of different files and readouts. Its vibrant color display allowed quick read and comparative evaluations between inputs.

Several programs have windows that include the spectrograph, oscilloscope and real-time frequency analysis. *SignalScope Pro* and *Room EQ Wizard* include multiple analysis tools, such as the above, with SPL measuring, dedicated FFT analyzer, octave band analyzer, etc., based upon the marketing status (e.g., freeware, shareware, purchase or commercial grade versions). *SignalScope Pro* will be used in the analysis of the tones below to generate a real-time progressive spectrogram. While the generation of the tones in this case exclude tristimulus and envelope analyses,[2] its FFT analyzer is very detailed and will provide readouts on a commercial level.

The program best suited for many parts of the project was *Room EQ Wizard* (v. 5, updated to v. 5.20 in beta), freeware primarily used in analyzing live sound amplification situations, where the audio characteristics change from venue to venue. It identifies elements within the venue to prevent "feedback" and other room anomalies from interfering with performance audio. Its various elements include a parametric equalization readout, an SPL display and more relevant to this paper, a real time frequency analysis. Although a freeware, its uses are far more extensive and would be worth every penny as a commercial software; the RTA element is the primary analysis method used in this paper. The program settings are as follows for the resulting analyses:

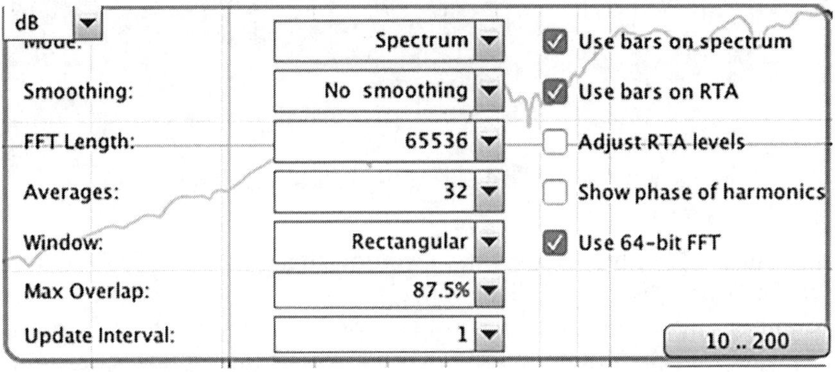

Figure 187. REW Program settings screenshot

The last class of software includes the "plugins" found in the digital audio workstation (DAW) software that generated the initial tones, Logic Pro, by Apple, Inc. These were used to generate and identify the tones within the digital domain of the software and thus ensured that the tones would not be affected by any exterior system anomalies, whether acoustic, electric or even digital processing. Those related to FFT frequency analysis were designed to be no higher resolution than would be normally used in a mixing/mastering commercial recording situation. As a result, frequency analysis generated within such a system and with these measurement tools may be called into question, without its help establishing a baseline for measurement. The oscilloscope elements were valuable, being comparable to any of the above-named software. The generation of tones, processing and analysis were separable to aid in fine tuning elements within the entire system.

Generating Tones

The calibration used the tones, sweeps and noise generators inherent within each software program. To generate multiple tones, the computer-generated sine waves through digital audio production software, Logic, to ensure level adjustment, acoustic isolation, and tone controllability. The software's *Test Wave* generator plug-in was used to generate and control frequencies within the closed system of the Logic software. This also ensured unfiltered sound up to the point of the audio output in the software. Each frequency was produced using a sine wave to eliminate timbre as a consideration for the initial tests and to support the overall premise of the theory. Pure, computer-generated and -limited sine waves have no inherent timbre and using them allowed the process to focus on single frequencies to eliminate sidebands, anomalies and aberrant phasing. There are no other filters run through the system, so the initial sine waves have no modifiers beyond initial generation and subsequent resonance within the system, if any.

Asmus used a binaural perspective by directing primary tones (f_1 and f_2) each to its own speaker to determine the physical properties of difference tones to the listener(s).[3] As the focus of this project dealt with multiple tones within a chordal environment, all primary tones were directed in monophonic speaker presentation; any additional blending of the tones beyond amplification (which was even distributed according to the presenting software) was due to the acoustic environment after the speaker output.

Audio Systems and Recording

The system for producing and recording tones generally follows that of Asmus, using various methods for producing, propagating, recording and analyzing the tones. The entire system is as follows:

sound source—output—harmonic processing (if any)*—input—analysis*

The project used a system of progressive conditions to determine at what point of the electrical or acoustical processing the difference tones actually occur. With an entirely closed system, that is, one with no processing, artificial or natural, beyond the addition of the pure sine waves together, we isolate any anomalies introduced by exterior elements.

The second system added software processing and produced artificial environments in which the signal may be processed but without additional resonances outside the control of the plug-ins themselves. Third, the process used a close electrical loop with a lead line directly from the computer's output to its input, which isolated acoustic influences and included electronic sources but processed the signal through the computer's ADDA converter at both ends of the system.

A fourth process consisted of processing the system through the ADDA converter, into a standard soundboard, feeding directly and electronically through the computer's internal microphone input. This added the possibilities of aspects of noise and internal resonance that were strictly electrically based, such as RF, any 60 Hz ground looping (this is significant as later shown), heat-sourced resonance, or electrical power residue (EPR). Finally, the fifth process fed the output through the speakers and allowed to permeate the studio control room for the addition of random and physical acoustic properties, then recorded into the computer's microphone or input.

No attempt was made to use exterior or post-production equalization to attenuate any spikes inherent in the calibration readings. Part of the reason for this was to provide raw data to the critical reader, and also to begin with the original frequency signature of the system itself. All subsequent data readout would be considered against the benchmark readings.

Closed Systems

Internal Feed

The project implemented the analysis for internal feed with AU "plugins" added on to the end of the Logic test wave generator. There were two basic oscilloscopes and several similar RTA frequency plugins. The RTAs were limited in evaluative resolution, all readouts were 30-band from 20 Hz to 20 kHz or less. The calibration in this case resulted in a 0 reading for all frequencies tested, using white noise as the source. Any post-fader processing shows a uniform frequency readout, aside from any frequency-specific processing within any added plugin (see Figure 188).

Opposite, bottom: **Figure 189. Closed electrical loop system**

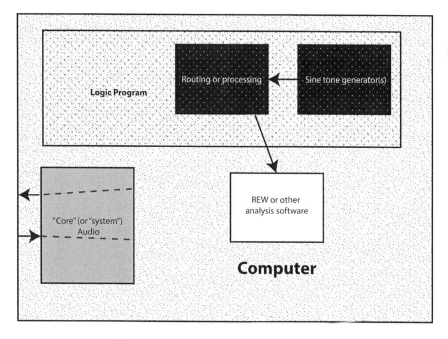

Figure 188. Internal closed loop system

Closed Electrical Loop

The closed electrical loop system is shown as follows, with the following baseline readout. Because the signal is processed (digital-to-electrical audio) and reprocessed (electrical audio-to-digital), an electrical influence and its resonating components are introduced to the system (Figure 189).

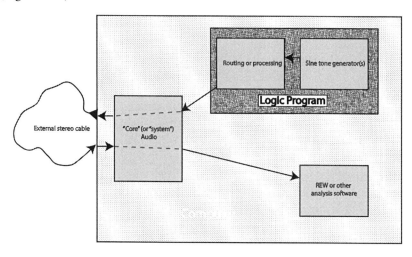

Looped Through Soundboard

To generate tones through the soundboard (Figure 190), we routed from the audio output of the computer into the line inputs of the 'board, thence to a pre-amplifier auxiliary send and into the computer's microphone input:

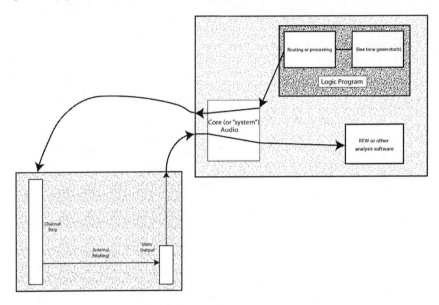

Figure 190. Soundboard routing

This guaranteed a "closed" but electronic system with no room or other exterior acoustics influence. Although electronic noise floor may be present, outside or acoustic harmonic anomalies in this case should be kept to a minimum, with response only occurring through electronic analog means. Similar readouts, using the same criteria as above, are below.

Below shows a spectrogram response to pink noise generated by the computer, fed through the 'board, and brought directly into the computer through its stereo microphone input (unbalanced) (see Figure 191 on next page).

While the above waterfall display shows a uniform response to a pink noise test, the response of a sweep test showed a slow response in frequencies 100 Hz and under. The basic readout of the system through a 20 Hz–20 kHz sine wave sweep was as follows, displaying again a drop below 50Hz. There were four variable sweeps, plus an average readout of all four, which is shown:

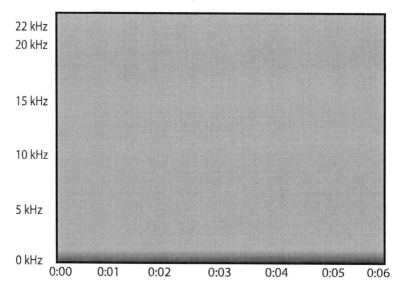

Figure 191. Pink noise generated through a soundboard

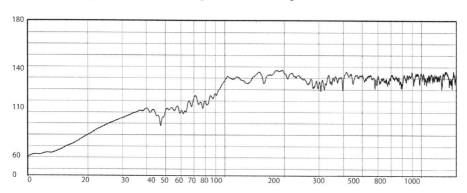

Figure 192. Sine wave sweep through soundboard

Open Systems

The first calibration assessment in an open system was the sound card test through the computer speakers to identify potential issues within the sound card alone. Rather than working through concept of complete flatline generation or regeneration, the focus was to identify latent frequencies that may compromise the identification of difference, harmonic and other tones coincidental with the generated tones. There is no subsequent equalization to ensure a flat response but results are from raw data.

One approach used the computer's stock or factory system to generate and record tones acoustically:

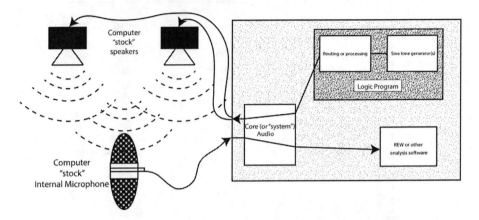

Figure 193. Computer external speakers/microphone

The system may generate side elements such as hardware resonance, room acoustic anomalies, or imaging bias. Using the computer speakers and the internal microphone also allow other variables contribute to the results. First, the speakers are limited in response and were not artificially adjusted to reflect any aural preferences or compensate for speaker prejudice. The readouts for these speakers' frequency response are as follows, again using the REW software speaker analysis system. The display indicates average readout, using 8 sweeps from 0 Hz–22050 kHz at three speeds of 5.6s, 11.25s, and 23.7s each, totaling 45s, 90s, and 190s, respectively (see Figure 194).

The following readout includes a snapshot of the RTA relative frequency response to pink noise input. The average from the sweeps is also given for comparison (see Figure 195).

Note the spikes and notches in both the average from the sweeps and the RTA readout. This is significant to show that the frequencies generated during the testing are not inherent anomalies from the computer's hardware system but unique in themselves and compared to this baseline. It is consistent with the response tests run through the closed electronic system described above.

Played Through Studio Speakers

The final processing involved playing the sine waves through the studio system, as per the following diagram (see Figure 196).

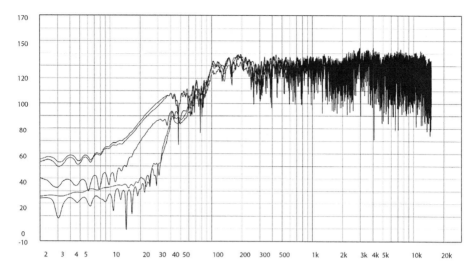

Figure 194. Sine wave sweep through computer speakers and microphone

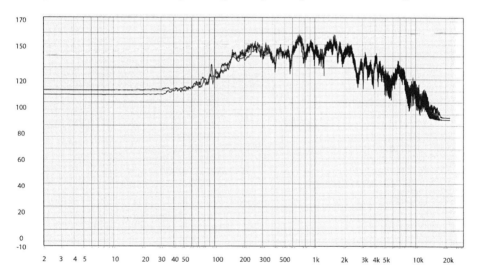

Figure 195. Sine wave sweep and pink noise output: speakers and microphone

The following graph (Figure 197) shows the RTA for similar sweeps played through studio speakers. There is still consistency in the readout, again without artificial compensation. There is still a spike at around 100 Hz with a small boost of frequencies in the mid-range.

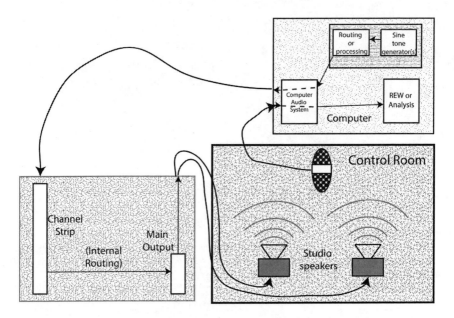

Figure 196. Control room system

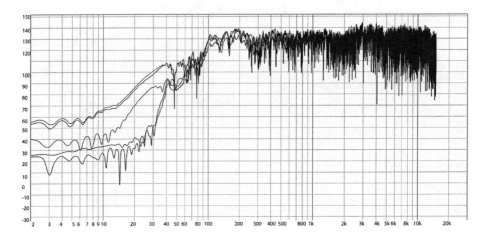

Figure 197. Sine wave sweeps through control room system

Test Results

Closed Systems

The RTA plugins for Logic failed to identify any difference tones when analyzed directly through the DAW system. While this may be due to the low resolution of the plugins, it must not be inferred that they exist (or not) within the virtual world of the software. This is also consistent with the findings of multiple experimenters.[4] White and Grieshaber pointed out the possibility of intrusion of intermodulation into acoustic data but the addition of sine waves guarantees a linear situation. Thus, no intermodulation will interfere with the output analysis in this situation. To ameliorate this further, the above baseline readings show inherent spikes that are to be taken into consideration as the initial and combination frequencies are presented.

However, even as the internal systems exclude outward resonance, the oscilloscopes for several plugins show measurable phasing that correspond to the frequencies as shown in the figures above. The time stamps on an oscilloscope picture produced by the software *AudioXplorer* upon an AIFF file recorded from C triad shows the wavelength corresponding to C_{132} within a higher frequency readout. The spikes at C_{132} may be thought of as a series of pulses whose amplitude allows it to rise above a background, comparative, "noise," that is, the higher frequencies. This is analogous to the frequency of a note played by an instrument rising above higher noise, in that case, "timbre."

Note that each pulse may have variable amplitudes due to phasing (e.g., each may "share" amplitudes and timing):

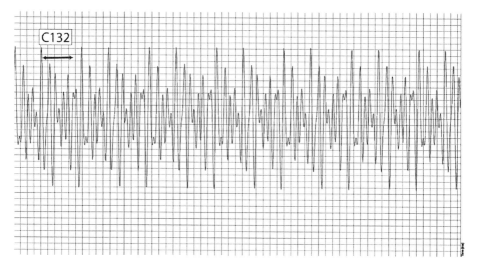

Figure 198. Noting difference tones as they appear in oscilloscope displays

The pulses produced by phasing are lower in frequency and audibly produce a tone lower than either f_1 or f_2 from the original chord.

Using an electrical loop that exits the digital domain and returns to it, thus adding ADD and DDA processing and their respective electronic/electric resonances to the mix, as shown resulted in the same readouts at three different levels. Note the increase in difference tones and harmonics as overall amplitude increases the virtual and electrical potential for resonance[5]:

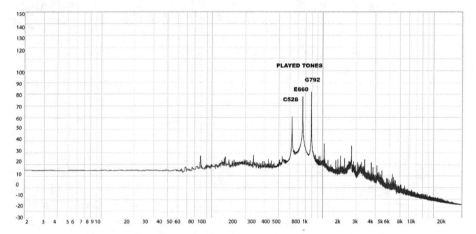

Figure 199. Closed electrical response at -40 dB relative input

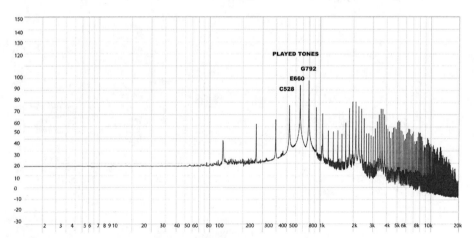

Figure 200. At -25 dB relative input

As the input level increases, resonant effects begin, probably as a result of the induced electrical or virtual environments. On a strictly acoustics basis, the discussion between the difference tone phenomenon as a psychoacoustic issue or an acoustics source must introduce a third issue: that of acoustic or electronic resonance, whether inside or outside the ear system. While it seems that phasing occurs even within a

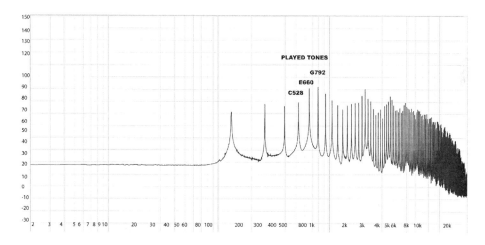

Figure 201. At 0 dB relative input

virtual system based upon the oscilloscope readouts, the audible difference tones are enhanced when the opportunity includes outside acoustic and environmental resonating contributors.

Once the output is processed through the AD/DA converters, the electronic/electric environment produces measurable difference tones and harmonics. The curious thing is that they do not register within the program itself, except as an oscilloscope readout of phasing: the frequencies of difference tones and harmonics are not manifest. The following diagram shows the progression:

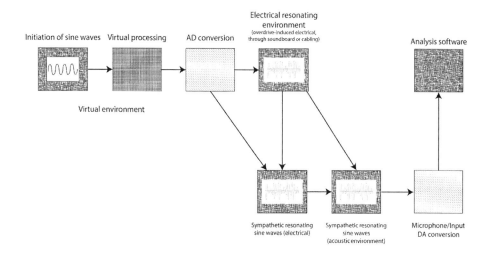

Figure 202. Progression of components that influence phasing

Open Systems

Keeping the loop within the soundboard produced the following RTA readout. This confirms that combination wave generation is not just dependent upon room acoustics and are inherent within certain electrical systems. On a practical basis, this has implications in live reinforcement and recording, where at least part of the transition to audible signals is analog within the electrical domain.

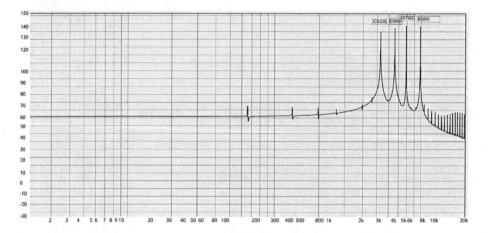

Figure 203. Soundboard readout of generated C major 7 chord

The following readout is an analysis using the studio room system as described above. It adds a room dynamic, even though the room is a minimal reflection control booth used for audio monitoring (played notes are an octave higher for clarity).

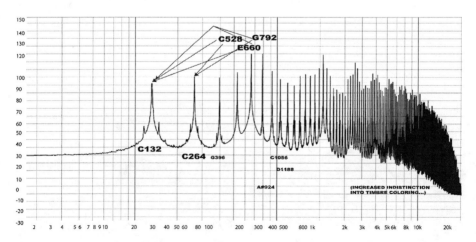

Even with 32 averages being calculated, one can see the addition of frequency anomalies produced by the room. The main difference tones and harmonics remain the same. Compare the above with the following readouts of the first and second inversions, respectively. Notice that additional harmonics are generated that exist *below* the played tones, and cannot be a direct result of them or those generated from primary harmonics but of difference tones. The third and seventh harmonics of C_{132} are prominent as G_{396} and $A\#_{924}$ respectively, proving that they cannot come from played notes but must be additional resonances from C_{132} as a difference tone.

All readouts show that phasing due to acoustic resonance occurs, in constructive and destructive modes. As part of the study involves the presence of difference tones that are the result of, and contribute to the phasing, they cannot be eliminated to show exact attenuation consequences. Therefore, determining the exact amount of phasing due to these interactions goes beyond the scope of this project. However, one can see by the graphs how the played frequencies may be attenuated by the presentation of the difference tones, and their varying degrees. For example, the original sine waves are presented (played) at equal levels but the following detail shows the clear attenuation of C_{528}, as compared to E_{660} and G_{792}. As this phasing occurs with interactions of all three tones, one can only assume that this frequency-specific attenuation is a result of phasing with additional harmonic tones peculiar to the order in the root position and the redistribution of the original sound pressure level energy.

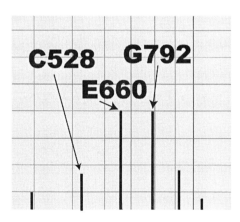

Figure 205. C triad, destructive phasing of C_{528}

Opposite, bottom: **Figure 204. Control room readout of C major triad**

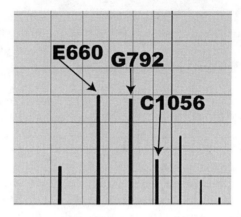

Figure 206. C triad, 1st inversion, destructive phasing

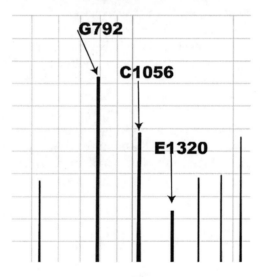

Figure 207. C triad, 2nd inversion, destructive phasing

Chapter Notes

Introduction

1. See Heinrich Schenker, *Harmony*, vol. 1 (Chicago: University of Chicago Press, 1954); and Olivier Messiaen, *Technique de mon langage musical* (Paris: Leduc, 1944).

2. Maurice Ravel, *Orchestra Music Selections: Four Orchestral Works* (New York: Dover Publications, 1989), 225.

3. Hermann von Helmholtz, *On the Sensations of Tone as a Physiological Basis for the Theory of Music*, 1863, trans. Alexander J. Ellis (New York: Dover Publications, 1954).

4. Jack DW Ballard, Jr., *Principles of Music: Harmony, Melody, Rhythm and Form for the Working Musician* (Alliance, OH: Kiwibird Creative Services, 2005, 2020), 92–94. Used by permission.

5. Robert W. Wason, and Elizabeth West Marvin, "Riemann's 'Ideen zu Einer «Lehre von den Tonvorstellungen»': An Annotated Translation," *Journal of Music Theory* 36, no. 1 (1992): 69–79.

6. Merriam-Webster, "Harmonic," *Merriam-Webster Online Dictionary*, http://www.merriam-webster.com/dictionary/harmonic (accessed May 19, 2008).

Chapter 1

1. The major sixth shows in the 5:3 ratio as this harmonic appears but for order's sake and considering 16th c. counterpoint as a guideline, we will adhere to the order here. It should also be noted that the minor sixth does not show as a naturally occurring ratio until later, at 8:5.

2. Johann Lippius, *Synopsis of New Music*, vol. 8, 1612, trans. by Benito V. Rivera (Colorado Springs: Colorado College Music Press, 1977), 18, 65.

3. Lippius, *Synopsis,* 14.

4. George J. Buelow, *Thorough-Bass Accompaniment According to Johann David Heinichen* (Berkeley: University of California Press, 1966), 24–25.

5. Ian D. Bent and Anthony Pople, "Analysis," in *Grove Music Online, Oxford Music Online*, http://www.oxfordmusiconline.com/subscriber/article/grove/music/41862pg1 (accessed November 14, 2008).

6. Herbert Westerby, "The Dual Theory in Harmony," *The Musical Association* (29th Session, 1902–1903): 62.

7. Lippius, *Synopsis,* 41, 65.

8. Jean-Philippe Rameau, *Treatise on Harmony*, 1722, trans. Philip Gossett (reprint, New York: Dover Publications, 1971).

9. Hugo Riemann, "Ideas for a Study 'On the Imagination of Tone,'" *Journal of Music Theory* 36, no. 1 (1992): 98–101.

10. David M. Howard and Jamie Angus, *Acoustics and Psychoacoustics*, 3rd ed. (London: Focal Press, 2007), 139.

11. Westerby, "The Dual Theory," 57.

12. Walter Piston and Mark DeVoto, *Harmony*, 5th ed. (New York: Norton, 1987), 231, 575.

13. Schenker, *Harmony*, 191, 359.

14. Piston and DeVoto, 309, 575. This idea of "sub-position" is derived from the "missing" functional root of perceptibly incomplete chords. In this case, the vii° is considered by Piston to be an "incomplete" V7: merely an extension of an implied $\hat{5}$ root.

15. Schenker, *Harmony*, 205, 359.

16. David W. Bernstein, "Georg Capellen's Theory of Reduction: Radical Harmonic Theory at the Turn of the Twentieth Century," *Journal of Music Theory* 37, no. 1 (1993): 106.

17. Bernstein, "Georg Capellen's," 106.

Chapter 2

1. William J. Mitchell, "The Study of Chromaticism," *Journal of Music Theory* 6, no. 1 (1962): 11.

2. David Lewin, *Generalized Musical Intervals and Transformations* (New York: Oxford University Press, 2007), 177.

Chapter 3

1. Ballard, Jack. *Blues Intonation in an Equal Tempered World*. Paper presentation at the Ben Johnson Colloquium; Wayne State University. Dayton, Ohio, March 13, 2010. Content © by Kiwibird Creative Services. Used by permission.

2. Gioseffo Zarlino, *Istitutioni*. Part III, Chapter 61, p. 293. Quoted in Rameau, *Treatise on Harmony* (Gossett, ed.) Dover Publications, 1971.

3. Ballard, Jack. *Principles of Music*. MS. Unpublished, Kiwibird Creative Services, 2003, 2015, 2020.

Chapter 4

1. J. Murray Barbour, *Tuning and Temperament: A Historical Survey* (East Lansing: Michigan State College Press, 1953), 57–59.

2. Christopher Page, "Jerome of Moravia on the Rubeba and Viella," *The Galpin Society Journal* 32 (1979): 82–83. See also Barbour, 12.

3. Mitchell, "The Study," 21.

4. This does not include extended techniques such as bending strings, "whammy" bars, etc.

5. Barbour, *Tuning*, 198–200. See Chapter VIII for his full commentary on modern practice.

6. Olivier Messiaen, *Technique de mon langage musical* (Paris: A. Leduc, 1944), 47–53.

7. Messiaen, *Technique*, 43.

8. Messiaen, *Technique*, 55.

9. Giselher Schubert, «Hindemith, Paul,» in *Grove Music Online. Oxford Music Online*, http://www.oxfordmusiconline.com/subscriber/article/grove/music/13053 (accessed November 14, 2008).

10. Paul Hindemith, *Traditional Harmony* (New York: Associated Music Publishers, 1944).

11. Schenker does not include the octave redundancies but new, different tones.

12. Schenker, *Harmony*, 29.

13. Matthew Shirlaw, *The Theory and Nature of Harmony* (Sarasota, FL: Birchard Coar, 1970), 498.

14. Suzannah Clark, "Schenker's Mysterious Five," *19th-Century Music* 23, no. 1 (1999): 8.

15. Shirlaw, *The Theory*, 500.

16. Benoit B. Mandelbrot, *The Fractal Geometry of Nature* (New York: W. H. Freeman, 1983), 468.

17. Messiaen, *Technique*, 47.

Chapter 5

1. Enrico Fubini, *Music and Culture in Eighteenth-Century Europe: A Source Book* (Chicago: University of Chicago Press, 1994), 153.

2. Hermann von Helmholtz, *On the Sensations of Tone as a Physiological Basis for the Theory of Music, 1821–1894*, trans. Ellis J. Alexander (New York: Dover Publications, 1954), 49.

3. Robert W. Wason and Elizabeth West Marvin, "Riemann's 'Ideen zu einer...'" *Journal of Music Theory* 36, no. 1 (1992): 69–79.

4. Hugo Riemann, "Ideas for a Study 'On the Imagination of Tone'," *Journal of Music Theory* 36, no. 1 (1992): 99–100.

5. Helmholtz, *On the Sensations*, 18.

6. Riemann, "Ideas," 94.

7. David Miles Huber and Robert E. Runstein, *Modern Recording Techniques*, 4th ed. (Indianapolis, IN: Sams Publishing, 1995), 59, 496.

8. Leo L. Beranek, *Acoustics* (New York: McGraw-Hill, 1954), 404.

9. Huber and Runstein, *Modern Recording*, chaps. XI and XV passim.

10. The so-called 12-string bass takes advantage of this principle by doubling

each standard bass string (tuned E_0-A_0-D_0-G_0) with a second and third string tuned an octave higher. Originally built by Jol Dantzig in 1977 for Cheap Trick's bass player, Tom Petersson, it has appeared in various tunings and formats, such as a six-string bass-guitar hybrid. See M. Wright, et al., *Vintage Guitar Magazine*, "The History of Hamer, Part One."

11. David Bernstein, "Georg Capellen's Theory of Reduction: Radical Harmonic Theory at the Turn of the Twentieth Century," *Journal of Music Theory* 37, no. 1 (1993): 87–88.

12. Beranek, *Acoustics*, 401–402.

13. Howard and Angus, *Acoustics*, 121–33.

14. Riemann, "Ideas," 86.

15. Ballard, Jack DW, Jr., and Mark A. Changizi. *Re: Musical Continuity*, Email correspondence, 2008.

16. See Steve Larson, "The Problem of Prolongation in 'Tonal' Music: Terminology, Perception, and Expressive Meaning," *Journal of Music Theory* 41, no. 1 (1997): 101–136.

Chapter 6

1. Smith, Charles J. "Musical Form and Fundamental Structure: An Investigation of Schenker's *Formenlehre*." *Music Analysis* 15 (1996): 191–297.

2. Ballard, *Part One: The Castle. Part Two: Hyperextended Chord Tones: Chromatic Consonance in a Tertian Context* (PhD diss., Kent State University, 2008), 334–335.

3. See Larson, "The Problem."

4. Morgan 1978, Morgan, Robert P. "The Theory and Analysis of Tonal Rhythm." *The Musical Quarterly* 64, no. 4 (Oct., 1978), 430–433.

5. See Schenker, *Harmony*, 1954; Schoenberg, Arnold and Gerald Strang. *Fundamentals of Musical Composition*. New York: St. Martin's Press, 1967.

6. Larson, "The Problem," 105.

7. The B may have not been in the original. See Ballard, 2006, and Johnston, 1984.

8. See Fobel, Oliver, and Torsten Dau. "Searching for the optimal stimulus eliciting auditory brainstem responses in humans." *The Journal of the Acoustical*

Society of America vol. 116,4 Pt 1 (2004): 2213–22. doi:10.1121/1.1787523, Ballard and Changizi, 2008, Ballard, "Part One," 2008.

Chapter 7

1. See the author's MS, *Avenues of Vision*, for discussions on context and reactions to aesthetic stimuli.

2. Technically, a human should be able to "hear" 20Hz or above. However, "hear," and "perceive" are subjective terms, and dependent upon amplitude as well as pitch. Below 30Hz, a sine wave may be only perceived as a source of pressure and sometimes pressure pulses, if that. 30Hz gives us a margin of error and perceivability.

3. General MIDI (or "GM") is a standard developed by the music keyboard/synthesizer industry to provide a standard set of 128 sounds. Its purpose was to ensure that any MIDI, or synthesizer song built on MIDI, would sound exactly the same on any GM instrument, regardless of the manufacturer or model. See https://www.midi.org/specifications-old/item/gm-level-1-sound-set. "Orchestra Hit" is number 56.

4. Howard and Angus do an excellent job of describing acoustic physics within the context of musical application. Howard and Angus, *Acoustics* 2017.

5. Sirr, Steven A., and Waddle, John R. "Use of CT in Detection of Internal Damage and Repair and Determination of Authenticity in High-Quality Bowed Stringed Instruments." RadioGraphics. 1999. 19:3, 639–646. See also their "CT analysis of bowed stringed instruments." Radiology 1997 203:3, 801–805, and Sacconi's work on violin construction and an analysis of Stradivari violin, The 'Secrets' of Stradivari.

6. Vaughan Williams, *Fantasia on a Theme of Thomas Tallis*. 1910.

Chapter 8

1. Ballard, Jack. *Cherubim Bells*, 2010, Alliance, OH: Kiwibird Music (ASCAP). Used by permission.

2. Referenced in Howard and Angus, *Acoustics*, 2017.

3. See Howard and Angus, *Acoustics,* 2017.

Chapter 9

1. T.D. Rossing and A.J.M. Houtsma (1986), "Effects of signal envelope on the pitch of short sinusoidal tones," J. Acoust. Soc. Am. 79, 1926–33, and S.S. Stevens (1935), "The relation of pitch to intensity," J. Acoust. Soc. Am. 6, 150–54.

2. Malcolm Slaney and Richard F. Lyon, Apple Hearing Demo Reel, Apple Computer Technical Report #25. Video. Cupertino, CA 95014 (c) 1991. https://ccrma.stanford.edu/~malcolm/correlograms/.

3. Rossing and Houtsma, "Effects," (1986) 150–54 .

4. Falstad, Paul. *falstad.com.* Accessed August 13, 2020.

5. "Complaint," in *Concerto No. 2 for Piano, Orchestra and Jazz Continuo.* Alliance, OH: Kiwibird Music. 1994.

Chapter 10

1. Asmus, Jr., Edward P. 1978. "Perception and Analysis of the Difference Tone Phenomenon as an Environmental Event." *Journal of Research in Music Education,* Vol. 26, No. 2, pp. 82–89. Published by: Sage Publications, Inc. on behalf of MENC: The National Association for Music Education. 88–89.

2. Ballard, Jack. *Journal of Kenyan Fulbright Studies.* Unpublished, 2012–2013. Alliance, OH: Kiwibird Creative Services. Used by permission.

3. Norman Cazden, "The Definition of Consonance and Dissonance." *International Review of the Aesthetics and Sociology of Music,* Vol. 11, No. 2 (1980): 123–168.

4. Cazden, "Definition of Consonance," 130.

5. Patterson, Roy D. 1990. "The Tone Height of Multiharmonic Sounds." *Music Perception: An Interdisciplinary Journal.* Vol. 8, No. 2. 203–213. University of California Press. 207.

6. Cazden, "The systematic reference of musical consonance response," *International Review of the Aesthetics and Sociology of Music,* 3 (1972). 133.

7. "FM Tone Generators and the Dawn of Home Music Production." *Yamaha Synth 40th Anniversary.* Yamaha Corporation, 2019. Accessed October 24, 2019.

8. Schenker, *Harmony,* 26–28.

9. Cazden, "Definition of Consonance."

10. These types may also be a function of different types of sub-position.

11. Helmholtz, *On the Sensations.* 66.

Chapter 11

1. Schenker, *Harmony,* 29.

2. Howard and Angus, *Acoustics* (see section 2.2).

Chapter 12

1. This aspect of the Nyquist theorem basically dictates that a sampling frequency must be double the highest audible frequency to accurately replicate it, as each cycle consists of a high point and a corresponding "low" point (+180° and -180°), and thus requires *two* measurements of amplitude in given time for each sine wave involved (see Fourier analysis for reduction of complex waves into aggregate sine frequencies). The "odd" point of 44.1kHz has had multiple explanations, the most logical its being the result of a programming issue and limited data storage/processing capabilities.

2. Online discussions.

3. Hughes, Matthew. "Four reasons why vinyl is better than digital." *Make Use Of.* April 18, 2015. https://www.makeuseof.com/tag/reasons-why-vinyl-better-digital/.

4. Haeff, A., & Knox, C. (1963). Perception of Ultrasound. *Science, 139*(3555), 590–592. Retrieved from http://www.jstor.org/stable/1709911.

5. Qin, Michael; Schwaller, Derek; Babina, Matthew; Cudahy, Edward. Human underwater and bone conduction hearing in the sonic and ultrasonic range. *The Journal of the Acoustical Society of America.* 129 (2011). https://doi.org/10.1121/1.3588185

6. Haeff, A., & Knox, C. «Perception.»

Chapter 14

1. Sotorrio, José A. 2013. The Undertone Series. May 29, 2012. http://www.youtube.com/watch?v=R_0s33fMOPI. Accessed, December 28, 2018.

2. Christiansen, Thomas. 2004. *Rameau and Musical Thought in the Enlightenment*. London: Cambridge University Press. 99–100.

Chapter 16

1. Messiaen, Olivier. *Technique de mon langage musical*. Paris: A. Leduc, 1944. 47–53.

2. As there are often several perspectives and reference points regarding the notes as present in the harmonic series and ratios, a couple of things need to be mentioned. First, ratios here are not given with regard to simple intervals but to each harmonic's relationship with the fundamental and to each other (e.g., 5:4 is the ratio of the fifth harmonic tone to the fourth harmonic tone as they relate to the fundamental). Second, designation of harmonics, partials or overtones are referred to with the fundamental as f_1. Therefore, the first harmonic as produced by f_1 is designated f_2, the second as f_3, etc.

3. Bais, Reginald, *A Pythagorean Tuning of the Diatonic Scale* (Sept 24, 2002) in.music.sc.edu › bain › atmi02 › pst. Accessed Sept 2, 2020. Although this is Pythagorean tuning, nonetheless, the intonation differences between the different tunings are enough to be argumentative. We are looking, after all, at the development of the half step and the justification of the major fifteenth, not comparing the various measurements by which each philosophy is derived. The 25/24 is also considered but this is too high to be considered the first source for the justification of the minor second. See also Allen, John S. "Matrix Tunings and the Permutation Lattice." http://www.bikexprt.com/tunings/tunings3.htm (accessed March 20, 2006); and Monzo, Joe. "A Table of the Log(2) Harmonic-Distance for Some Intervals in the 11-Limit." *Tonalsoft Encyclopedia of Microtonal Music Theory*. http://www.tonalsoft.com.

4. Monzo, *Tonalsoft Encyclopedia of Microtonal Music Theory*.

5. Guy Oldham, Murray Campbell and Clive Greated. "Harmonics." *Grove Music Online*. https://doi.org/10.1093/gmo/9781561592630.article.50023. (accessed Jan 24, 2006, Sept 02, 2020).

6. In Schenker's time, the technology did not necessarily allow a controlled atmosphere with the extreme amplitude that makes the highest resonating harmonics "audible, a subjective term in itself. Even today, we *can* actually hear (very strongly, in fact) an amazing number of partials in, say, a train "whistle," whose fundamental oscillator nonetheless emits very audible partials at least past f_9 and beyond, to the discerning ear. This has little to do with timbre up to this point (f_9).

7. Oldham, "Harmonics."

8. Gunther Schuller. *The Visitation: Opera in Three Acts*. New York: Associated Music Publishers, 1967.

9. Schuller, *The Visitation*.

10. Oldham, etc. "Harmonics." These are my calculations, based upon the table provided in Groves.

11. The "natural minor" as depicted above is derived from deducting 100 cents from the naturally occurring major (f_5). This perspective is in response to a Schenker perspective that the minor third is an anomalous chromatic neighbor to the major third, rather than a consonant tonality by itself.

12. Maurice Ravel, *Pavane pour une infante défunte pour un petite orchestre*. Mineola: Dover Publications, Inc., 1899, Orch. 1910, 1989.

Chapter 17

1. Rameau, *Treatise*. 48,444; Shirlaw, *The Theory of Harmony: An Inquiry into the Natural Principles of Harmony, with an Examination of the Chief Systems of Harmony from Rameau to the Present Day*. Reprint, Sarasota, FL: Birchard Coar, 1970. 509–517; Piston and DeVoto, *Harmony*. 5th ed. New York: W. W. Norton, 1987. 309–312, 575.

2. See Shirlaw's commentary on Rameau in *The Theory*. 127, 149, 193.

3. Gridley, Mark C., and Cutler, David. *Jazz Styles: History & Analysis*, 8th ed. (Upper Saddle River, NJ: Prentice Hall, 2003), 442.

4. Powell, Jonathan, "Skryabin [Scriabin], Aleksandr Nikolayevich," *Groves Music Online*, https://doi.org/10.1093/gmo/9781561592630.article.25946. Accessed Sept 2, 2020.

5. Powell, and Dernova, quoted in Ballard, "Part One," 2008.

6. Messiaen, *Techniques*, 47–53.

Chapter 18

1. For more on the concept of "non-progressive chords," see Ballard, *Principles of Music for the Working Musician*. Unpublished. Kiwibird Creative Services. http://www.kiwibirdcreativeservices.com/principles-of-music-for-the-working-musician-2015/?preview=true. Accessed August 13, 2020. Used by permission.

Chapter 20

1. Roger F. T. Bullivant and Elizabeth Godley, "The Minor Triad," *Music & Letters* 34, no. 1 (1953): 86–88, 294.

2. Barry Mann, Cynthia Weill, and Brenda Russell, *None of Us Are Free*, Solomon Burke and Five Blind Boys of Alabama, Compact Disc (DLC) 2003572955, 2002 Fat Possum Records (accessed May 12, 2008); "xykep," "Solomon Burke—None of Us are Free (2002)," YouTube, http://www.youtube.com/watch?v=kfzVeTaSAsQ (accessed May 12, 2008).

Chapter 21

1. Amnon Shiloah, "The Arabic Concept of Mode," *Journal of the American Musicological Society*, Vol., 34, No. 1. (Spring, 1981), 29.

2. Shiloah, "The Arabic Concept," 20

3. Lois Ibsen al Faruqi, "The Modal System of Arab and Persian Music, A.D. 1250–1300 by O. Wright," *Ethnomusicology*, Vol. 24, No. 1. (Jan., 1980), 126

4. Henry George Farmer, "The Influence of Music: From Arabic Sources," *Proceedings of the Musical Association*, 52nd Sess. (1925–1926), 103.

5. Shiloah, "The Arabic Concept," 30.

6. Lois Ibsen al Faruqi, review on "The Theory of Music in Arabic Writings (c.

900–1200): Descriptive Catalogue of Manuscripts in Libraries of Europe and the U.S. A., Vol. Bx, Repertoire International des Sources musicales (RISM) by Amnon Shiloah," *Asian Music*. Vol. 14, No. 2, chines Music History. (1983), 183.

7. Shiloah, "The Arabic Concept," 29

8. H. J. W. Tillyard, "A Byzantine Musical Handbook at Milan," *The Journal of Hellenic Studies*, Vol., 46, Part 2. (1926), 222.

9. H. G. Farmer, *Historical Facts for the Arabian Musical Influence*. London: William Reeves Bookseller Limited, 1928. 60.

10. Farmer, *Historical Facts*, 72–73.

11. Christopher Page, "Jerome of Moravia on the Rubeba and Viella," *The Galpin Society Journal*, Vol. 32. (May, 1979), 82.

12. Xavier Maurice Collangettes, *Étude sur la musique arabe*, Paris: Société asiatique (1904–1906), 419.

13. Hassan Habib Touma, *La musique arabe*, Paris: Buchet chastel, 30–31.

14. Owen Wright, "Ibn al-Munajjim and the Early Arabian Modes," *The Galpin Society Journal*, Vol. 19. (Apr., 1966), 31.

15. In fact, there are several "sub-progressions" or "non-progressive chord patterns" that may be jazz's analogous response to such "preset" modes. See the author's MS *Principles of Music*.

16. Wright, "Ibn al-Munajjim," 33.

17. Farmer, *Historical Facts*, 60.

18. Farmer, Arab Influences (p. 60) (see Bar Hebraeus, "Ethikon" (Bedjan Edit.), p. 69, and Guillaume André Villoteau, "De l'état actuel de l'art musical en Égypte, ou relation historique" in *l'Egypte ou recueil des observations et des recherches* (2nd ed., 1826), Paris: Pankoucke. 613.

19. Wright, "Ibn al-Munajjim," 30.

20. "The short *risala* of Yahya b. "Ali b. Yahya al-Munajjim al-Nadim is the only extant document to contain an appreciable amount of information about the modal structure of Arabian art-music in the eighth and ninth centuries." Wright, "Ibn al-Munajjim," 27.

21. Peter Manuel, "Modal Harmony in Andalusian, Eastern European, and Turkish Syncretic Musics," *Yearbook for Traditional Music*, vol. 21. (1989), 55.

22. Wright's example, taken from Arabic sources were in B♭. For the sake of continued clarity, we will proceed in the key of C (no key signature).

23. Manuel, "Modal Harmony," 72.

24. Shiloah, "The Arabic Concept," 30.

25. Owen Wright, The Modal System of Arab and Persian Music A.D. 1250–1300. (London. Oxford Univ. Press, 1978), 31.

26. Ikhwān al-Ṣafāʾ, Shiloah, A., World Congress on Jewish Music (1978 : Jerusalem). (19781976). *The epistle on music of the Ikhwān al-Ṣafāʾ: (Bagdad, 10th century).* English ed. Tel-Aviv: Tel-Aviv University, Faculty of Fine Arts, School of Jewish Studies, Stanza 18, 68.

27. Ikhwān al-Safā,' 69.

28. See his *Space Trilogy*, especially *Perelandra* for more on this philosophy.

29. Note, also, how many polyphonic pieces progressed harmonically through their performances, producing lush [major] triads and non-harmonic tones, only to end on a perfect fifth. Analogously, it seems that the relationship of a perfect fifth to the major triad in the Renaissance—e.g., more "consonant"—relates to a similar relationship in the Picardy third of a major triad.

Chapter 22

1. See Schenker, *Harmony,* 34–46.

2. Paul Hindemith, *Sonate für Flöte und Klavier (1936)* (New York: Schott, 1965).

3. Resolution *within* the chord has more to do with linear resolution of melodies (e.g., "non-harmonic" tones, although, of course, these are relevant) than resolution of the sonority itself.

4. Darius Milhaud, *Sonate pour flute, hautbois, clarinet en si bémol et piano* (Paris: Durand, 1923), 13.

Chapter 23

1. 1931 July 3, *The Daily Times*, Life Is Full of Things–But They Don't Mean Anything by Will Rogers (McNaught Syndicate), Quote Page 2, Column 2, Davenport, Iowa. (Newspapers_com).

2. Kadosh, Roi and Terhune, David. Redefining synesthaesia?. *British Journal of Psychology.* 2012, 103: 20–23. http://research.gold.ac.uk/17077/1/Cohen%20Kadosh%20%26%20Terhune%202010%20BJP.pdf

3. Dael, N., Sierro, G., & Mohr, C. (2013). Affect-related synesthesias: a prospective view on their existence, expression and underlying mechanisms. *Frontiers in psychology, 4,* 754. doi:10.3389/fpsyg.2013.00754

4. Bragança, G., Fonseca, J., & Caramelli, P. (2015). Synesthesia and music perception. *Dementia & neuropsychologia, 9*(1), 16–23. doi:10.1590/S1980-57642015DN91000004

5. Goss, Clint. *The Color of Sound.* Flutopedia: an Encyclopedia for the Native American Flute. https://www.flutopedia.com/sound_color.htm

6. Where $c=299792458ms^{-1}$

7. Australian Telescope National Facility web page. https://www.atnf.csiro.au

8. $3.9924e+16_m$ is the distance in meters to Proxima Centauri, our nearest star besides the Sun. If we were able to measure a sweep (arc length) of 3000_m with two or more telescopes (for the sake of argument), the angle or sweep of the pulsar emission would be: $4.3054e\text{-}12^\circ$ or $.0000000000043^\circ$. If we were to extend our telescopes to Australia and Arizona (12.6km, considering the rotation and curve of the Earth and assuming we have the clock to accurately compare sightings), our angle is only improved to $1.8083e\text{-}10$ or $.00000000018^\circ$. The "Geriatric Pulsar" is 770 light years, or $7.285e+18$ with our arc length at 12.6km, has a resulting sweep arc of $9.9098e\text{-}13^\circ$.

9. Kapitza, P. (1979). Plasma and the Controlled Thermonuclear Reaction. *Science, 205*(4410), 959–964. Retrieved from http://www.jstor.org.ma.opal-libraries.org/stable/1748323

Appendix C

1. Keeping in mind that *any* transient or jump in amplitude that repeats consistently is "frequent" and by definition produces a tone.

2. Howard and Angus, 2011.

3. Asmus, 1978, 84.

4. Asmus (1978); White and Grieshaber (1980).

5. APP 31–38 are reconstructed from the original screenshots for image conformity.

Sources and Further Reading

Allen, John S. "A Bibliography on Musical Tunings and Temperaments." http://www.bikexprt.com/music/tunebibl.htm (accessed March 20, 2006).

_____. "Matrix Tunings and the Permutation Lattice." http://www.bikexprt.com/tunings/tunings3.htm (accessed March 20, 2006).

Archibald, R. C. "Mathematicians and Music." _The American Mathematical Monthly_ 31, no. 1 (1924): 1–25.

Asmus, Jr., Edward P. "Perception and Analysis of the Difference Tone Phenomenon as an Environmental Event." _Journal of Research in Music Education_, Vol. 26, No. 2, pp. 82–89. Published by Sage Publications, Inc. on behalf of MENC: The National Association for Music Education, 1978.

Bach, J.S. _Praeludium._ MS. http://ks4.imslp.net/files/imglnks/usimg/9/98/IMSLP81768-PMLP05948-BWV_851.pdf.

Backus, John. _The Acoustical Foundations of Music._ New York: W. W. Norton and Company, 1969.

Bain, Reginald. "A Pythagorean Tuning of the Diatonic Scale: A Tuning System Based on the Line of Fifths…" http://www.music.sc.edu/fs/bain/atmi02/pst/index.html (accessed May 20, 2008).

Ballard, Jr., Jack D.W. _Basic Arranging._ Power Point presentation. Alliance, OH: Kiwibird Creative Services, 2005. Used by permission.

_____. _The Castle._ Alliance, OH: Kiwibird Music, 2008. Used by permission.

_____. _Cherubim Bells._ Alliance, OH: Kiwibird Music, 2011. Used by permission.

_____. "Complaint," in _Concerto No. 2 for Piano, Orchestra and Jazz Continuo._ Alliance, OH: Kiwibird Music, 1994. Used by permission.

_____. _Concerto for Piano, no. 2._ Portland, OR: Kiwibird Music, 1994. Used by permission.

_____. "From Manuel de Falla to The Gipsy Kings: Flamenco, Andalusian and Gypsy Influences in Classical and Popular Music." Unpublished, 2007.

_____. "Part One: The Castle. Part Two: Hyperextended Chord Tones: Chromatic Consonance in a Tertian Context." Electronic Thesis or Dissertation. Kent State University, 2008. https://etd.ohiolink.edu/.

_____. _Principles of Music: Harmony, Melody, Rhythm and Form for the Working Musician._ Alliance, OH: Kiwibird Creative Services, 2005, 2015, 2020. Used by permission.

_____. _Symphony No. 5 (Spanish)._ Alliance, OH: Kiwibird Music (ASCAP), 2016.

_____, and Mark A. Changizi. _Re: Musical Continuity_, Email correspondence, 2008.

Balsach, Lorenç. "Application of Virtual Pitch Theory in Music Analysis." http://www.teoria.com/ (accessed November 15, 2007).

Barbour, J. Murray. "Just Intonation Confuted." _Music & Letters_ 19, no. 1 (1938): 48–60.

_____. _Tuning and Temperament: A Historical Survey._ 1952. Reprint, New York: Dover Publications, 2004.

Bartholomew, Wilmer T. _Acoustics of Music._ New York: Prentice Hall, 1942.

Bartók, Béla, Wilhelm Ziegler, and Béla Balázs. _Bluebeard's Castle, Op. 11: Piano Reduction by the Composer._ 1921. Reprint, Mineola, NY: Dover, 2001.

Beach, David. "The Current State of Schenkerian Research." *Acta Musicologica* 57 (1985): 275–307.

Bellan, P. "Simulating Solar Prominences in the Laboratory: The Techniques Used to Advance Fusion Research Can Be Fruitfully Applied to Some Basic Problems in Astrophysics." *American Scientist*, 88(2), (2000): 136–143. Retrieved from http://www.jstor.org.ma.opal-libraries.org/stable/27857993.

Bent, Ian D., and Anthony Pople. "Analysis." In *Grove Music Online. Oxford Music Online*, http://www.oxfordmusiconline.com/subscriber/article/grove/music/ 41862pg2 (accessed October 18, 2008).

Beranek, Leo L. *Acoustics*. New York: McGraw-Hill Book Company, 1954.

Bernstein, David W. "Georg Capellen's Theory of Reduction: Radical Harmonic Theory at the Turn of the Twentieth Century." *Journal of Music Theory* 37, no. 1 (1993): 85–116.

Bernstein, Leonard. *Symphonic Dances from "West Side Story."* New York: Boosey & Hawkes, 1990.

Beskin, V.S., A.V. Gurevich, and Y.N. Istomin." Theory of the Radio-Emission of Pulsars." *Astrophysics and Space Science*. Vol. 146, No. 2 (July 1988). Kluwer Academic Publishing. Dordrecht, Netherlands. pp. 205–281.

Bickerton, R. Introduction to High Temperature Plasma Physics. *Philosophical Transactions of the Royal Society of London. Series A, Mathematical and Physical Sciences*, 300(1456), (1981): 475–488. Retrieved from http://www.jstor.org.ma. opal-libraries.org/stable/36841.

Bobbitt, Richard. "The Physical Basis of Intervallic Quality and Its Application to the Problem of Dissonance." *Journal of Music Theory* 3, no. 2 (1959): 173–207.

Boomsliter, Paul C., and Warren Creel. "Extended Reference: An Unrecognized Dynamic in Melody," *Journal of Music Theory*, 7, (1963): 2–22.

_____. "The Long Pattern Hypothesis in Harmony and Hearing," *Journal of Music Theory*, 5, (1961): 2–31.

Bowling, D., and D. Purves. "A Biological Rationale for Musical Consonance." *Proceedings of the National Academy of Sciences of the United States of America*, 112(36), (2015): 11155–11160. Retrieved from https://www-jstor-org.ma.opal-libraries.org/stable/26464962.

Brown, Matthew. "The Diatonic and the Chromatic in Schenker's 'Theory of Harmonic Relations.'" *Journal of Music Theory* 30, no. 1 (1986): 1–33.

Buelow, George J. *Thorough-Bass Accompaniment According to Johann David Heinichen*. Berkeley: University of California Press, 1966.

Bullivant, Roger F. T., and Elizabeth Godley. "The Minor Triad." *Music & Letters* 34, no. 1 (1953): 86–88.

Burch, J., and J. Drake. "Reconnecting Magnetic Fields: The Huge Amounts of Energy Released from the Relinking of Magnetic Fields in Outer Space Are Both Mysterious and Potentially Destructive." *American Scientist*, 97(5), (2009): 392–399. Retrieved from http://www.jstor.org.ma.opal-libraries.org/stable/27859391.

Campbell, Murray, and Clive Greated. *The Musicians' Guide to Acoustics*. New York: Schirmer Books, 1987.

Carey, Norman, and David Clampitt. "Aspects of Well-Formed Scales." *Music Theory Spectrum* 11, no. 2 (1989): 187–206.

Cazden, Norman. "The Systemic Reference of Musical Consonance Response," *International Review of the Aesthetics and Sociology of Music*, 3 (1972): 217–242.

_____. "The Definition of Consonance and Dissonance." *International Review of the Aesthetics and Sociology of Music*, Vol. 11, No. 2 (1980): 123–168.

Christiansen, Thomas. *Rameau and Musical Thought in the Enlightenment*. London: Cambridge University Press, 2004.

_____. "The Systemic Reference of Musical Consonance Response." *International Review of the Aesthetics and Sociology of Music* 3, no. 2 (1972): 217–245.

Clark, Suzannah. "Schenker's Mysterious Five." *19th-Century Music* 23, no. 1 (1999): 84–102.

Clayton-Thomas, David. *Blood, Sweat and Tears.* 1996. Mobile Fidelity. B000000EPN (Compact Disc).

Clutsam, George H. "The Harmonies of Scriabine." *Music Theory* (1913): 156–158, 441–443, 521–524.

Condon, Jim, *Essential Radio Astronomy.* https://science.nrao.edu/opportunities/courses/era/j (accessed September 2, 2019).

DeBellis, Mark. *Music and Conceptualization.* New York: Cambridge University Press, 1995.

D'erlanger, Baron Rodolphe. *La Musique Arabe, etc.* Vol. 1. Paris: Librairie Orientaliste Paul Geuthner, 1930.

Dyson, George. *The New Music.* 2nd ed. London: Oxford University Press, 1926.

Elert, Glenn. *The Physics Hypertextbook.* Internet. 1990–2019. https://physics.info/.

Ellis, Alexander J. "On the Physical Constitution and Relations of Musical Chords." *Proceedings of the Royal Society of London* 13 (1863): 392–404.

_____. "On the Temperament of Musical Instruments with Fixed Tones." *Proceedings of the Royal Society of London* 13 (1863): 404–422.

Farmer, Henry George. *Historical Facts for the Arabian Musical Influence.* London: William Reeves Bookseller Limited, 1928.

_____. "The Influence of Music: From Arabic Sources," *Proceedings of the Musical Association,* 52nd Sess. (1925–1926), pp. 89–124.

Fobel, Oliver, and Torsten Dau. "Searching for the Optimal Stimulus Eliciting Auditory Brainstem Responses in Humans." *The Journal of the Acoustical Society of America* vol. 116,4 Pt 1 (2004): 2213–22. doi:10.1121/1.1787523.

Forster, Cristiano M. L. *Musical Mathematics: A Practice in the Mathematics of Tuning Instruments and Analyzing Scales.* San Francisco: The Chrysalis Foundation, 2000–2008. http://www.chrysalis-foundation.org/just_intonation.htm (accessed November 11, 2008).

Forte, Allen. *Tonal Harmony in Concept and Practice,* New York: Holt, Rinehart and Winston, 1962.

_____. "Secrets of Melody: Line and Design in the Songs of Cole Porter." *The Musical Quarterly* 77, no. 4 (Winter 1993): 607–647.

Frisk, George V. *Ocean and Seabed Acoustics: A Theory of Wave Propagation.* Englewood Cliffs, NJ: Prentice-Hall, 1994.

Fubini, Enrico. *Music and Culture in Eighteenth-Century Europe: A Source Book.* Chicago: University of Chicago Press, 1994.

Gershwin, George. *An American in Paris.* 1928. Reprint, Secaucus, NJ: Warner Bros. Publications, 1987.

_____. *Complete Gershwin Keyboard Works: Seven Major Compositions in One Volume.* Miami: Warner Bros. Publications, 1996.

_____. *Preludes for Piano.* New York: New World Music Corp., 1927.

Gilbert, Steven E. *The Music of Gershwin.* Composers of the Twentieth Century. New Haven: Yale University Press, 1995.

Goddard, Joseph. "The Philosophy of Our Tempered System." *Proceedings of the Musical Association* 28 (1901): 45–65.

Green, Joseph. "Harmony Modes." *The Musical Times and Singing Class Circular* 20, no. 435 (1879): 250–254.

_____. "On the Value of the Dissonance in Musical Theory." *The Musical Times and Singing Class Circular* 15, no. 341 (1871): 135–138.

_____. "On the Value of the Dissonance in Musical Theory (Concluded)." *The Musical Times and Singing Class Circular* 15, no. 342 (1871): 167–170.

Gridley, Mark C., and David Cutler. *Jazz Styles: History & Analysis.* 8th ed. Upper Saddle River, NJ: Prentice Hall, 2003.

Guernsey, Martha. "The Rôle of Consonance and Dissonance in Music." *The American Journal of Psychology* 40, no. 2 (1928): 173–204.

Haeff, A., and C. Knox. "Perception of Ultrasound." *Science, 139*(3555), (1963): 590–592. Retrieved from http://www.jstor.org/stable/1709911.

Hall, Robert A., Jr. "How Picard Was the Picardy Third?" *Current Musicology* 19 (1975): 78–80.

Hanžek, Branko. "The Genealogy of Science and Acoustics: A Supplement to the Description of the Role of Vinko Dvořák." *International Review of the Aesthetics and Sociology of Music* , Vol. 35, No. 2. 183–210, 2004. Croatian Musicological Society.

Haydn, Joseph, and H. C. Robbins Landon. Symphony no. 92, G Major : (*Oxford* Symphony). Edition Eulenburg. [Symphonies,]. Vol. 436. London; New York: E. Eulenburg, 1950.

Haydon, Glen. *The Evolution of the Six-Four Chord,* Berkeley: University of California Press, 1933.

Hermann, Helmholtz. *On the Sensations of Tone.* 2nd English Ed., Alexander J. Ellis, trans. New York: Dover Publications, 1954.

Hindemith, Paul. *Sonate für Flöte und Klavier (1936).* New York: Schott, 1965.

_____. *Traditional Harmony.* New York: Associated Music Publishers, 1943.

_____. *Unterweisung im Tonsatz* . Translated by Arthur Mendel. New York: Associated Music Publishers, 1937.

_____, and Arthur Mendel. "Methods of Music Theory." *The Musical Quarterly* 30, no. 1 (1944): 20–28.

Hjviri, Ali ibn Usman, *The Kashf al mahjub.* Translated by Reynold A. Nicholson. London: Messrs. Luzac and Company, Ltd., 1967.

Hodgson, J. "A Field Guide to Equalization and Dynamics Processing on Rock and Electronica Records." *Popular Music* 29(2), 283–297 (2010). Retrieved from http://www.jstor.org.ma.opal-libraries.org/stable/40926923.

Holst, Gustav. *The Planets.* Mineola, NY: Dover, 1996.

Howard, David M., and Jamie Angus. *Acoustics and Psychoacoustics.* 3rd ed. London: Focal Press, 2007.

Hsu, Kenneth J., and Andreas J. Hsu. "Fractal Geometry of Music." *Proceedings of the National Academy of Sciences of the United States of America* 87, no. 3 (1990): 938–941.

Huber, David Miles, and Robert E. Runstein. *Modern Recording Techniques.* 4th ed. Indianapolis: Sams Publishing, 1995.

Hughes, Matthew. "Four Reasons Why Vinyl Is Better Than Digital." *Make Use Of.* April 18, 2015. https://www.makeuseof.com/tag/reasons-why-vinyl-better-digital/.

Hull, A. Eaglefield. "Scriabin's Scientific Derivation of Harmony Versus Empirical Methods." *Proceedings of the Musical Assn.* 43rd Sess. (1916–1917): 17–28.

Ibsen al Faruqi, Lois. "The Modal System of Arab and Persian Music, A.D. 1250–1300 by O. Wright." *Ethnomusicology* 24, no. 1 (1980): 126–128.

Ives, Charles. *Hymn (Largo Cantabile), for String Orchestra.* 1935. Reprint. New York: Peer International, 1966.

Johnston, Richard. *Folk Songs North America Sings: A Source Book for All Teachers.* Toronto, Ont.: E.C. Kerby, 1984.

Jülicher, Frank, Daniel Andor, and Thomas Duke. "Physical Basis of Two-Tone Interference in Hearing." *Proceedings of the National Academy of Sciences of the United States of America* , Vol. 98, No. 16. (2001): 9080–9085.

Kapitza, P. "Plasma and the Controlled Thermonuclear Reaction." *Science,* 205(4410) (1979): 959–964. Retrieved from http://www.jstor.org.ma.opal-libraries.org/stable/1748323.

Karrick, Brant. "An Examination of the Intonation Tendencies of Wind Instrumentalists Based on Their Performance of Selected Harmonic Musical Intervals." *Journal of Research in Music Education* 46, no. 1 (1998): 112–127.

Katz, Adele T. *Challenge to Musical Tradition: A New Concept of Tonality.* New York: Alfred A. Knopf, 1945.

Kebede, Ashenafi. "The Bowl-Lyre of Northeast Africa. Krar: The Devil's Instrument." *Ethnomusicology* 21, no. 3 (1977): 379–395.

Kinsler, Lawrence E., and Austin Rogers Frey. *Fundamentals of Acoustics.* 2nd ed. New York: Wiley, 1962.

Kocharovsky, V.I.V., V.V. Zheleznyakov, E.R. Kocharovskay, and V.V. Kocharovsky. "Superradiance: The Principles of Generation and Implementation in Lasers." *Physics-Uspekhi* Vol. 50, no. 4; April 2017.

Komar, Arthur J. *Theory of Suspensions: A Study of Metrical and Pitch Relations in Tonal Music.* Princeton Studies in Music, vol. 5. Princeton: Princeton University Press, 1971.

Krumhansl, Carol L. "Music Psychology and Music Theory: Problems and Prospects." *Music Theory Spectrum* 17, no. 1 (1995): 53–80.

Kulsrud, R. "Plasma Physics." *American Scientist,* 48(4), (1960): 581–598. Retrieved from http://www.jstor.org.ma.opal-libraries.org/stable/27827651.

Larson, Steve. "The Problem of Prolongation in 'Tonal' Music: Terminology, Perception, and Expressive Meaning." *Journal of Music Theory* 41, no. 1 (1997): 101–136.

_____. "Schenkerian Analysis of Modern Jazz." PhD diss., University of Michigan, 1987.

_____. "Schenkerian Analysis of Modern Jazz: Questions about Method." *Music Theory Spectrum* 20, no. 2 (1998): 209–241.

Lerdahl, Fred. "Issues in Prolongational Theory: A Response to Larson." *Journal of Music Theory* 41, no. 1 (1997): 141–155.

Lester, Joel. *Between Modes and Keys: German Theory 1592–1802.* Harmonologia Series, no. 3. Stuyvesant, NY: Pendragon Press, 1989.

Lewin, David, *Generalized Musical Intervals and Transformations.* New York: Oxford University Press, 2007.

Lippius, Johann. *Synopsis of New Music (Synopsis Musicae Novae).* 1612. Colorado College Music Press Translations, vol. 8. Translated by Benito V. Rivera, Colorado Springs, CO: Colorado College Music Press, 1977.

MacDonald, George. *Adela Cathcart.* London: Strahan & Co., 1864.

Mandelbrot, Benoit B. *The Fractal Geometry of Nature.* New York· W. H. Freeman, 1983.

Mann, Barry, Cynthia Weill, and Brenda Russell. *None of Us Are Free.* Solomon Burke and Five Blind Boys of Alabama. 2002. Fat Possum Records. (DLC) 2003572955 (Compact Disc).

Manuel, Peter. "Andalusian, Gypsy, and Class Identity in the Contemporary Flamenco Complex," *Ethnomusicology,* Vol. 33, No. 1. (Winter, 1989), pp. 47–65.

_____. "From Scarlatti to 'Guantanamera': Dual Tonicity in Spanish and Latin American Musics." *Journal of the American Musicological Society* 55, no. 2 (2002): 311–336.

_____. "Modal Harmony in Andalusian, Eastern European, and Turkish Syncretic Musics." *Yearbook for Traditional Music* 21 (1989): 70–94.

Margon, B., J. Prochaska, N. Tejos, and T. Monroe. The Bright Symbiotic Mira EF Aquilae. *Publications of the Astronomical Society of the Pacific,* 128(960), (2016): 1–2. Retrieved from https://www-jstor-org.ma.opal-libraries.org/stable/26659923.

Mendel, Arthur. "Pitch in Western Music Since 1500: A Re-Examination." *Acta Musicologica* 50, no. 1/2 (1978): 1–328.

Merriam-Webster Incorporated. "Harmonic." *Merriam-Webster Online Dictionary.* http://www.merriam-webster.com/dictionary/harmonic.

Messiaen, Olivier. *Technique de mon langage musical.* Paris: A. Leduc, 1944.

_____, and Claude Samuel. *Music and Color: Conversations with Claude Samuel.* Portland, OR: Amadeus Press, 1994.

Mickelsen, William C., and Hugo Riemann. *Hugo Riemann's Theory of Harmony: A Study.* Lincoln: University of Nebraska Press, 1977.

Milhaud, Darius. *La création du monde.* Paris: M. Eschig, 1929.

_____. *Serenades, Orchestra, Op 62: Sérénade pour orchestre.* 1920/1921. Reprint. Munich: MPH, 2003.

_____. *Sonate pour flûte, hautbois, clarinette en sib et piano.* Paris: Durand, 1923. *Music Theory,* Vol. 36, No. 1 (Spring, 1992), pp. 81–117.

Mitchell, William J. "The Study of Chromaticism." *Journal of Music Theory* 6 no. 1 (1962): 2–31.

Monzo, Joe. "A Table of the Log(2) Harmonic-Distance for Some Intervals in the 11-Limit." *Tonalsoft Encyclopedia of Microtonal Music Theory.* http://www.tonalsoft.com.

Morgan, Robert P. "The Theory and Analysis of Tonal Rhythm." *The Musical Quarterly* 64, no. 4 (Oct. 1978): 435–473.

Mourning to Dancing. Audio recording. *Great Mystery*. 2007, 2015. "Sigh As You Close the Book." Music and Lyrics by Jack Ballard, Alliance, OH: Kiwibird Music. Used by permission. https://itunes.apple.com/us/artist/mourning-to-dancing/978324234 (accessed Sept 2, 2020).

Oldham, Guy, Clive Greated, and Murray Campbell. "Harmonics." In *Grove Music Online. Oxford Music Online*, http://www.oxfordmusiconline.com/subscriber/article/grove/music/50023 (accessed October 18, 2008).

Ortmann, Otto. "The Fallacy of Harmonic Dualism." *The Musical Quarterly* 10, no. 3 (1924): 369–383.

Page, Christopher. "Jerome of Moravia on the Rubeba and Viella." *The Galpin Society Journal* 32 (1979): 77–98.

Parker, Charlie. "Confirmation." *The Real Book*, 6th ed. New York: Atlantic Music Corp., 1946.

Patterson, Roy D. "The Tone Height of Multiharmonic Sounds." *Music Perception: An Interdisciplinary Journal*. Vol. 8, No. 2 (1990): 203–213.

Pikler, Andrew G. "History of Experiments on the Musical Interval Sense." *Journal of Music Theory* 10, no. 1 (1966): 54–95.

Piston, Walter, and Mark DeVoto. *Harmony*. 5th ed. New York: W. W. Norton, 1987.

Pole, W. "On the Philosophy of Harmony." *Proceedings of the Musical Association* 3 (1876): 74–83.

Porter, Lewis. "John Coltrane's 'A Love Supreme': Jazz Improvisation as Composition." *Journal of the American Musicological Society* Vol. 38, no. No. 3 (Autumn 1985): 593–621.

Powell, Jonathan. "Scriabin, Aleksandr Nikolayevich." In *Grove Music Online. Oxford Music Online*. http://www.grovemusic.com/shared/views/article.html?section=music.25946#music.25946 (accessed May 15, 2008).

Puterbaugh, John David. "Between Location and Place: A View of Timbre through Auditory Models and Sonopoietic Space." PhD diss., Princeton University, 1999.

Qin, Michael, Derek Schwaller, Matthew Babina, and Edward Cudahy. "Human Underwater and Bone Conduction Hearing in the Sonic and Ultrasonic Range." *The Journal of the Acoustical Society of America*. 129 (2011). https://doi.org/10.1121/1.3588185.

Rachmaninoff, Sergei. *The Complete Works for Piano and Orchestra: Second and Third Symphonies, Symphonic Dances*. Melville, NY: Belwin-Mills, 1973.

Racy, Ali Jihad. "A Dialectical Perspective on Musical Instruments: The East-Mediterranean Mijqiz." *Ethnomusicology* 38, no. 1 (1994): 37–57.

Rameau, Jean-Philippe. *Treatise on Harmony*. 1722. Phillip Grosset, trans. New York: Dover Publications. 1971.

Ravel, Maurice. *Boléro* (1928) [Bolero]. Paris: Editions Durand, 1998.

_____. *Four Orchestral Works*. New York: Dover Publications, 1989.

_____. *Pavane Pour Une Infante Défunte*. Edited by Paolo Gallico [Pavane on the Death of An Infant]. Vol. G. New York: Edward B. Marks Music Corporation, 1930.

_____. *Piano Masterpieces of Maurice Ravel*. New York: Dover, 1986.

_____. *Valses nobles et sentimentales pour orchestre*. New York: C. F. Peters, 1912.

Richter, E. F., and Alfred Richter. *Manual of Harmony: A Practical Guide to Its Study Prepared Especially for the Conservatory of Music at Leipzig*. New York: G. Schirmer, 1912.

Riemann, Hugo. *History of Music Theory, Books I and II: Polyphonic Theory to the Sixteenth Century*. Lincoln: University of Nebraska Press, 1962.

_____. "Ideas for a Study 'On the Imagination of Tone.'" *Journal of Music Theory* 36, no. 1 (1992): 81–117.

Rivera, Benito V. "The Seventeenth-Century Theory of Triadic Generation and Invertibility and Its Application in Contemporaneous Rules of Composition." *Music Theory Spectrum* 6 (1984): 63–78.

Roeder, John. "Beat-Class Modulation in Steve Reich's Music." *Music Theory Spectrum*, Vol. 25, No. 2 (2003): 275–304.

Rosenblatt, Bill. "Vinyl Is Bigger Than We Thought. Much Bigger." *Forbes*. September 18, 2018. https://www.forbes.com/sites/billrosenblatt/2018/09/18/vinyl-is-bigger-than-we-thought-much-bigger/#2d2614fc1c9c.

Rothgeb, John. "Motive and Text in Four Schubert Songs." In *Aspects of Schenkerian Theory*. edited by David Beach, 39–60. New Haven: Yale University Press, 1983.

Rothstein, William. "On Implied Tones." *Music Analysis* 10, no. 3 (Oct. 1991): 289–328.

Samson, Jim. "Scriabin: The Evolution of a Method." *Soundings* 4 (1974): 64–75.

Schenker, Heinrich. 1954. *Harmony*. Edited by Oswald Jonas. Translated by Elisabeth Mann Borgese. Chicago: University of Chicago Press, 1954.

Schmidt-Jones, Catherine. "Musical Intervals, Frequency, and Ratio." http://cnx.rice.edu/content/m11808/latest/mime text/html (accessed January 26, 2006).

Schneider, Marius. "A propósito del influjo árabe; ensayo de etnografía musical de la España medieval." *Anuario Musical, Instituto España de Musicología* (1946) 1:31–141.

Schoenberg, Arnold. *Theory of Harmony*. 1922. 3rd ed. Translated by Roy E. Carter. Berkeley: University of California Press, 1978.

_____, and Gerald Strang. *Fundamentals of Musical Composition*. New York: St. Martin's Press, 1967.

Scholz, Tom. "Something About You." New York: Epic/Sony, 1976.

Schubert, Franz. *200 Songs in Three Volumes*. Volume III. Edited by Sergius Kagen. Translated by Gerard Mackworth-Young. New York: International Music Company, 1961.

Schubert, Giselher. "Hindemith, Paul." In *Grove Music Online. Oxford Music Online*, http://www.oxfordmusiconline.com/subscriber/article/grove/music/13053 (accessed October 18, 2008).

Schuller, Gunther. *Seven Studies on Themes of Paul Klee*. London: Universal Edition, 1962.

_____. *The Visitation: Opera in Three Acts*. New York: Associated Music Publishers, 1967.

Scott, Thomas More. Book Defense. Committee: Ralph Lorenz, Frank Wiley, C. M. Shearer and David Odell-Scott, 2008.

Scriàbine, Alexander. *Poema ekstaza: le poème de l'extase pour grand orchestre Opus 54*. London, New York: Boosey & Hawkes, 1900.

Shackford, Charles. "Some Aspects of Perception. I: Sizes of Harmonic Intervals in Performance." *Journal of Music Theory* 5, no. 2 (1961): 162–202.

Shiloah, Amnon, "The Arabic Concept of Mode." *Journal of the American Musicological Society* 34, no. 1 (1981): 19–42.

_____. *The Dimension of Music in Islamic and Jewish Culture*. Brookfield, VT: Ashgate Publishing Limited, 1993.

Shirlaw, Matthew. "The Science of Harmony: The Harmonic Generation of Chords." *Journal of Music Theory* 4, no. 1 (1960): 1–18.

_____. *The Theory of Harmony: An Inquiry into the Natural Principles of Harmony*. 1917. Reprint, Sarasota, FL: Birchard Coar, 1970.

Shorter, Wayne. *E.S.P.* New York: Miyako Music, 1965.

Shostakovich, Dmitri Dmitrievich. *Quartets, Strings, no 8, Op 110, C Minor*. Edited by Lucas Drew. Boca Raton, FL: E. F. Kalmus, 1984.

Simms, Bryan. "Choron, Fétis, and the Theory of Tonality." *Journal of Music Theory* 19, no. 1 (1975): 112–138.

Slatin, Sonia. "The Theories of Heinrich Schenker in Perspective." PhD diss., Columbia University, 1967.

Smith, Charles J. "Musical Form and Fundamental Structure: An Investigation of Schenker's *Formenlehre*." *Music Analysis* 15 (1996): 191–297.

Soriano-Fuertes y Piqueras, Mariano. *Historia de la musica expañola desde la venida de los Fenicos hasta el año de 1850*. Madrid: Martin y Salazar, 1855–1859.

_____. *Música árabe-española...y conexion de la musica con la astronomía, medicina y arquitectura*. Barcelona: Juan Oliveres, 1853.

Spreadbury, Daniel, Michael Eastwood, Ben Finn, and Jonathan Finn. *Sibelius Reference*, vol. 5.2. London: Sibelius Software, 2008.

Steedman, Mark, T. N. Rutherford, T. Addis, R. Cahn, B. Larvor, and E. Clarke. "The Well-Tempered Computer [and Discussion]." *Philosophical Transactions: Physical Sciences and Engineering* 349, no. 1689 (1994): 115–131.

Stewart, Madeau. "The Echoing Corridor," *Early Music*. Vol. 8, No. 3. (Jul. 1980), pp. 339–357.

Stoll, Dennis, "The Eastern Modal Influence," *Music & Letters*, Vol. 22, No. 2 (Apr. 1941), pp. 135–138.

Straus, Joseph N. *Introduction to Post-Tonal Theory*. 2nd ed. Upper Saddle River, NJ: Prentice Hall, 2000.

_____. "Response to Larson." *Journal of Music Theory* 41, no. 1 (1997): 137–139.

Stravinsky, Igor. *Zhar-Ptitsa; The Firebird*: Original 1910 Version. Mineola, NY: Dover, 2000.

Stumpf, Carl. "Konsonanz und Konkordanz?" *Beiträge zur Akustik und Musikwissenschaft*, 6 (1911), 116–150.

Tayler, R., and J. Morgan. "Thermonuclear Plasma Conditions in Stellar Interiors [and Discussion]." *Philosophical Transactions of the Royal Society of London. Series A, Mathematical and Physical Sciences*, 300(1456), (1981):641–648. Retrieved from http://www.jstor.org.ma.opal-libraries.org/stable/36857.

Taylor, J. "Plasma Containment and Stability Theory." *Proceedings of the Royal Society of London. Series A, Mathematical and Physical Sciences*, 304(1478), (1968): 335–360. Retrieved from http://www.jstor.org.ma.opal-libraries.org/stable/2415926.

Thomson, William. "Hindemith's Contribution to Music Theory." *Journal of Music Theory* 9, no. 1 (1965): 52–71.

Tillyard, H. J. W. "A Byzantine Musical Handbook at Milan," *The Journal of Hellenic Studies*, Vol. 46, Part 2. (1926), pp. 219–222.

Title, Alan. "Magnetic Fields Below, On and Above the Solar Surface." *Philosophical Transactions: Mathematical, Physical and Engineering Sciences* 358, no. 1767 (2000): 657–68. http://www.jstor.org.ma.opal-libraries.org/stable/2666906.

van Beethoven, Ludwig, Antonio Janigro, and Jörg Demus. *The Five Sonatas for Cello and Piano*. 1965. Vanguard. r 65003607; (OCoLC)ocm12408664; AMU2022CU; (NNC)2058466.

Vaughan Williams, Ralph. *The Lark Ascending: Romance for Violin and Orchestra*. London: Oxford University Press, 1925.

_____. *Song Album* [Vol. I]. London & New York: Boosey & Hawkes, 1985.

_____. *Symphonies, No 2, G Major: A London Symphony*. Rev. ed. London: Stainer & Bell, 1920.

Waterman, Richard A., William Lichtenwanger, Virginia Hitchcock Herrmann, Horace I. Poleman, and Cecil Hobbs. "Bibliography of Asiatic Musics, Sixth Installment," *Notes*, 2nd Ser., Vol. 6, No. 2 (Mar. 1949), pp. 281–296.

Watson, Robert W., and Elizabeth West Marvin. "Riemann's 'Ideen Zu Einer «Lehre Von Den Tonvorstellungen»': An Annotated Translation." *Journal of Music Theory* 36, no. 1 (1992): 69–79.

Weisberg, J., S. Johnston, B. Koribalski, and S. Stanimirović. „Discovery of Pulsed OH Maser Emission Stimulated by a Pulsar." *Science*, 309(5731), (2005): 106–110. Retrieved from http://www.jstor.org.ma.opal-libraries.org/stable/3842175.

Weisstein, Eric. "World of Physics: Acoustics/References." Wolfram Research, Inc. http://www.wolfram.com (accessed February 4, 2006).

Westbay Technology, Ltd. "Westbay Technology Fourier Analysis." Westbay Technology. http://www.westbay.ndirect.co.uk/periodic.htmmime text/htmlhvrs__data (accessed February 7, 2006).

Westerby, Herbert. "The Dual Theory in Harmony." *Proceedings of the Musical Assn*. 29th Sess. (1902–1903): 21–72.

White, Glenn, and Grieshaber, Kate. "On the Existence of Combination Tones as Physical Entities." *Journal of Research in Music Education* , Vol. 28, No. 2 (1980): 129–134. Published by: Sage Publications, Inc. on behalf of MENC: The National Association for Music Education.

Wright, Owen, "Ibn al-Munajjim and the Early Arabian Modes," *The Galpin Society Journal*, Vol. 19. (Apr. 1966): 27–48.

_____. *The Modal System of Arab and Persian Music, A.D. 1250–1300*. London: Oxford University Press, 1978.

Xenakis, Iannis, and Olivier Messiaen. *Arts-Sciences Alloys*. Monographs in Musicology, vol. 2. New York: Pendragon Press, 1985.

xykep. "Solomon Burke—None of Us Are Free (2002)." YouTube. http://www.youtube.com/watch?v=kfzVeTaSAsQ (accessed May 12, 2008).

Zarlino, Giuseppe. *On the Modes*. Part Four. Translated by Vered Cohen. London: Yale University Press, 1983.

Zheleznyakov, P.A. Bespalov. "A Model for the Source of Quasi-Harmonic Bursts on the Crab Pulsar." Original Russian Text © V.V. Zheleznyakov, P.A. Bespalov.

Internet Resources

"FM Tone Generators and the Dawn of Home Music Production." *Yamaha Synth 40th Anniversary*. Yamaha Corporation, 2019 (accessed October 24, 2019).

"Hugo," *Harmonics*. http://www.onmyphd.com/?p=intermodulation. 2013. Accessed December 28, 2018.

Lippius, Johannes. *Synopsis Musicæ Novæ Omnio Veræ atque Methodicæ Vniversæ* Argentorati : Ledertz, 1612. Facsimile. http://diglib.hab.de/drucke/2–12-musica-1s/start.htm. 2013. (accessed, March 14, 2015).

Oldham, Guy, C. Greated, and Murray Campbell. "Harmonics." Grove Music Online; Oxford University Press, 2008. http://www.grovemusic.com (accessed December 28, 2018).

Schulzrinne, Henning. *Explanation of 44.1 kHz Sampling Rate*. Columbia University. http://www.cs.columbia.edu/~hgs/audio/44.1.html (accessed September 17, 2019).

Sotorrio, José A. 2013. The Undertone Series. May 29, 2012. http://www.youtube.com/watch?v=R_0s33fMOPI (accessed, December 28, 2018).

Software

AudioXplorer. V. 1.3.1 (125). Arizona Software, 2018.

Beskow, Jonas, and Sjolander, Kare. 2001. *WaveSurfer*, v. 1.8.8p3–1102041121. ©2000–2001.

Kojevnikov, Alexander, et al. 2013. *Spek-Acoustic Spectrum Analyser*. ©2010–2015.

Mulcahy, John. 2011. *Room EQ Wizard*, ©2004–2011, v. 5.2 beta 2, ©2019. http://www.hometheatershack.com/roomeq. Accessed October 30, 2019.

SignalScope Pro. V. 3.1.2 (1233). Faber Acoustical, LLC, 2018.

2006 *iSpectrum*. V. 2.05 (2.05). End Productions and Dog Park Software Ltd., ©2002–2006, 2018.

2007. *AutoSampler*. V. 1.6.2 Demo.4211. Redmatica Srl, ©2004–2007, 2018.

Index

Numbers in **_bold italics_** indicate pages with illustrations